£5

D1807529

Mediating Institutions

Malcolm Torry

Mediating Institutions

Creating Relationships between Religion and an Urban World

palgrave
macmillan

Malcolm Torry
London School of Economics and Political Science
London, United Kingdom

ISBN 978-1-349-94912-0   ISBN 978-1-349-94913-7   (eBook)
DOI 10.1057/978-1-349-94913-7

Library of Congress Control Number: 2016940611

© The Editor(s) (if applicable) and The Author(s) 2016
The author(s) has/have asserted their right(s) to be identified as the author(s) of this work in accordance with the Copyright, Designs and Patents Act 1988.
This work is subject to copyright. All rights are solely and exclusively licensed by the Publisher, whether the whole or part of the material is concerned, specifically the rights of translation, reprinting, reuse of illustrations, recitation, broadcasting, reproduction on microfilms or in any other physical way, and transmission or information storage and retrieval, electronic adaptation, computer software, or by similar or dissimilar methodology now known or hereafter developed.
The use of general descriptive names, registered names, trademarks, service marks, etc. in this publication does not imply, even in the absence of a specific statement, that such names are exempt from the relevant protective laws and regulations and therefore free for general use.
The publisher, the authors and the editors are safe to assume that the advice and information in this book are believed to be true and accurate at the date of publication. Neither the publisher nor the authors or the editors give a warranty, express or implied, with respect to the material contained herein or for any errors or omissions that may have been made.

Printed on acid-free paper

This Palgrave Macmillan imprint is published by Springer Nature
The registered company is Macmillan Publishers Ltd. London

Dedicated to those religious and faith-based organisations in which I have had the privilege to serve

Also by Malcolm Torry

Bridgebuilders: Workplace chaplaincy – a history
Diverse Gifts: Forms of ministry in the Church of England (ed.)
Managing God's Business: Religious and faith-based organizations and their management
Managing Religion: The management of Christian religious and faith-based organizations: Volume 1: Internal relationships; Volume 2: External relationships
Money for Everyone: Why we need a Citizen's Income
Ordained Local Ministry: A New shape for the Church's ministry (ed., with Jeffrey Heskins)
Regeneration and Renewal: New and changing communities and the Church (ed.)
The Feasibility of Citizen's Income
The Management of Religious and Faith-based Organisations: A guide to the literature (with Margaret Harris)
The Parish: People, Place and Ministry: A theological and practical exploration (ed.)
The Sermons of John Boys Smith: Theologian of integrity (ed.)
Together and Different: Christians engaging with people of other faiths (ed., with Sarah Thorley)
101 Reasons for a Citizen's Income: Arguments for giving everyone some money

Preface

Religion is an important social phenomenon. It always has been, of course. In Europe our attention might sometimes have been diverted, as it seemed that religion was becoming less significant in individuals' lives as well as in the public square: but for most of the world, religion has never gone away. Now that so many cities are multicultural – however contested that term might be (Ahmed et al. 2009) – and so many of our cities' many cultures are intrinsically religious, religion is everywhere demanding our attention. It rather looks as if 'God is back'. This might be because people are choosing religion rather than secularisation (Micklethwaite and Wooldridge 2009: 17, 23, 373, 139), or because religious leaders are employing a 'God is back' discourse to generate legitimacy for religion in the public square (Kettell 2015: 67), or because religion's association with political violence, and governments' increasing reliance on faith-based organisations for social welfare provision, are forcing religion on our attention (Hjelm 2015: 2, 9–11): but whatever the reason, religion is now a significant social fact, and to ignore it is to ignore an increasingly significant reality.

Often the presenting issue will be terrorist acts perpetrated by individuals or institutions claiming religious motives. Our attention is thus drawn to particular aspects of faith communities rather than to others – which makes it all the more important for us to understand the full breadth of religious belief and practice represented in the many different faith communities that increasingly shape our societies. It is too simplistic to say that religiously-motivated terrorists are somehow less religious than the more peace-loving members of their faith communities. Every relationship between every aspect of religion and every aspect of our societies will need to be understood if we are to answer the vital question facing us: How are we to build a peaceful world in which the many different aspects of religion can live together with every other aspect of our increasingly complex societies?

This book will not attempt to answer that vast question. It will, however, respond to a question that we shall need to consider if the broader question is ever to be understood and answered. Societies are composed of individuals, but they are also composed of institutions. Faith communities, too, are composed of both individuals and institutions. So if faith communities and all of the other aspects of our societies are to relate to each other, then religious institutions will need to relate to all of the other institutions in our societies – to other religious institutions, to non-religious institutions, and to all of those institutions that lie in between. Much of any individual's relationship with wider society is constituted by their participation in institutions of one sort or another, so if institutions are not relating well to each other, then individuals will not be relating well to each other either. Our societies will suffer relationship deficits, and it will become increasingly difficult to build coherent and peaceful societies. Conversely, if the institutions to which we belong are relating well to each other, then we shall find ourselves relating well to other individuals in society, at least in relation to our institutional aspects.

The thesis of this book is that what I shall call 'mediating institutions' – institutions that mediate between religious and secular institutions – can facilitate the kinds of relationships that we need between religious institutions and every other kind of institution. This is a simple and practical thesis, based on experience, that might be of use in communities and institutions anywhere, and that might be of benefit to the world's many different societies, as together we build the only kind of world that will now work: a multi faith and multicultural world in which institutions of all kinds can work together in the service of cohesive and peaceful societies.

Acknowledgements

For twenty years now I have researched and written about religious and faith-based organisations, so there is an increasing number of people to thank.

In 1996, a conversation took place between me and Margaret Harris, who was then on the staff of the Centre for Voluntary Organisation at the London School of Economics. We lamented the fact that Jewish rabbis and Christian ministers were going to business schools to learn how to manage their organisations, because we both thought this to be entirely inappropriate. Under Margaret's supervision I wrote *Managing Religious and Faith-based Organizations: A guide to the Literature* (published by Aston Business School in 2000) which revealed just how little literature there was on religious and faith-based organisations and their management.

Colin Rochester, Director of the Centre for Nonprofit and Voluntary Sector Management at Roehampton University, then invited me to take up an honorary visiting research fellowship at the Centre, and in that context I continued my research and wrote *Managing God's Business: Religious and faith-based organizations and their management*, which was published by Ashgate in 2005. I am still most grateful to Margaret, to Colin, to Sarah Lloyd and her colleagues at Ashgate, and to all of those who contributed to the research and writing that went into *Managing God's Business*.

Readers of *Managing God's Business* quite rightly commented that it contained rather more about the characteristics of religious and faith-based organisations than about their management, and while the literature on congregational studies and various other aspects of religious organisations was growing, there was still nothing further on the management of religious and faith-based organisations. Dr James Sweeney invited me to join the Department of Pastoral and Social Studies at Heythrop College, London, as a visiting research fellow for two years from 2010 to 2012, so that I could continue with my research in this field; and subsequently Professor Hartley Dean invited me to join the Social Policy Department at the London School of Economics as a Senior Visiting Fellow so that I could research both the feasibility of Citizen's Income (an unconditional, nonwithdrawable income for every individual as a right of citizenship) and the characteristics and management of religious and faith-based organisations. The outcome was a two volume book, *Managing Religion: The management of Christian religious and faith-based organizations*, published by Palgrave Macmillan in 2014. I continue to be enormously grateful to James Sweeney, to Hartley Dean, to Virginia Thorp and Liz Barlow and their colleagues at Palgrave Macmillan, and to everyone who assisted with the writing of *Managing Religion*.

In 2010 the Church Commissioners gave to the Parish of East Greenwich a grant to enable me to research the Church of England's and other churches' relationships to new housing and other developments in the Thames Gateway: the development area from Docklands to Southend on the north side of the Thames Estuary, and from Deptford to the River Swale on the south side. We employed a researcher, Deborah Dukes, to assist with the work, and in July 2011 I submitted a draft report to the Church Commissioners. That same year the M.B. Reckitt Trust gave the parish a grant to enable us to extend the research to cover the relationships between other faith communities and the Thames Gateway developments, and a report was submitted to the Trust, somewhat belatedly, in 2014. The reason for the delay was that I was finishing *Managing Religion* and was in the process of retiring early from the stipendiary ministry of the Church of England in order to devote more time to research, mainly in the social security field. But the M.B. Reckitt Trust report was written, and the Church Commissioners and M.B. Reckitt Trust reports between them constituted a useful account of how faith communities were relating to new housing and other developments in the Thames Gateway. In relation to these reports I am most grateful to Sue Hutson, Parish Development Officer in the Diocese of Southwark, and the Ven. Christine Hardman, then Archdeacon of Lewisham and Greenwich, and now Bishop of Newcastle, for negotiating the Church Commissioners' grant; to the Church Commissioners and to the M.B. Reckitt Trust for funding; to Deborah Dukes for carrying out and writing up visits and conversations; to the Parish of East Greenwich's officers for managing the research post; and to all of those working in new developments in the Thames Gateway who contributed to the research for the two reports.

In relation to this book, I am grateful to the Church Commissioners, the Diocese of Southwark, and the M.B. Reckitt Trust, for permission to use material from the reports written for them; to Deborah Dukes for permission to use material that she wrote for the reports; to all of those who took part in conversations with Deborah during the gathering of material for the reports; to those who have helped me with information that has enabled me to update the case studies and to add some new ones; and to those who have read and commented on parts of the typescript: Ray Borrett, Simon Boxall, Margaret Cave, Patrick Eggleston, Jeremy Fraser, Sheridan James, Mike Leader, Rob Ryan, Fiona Stewart-Darling, Jesse van der Valk, Bart Woodhouse, and Tim Yeager. I am also grateful to the Holy Trinity Greenwich Peninsula District Church Council for agreeing to the inclusion of its 2012 paper on relationships and sexuality as an appendix. I am enormously grateful to both Colin Rochester and Deborah Dukes for reading a draft of the book and for offering invaluable comments, and to Liz Barlow and Maddie Holder and their colleagues at Palgrave Macmillan for their encouragement and assistance throughout the project. So many people have been involved in one way or another with the preparation of the two research reports and of this book that it would be impossible to name all of them, and all I can do is say a corporate thank you to everyone who has contributed. If I have forgotten anyone whom I ought to have thanked by name then please accept my apologies. I shall right the wrong if there is a second edition. If I have misunderstood situations and events recounted in the case studies then that is my responsibility, and not that of any of those who have assisted with either the research reports or the book – so again, my apologies.

In relation to all of this research and writing, I am most grateful to St John's College, Cambridge, for hospitality while I used the Cambridge libraries, both during annual three day visits and for occasional longer periods of residence; to the Bishop of Southwark, the Rt. Rev'd Christopher Chessun, for permission to undertake significant research projects while being Team Rector of a demanding parish; and to the clergy and officers of the Parish of East Greenwich for taking on additional responsibilities while I spent time on research projects (and especially to the Rev'd Jeremy Fraser for taking on the co-ordinating role in the Greenwich Peninsula Chaplaincy for eighteen months). I am of course most grateful to my wife Rebecca who has put up with me using my days off for research and writing over a number of years, and for agreeing to my early retirement in 2014 so that I could continue to research and write and not burn out while doing so. While much of what you will find in this book is based on research literature and on researched case studies, a great deal is based on my own considerable experience of serving religious and faith-based organisations: so I would finally like to thank all of those people, whom I could not possibly count, with whom I have worked so happily in religious and faith-based organisations for nearly forty years, and particularly all those with whom I have worked in mediating institutions.

A Note on Sources

Chapters 2 to 5, Case Studies

The bulk of this book – Chaps. 2, 3, 4 and 5 – consists of case studies; and so as not to clutter the text of the book with notes on sources, I shall list here the sources of the information on which the case studies are based.

Some of the case studies appeared in an earlier form in a draft unpublished report written in 2011 for the Diocese of Southwark and based on research sponsored by the Church Commissioners, or in a draft unpublished report written for the M. B. Reckitt Trust in 2014 and based on research that it had sponsored. Where this is the case, the name of the case study will be followed by *MBRT* or *DS-CC*, and in some cases both. The Diocese of Southwark and the M.B. Reckitt Trust have given permission for the material to be used in this book, and Deborah Dukes, who wrote most of the case study material in the reports, has also given permission for material to be used.

Much of the information that appeared in the two reports was provided by Deborah Dukes on the basis of visits to the case study locations and conversations with numerous people in those locations. It would not be possible to list everyone Deborah met during her visits: hence the more general expression of gratitude in the acknowledgements. The research was conducted between 2009 and 2012, so additional information was required to bring the accounts up to date, and I needed to check that material in the two reports was still accurate. I have therefore held conversations with a number of individuals, and each one has been kind enough to read and comment on the text of the relevant case study. Other people as well have been kind enough to read and comment on sections of the text to check for accuracy. The names of the people who have contributed in either of these ways are listed in italics alongside the relevant case study.

Where information from a book, chapter, or website has been employed throughout a case study, it is listed here in brackets. Where a reference is required for a particular point in a case study then it will be found embedded in the text in the usual way.

Chapter 2

Workplace Chaplaincy in the UK (Torry 2010)
The Greenwich Peninsula in the Twenty-First Century, *DS-CC, MBRT, Mike Leader* (Torry 2007, 2009, 2010)
Bluewater, *DS-CC, Ray Borrett*
Stratford City, the Athletes' Village, and the Olympic Park, *DS-CC, MBRT, Jeremy Fraser*
Canary Wharf, *DS-CC, MBRT, Fiona Stewart-Darling* (Fiona Stewart-Darling, *Multifaith Chaplaincy in the Business Community* (working title) Jessica Kingsley, 2016: forthcoming, so not employed in the writing of the case study, but when it is published it will enable readers to further their understanding of the Canary Wharf chaplaincy.)
The Gossner Mission (Gossner Mission 2015; Starbuck 1966)
The United States of America: Interfaith Worker Justice – And Citizens UK, *Tim Yeager* (Interfaith Worker Justice 2015; Arise 2015)

Chapter 3

Thamesmead, *DS-CC, Patrick Eggleston, Simon Boxall* (Thorley 2004; Enoch-Onchere and Boxall 2007; Wigfall 2008: 96–104)
The Beacon Project, *DS-CC, Bart Woodhouse*

The Greenwich Millennium Village, *DS-CC, MBRT, Margaret Cave, Rob Ryan* (Torry 2007, 2009)
Other Faiths in the Thames Gateway, *MBRT*
Four Organisations in North Kent, *MBRT* (Thames Gateway Partnership 2010)

Chapter 4

Telegraph Hill, *Sheridan James* (Torry 2009)
OneSpace, Kidbrooke Village, *Margaret Cave* (Russell and Ingram 2007)
St. Mary's, Woolwich, *Jesse van der Valk* (Stacey 1971)
Christ Church Forum, *Margaret Cave* (Torry 2008)
Foodbanks, *Mike Leader* (Torry 2014b: 165–7)
Religious drama, *Sheridan James* (Torry 2009)
Across Europe: Faith-Based Organisations as Mediating Institutions (Bäckström and Davie 2010)
Housing Associations in the UK and the USA, *Tim Yeager* (Torry 2008)

Chapter 5

Educational Institutions (Torry 2016)
Established Religion
Reports, *DS-CC*
Chaplains (Ryan 2015)
State-Funded Mediating Institutions
Ecumenical Borough Deans, *Mike Leader* (Torry 2014b:132–4)
Inter Faith Fora, *MBRT, Jesse van der Valk* (Torry 2014b: 134–5; Weller 2009)
Inter Faith Network UK (Inter Faith Network UK 2015; Weller 2009)
Language
Marriage
The Clergy as a Mediating Institution (Torry 2005: 134–50, 2006, 2014a: 198–229; Torry and Heskins 2006)
The United States of America: The Episcopal Peace Fellowship, *Tim Yeager* (Episcopal Peace Fellowship 2015)

Much of the material is based on my own personal experience of the communities and institutions under discussion. Where this material has not been included in one of my previous publications it will not be referenced; where it has been, it will be.

Chapters 1 and 6

Some of the material in Chap. 1 on the Thames Gateway is an updated version of material found in *MBRT* and *DS-CC*, and some of the material in Chap. 7 appeared in an earlier form in *DS-CC*.

Additional Notes on Sources

Where research material that informed the writing of either *Managing God's Business* (Ashgate 2005) or *Managing Religion* (Palgrave Macmillan, 2014) is used in the same way as in those books, then those books are referenced. Where the research material is used to make a different point then those books are not referenced.

All biblical texts are taken from the New Revised Standard Version of the Bible, Anglicized Edition, copyright ©1989, 1995, the National Council of the Churches of Christ in the United States of America. Used by permission. All rights reserved.

Contents

List of Figures

Introduction

The world in which we live is intensely religious. Yes, secularisation is real: but that does not change the fact that religion is an important social fact. Two important facts about religion that will be central to the thesis of this book are that every religion is different, and that every religion is institutional. A subsequent fact is that there are two kinds of institution: organisations, and non-organisational institutions.

The essential religious organisation is the congregation: individual believers gathered for worship (Torry 2014a: 1–12). A second category of organisations related to religion is faith-based organisations. A faith-based organisation is an organisation with a purpose other than worship, but which is connected to a congregation or to a religious tradition. A faith school would be such a faith-based organisation (Torry 2014b: 50–86).

Non-organisational institutions are ordered activities that are not organisations. Money is an obvious example; and marriage is another. We can therefore conclude that religion is constituted by congregations, by connections with faith-based organisations, and by such institutions as rituals. Yes, religion is also constituted by sacred writings, religious experience, and much else: but all of these will either be institutions, or they will be intimately connected with them. Sacred writings have either been created or validated by an organisation; the words that we use in prayer are examples of religious language, which is an important institution; and the meaning that we attach to religious experience will have been mediated by a variety of organisations and other institutions. The rituals at the heart of a religion – for instance, the Eucharist at the heart of the Christian religion, and the prescribed words and actions of Muslim prayer – are institutions embedded in organisations. Religion is intrinsically institutional.

The same can be said of society, of course. Any community, whether local, regional, or national, is intensely institutional, and is frequently organisational. Whenever we speak to a neighbour, we are employing and shaping a shared language; when we buy something in a shop we are transacting a contract (an institution) using money (an institution) and language (an institution) in the context of an organisation.

As we shall discover in Chap. 1, secularisation as well as religion is an institutional reality; and relationships between religion and a secular urban world are always institutional, too. What this means is that if religious individuals are to relate to secular individuals, or the secular parts of ourselves are to relate to the religious parts of ourselves, or religious institutions are to relate to secular institutions – or religion and a secular society are to relate to each other – then we need to build relationships between institutions. It is here that mediating institutions are so important. Their task is to facilitate the relationships between religious institutions and secular institutions: relationships that would otherwise be difficult to build. Take an example that the reader will find in Chap. 2: it would not be easy for an individual Christian or a Christian congregation to develop a relationship with a large multinational entertainment company: but by establishing a workplace chaplains' team as an organisation, and by chaplains functioning in their institutional roles, both the chaplaincy as an organisation, and the chaplains as individuals, can relate both to the multinational company and to congregations of a variety of faiths to which the chaplaincy and the chaplains will relate. The chaplaincy and the chaplains can thus mediate a relationship between their faith communities and a multinational company: a relationship that would not be possible otherwise.

As this book will show, in workplaces, in residential areas, and in society at large, mediating institutions are hard at work, relating to secular institutions and religious institutions, and enabling them to relate to each other. The material gathered here will show how important both organ-isational and non-organisational mediating institutions are, with the clear implication that we need as many of them as we can get if religion and a secular world are to relate well to each other for the benefit of both.

The reason that this book has to be written is that there is no book on such mediating institutions. In 2009 I published an article on the sub-ject in *Theology* (Torry 2009), and I included a few references to mediat-ing institutions in *Managing Religion* (Torry 2014b: 69–70, 72, 109–11, 119, 134): but as far as I know there has been nothing else on the subject of institutions that mediate between religious and secular institutions. A literature search reveals multiple references to 'mediating institutions' and 'mediating structures' understood as institutions that stand between the individual and the State, whether conceptualised as enabling individuals to work together for community purposes, or as channels for élite influ-ence (De Tocqueville 2003/1840; Berger and Neuhaus 1977; Klimon 1992); and there is also some recent research on how political institutions mediate between religion and governments (den Dulk and Oldmixon 2014): but there appears to be no book that studies those institutions that stand between religious institutions and other institutions in order to facilitate relationships between them. Given the importance of the role that mediating institutions fulfil – and that they will increasingly need to fulfil – that gap in the literature demands to be filled. This book is a first attempt to fill it. I hope that other books will follow from other authors able to offer additional insights and research results.

Most of the book is taken up with case studies. These show just how many mediating institutions there are, how they emerge, what they do, and how they do it. Many of the case studies relate to the Thames Gateway. The entirely pragmatic reasons for this are that this is an area that I know well, and that in 2009 I was asked to undertake research into the ways in which faith communities were relating to the new housing and other developments in this massive regeneration area on the north and south sides of the Thames Estuary. An advantage of the book drawing a num-ber of its case studies from this single area is that it will enable the reader to identify with the place from which the case studies are drawn. But I have not restricted myself to the Gateway. I have been involved in a wide variety of mediating institutions elsewhere, and I include some of these where they have something to teach us about mediating institutions; and for comparison I also include material from elsewhere in Europe and from the United States. All of the contexts are urban. Again, this is partly because that is where my experience lies, but it is also because the city is a place of intensity, enabling us to see in the clearest possible light the importance of mediating institutions. (The fact that the case studies from the United States are drawn mainly from the Chicago area is again purely practical: the Rev'd Tim Yeager, now Vicar of St. George's, Westcombe Park, but previously from Chicago, has been able to provide me with information about relevant mediating institutions from that area.) Every selection of case studies will be biased in one direction or another, and while a variety of faith communities, a variety of places, and a variety of types of institution, will be discussed in this book, the case studies are biased towards the urban world, towards Christian organisations, and in particular towards the Church of England. This is the result of my own experience as an stipendiary minister in the Church of England for thirty-four years, and of the fact that about half of the case studies originally appeared in reports on the relationship between faith communities and new housing developments in the Thames Gateway. It would be a pleasure to see further research and further publications on mediating institutions that relate to other kinds of community.

Different readers might come to the book with different interests. Some might be seeking an understanding of mediating institutions and of their increasingly important role in our different societies; others might be seeking an understanding of how the Church and other faith communities might be able to relate to new developments, and might appreciate learning about the role that mediating institutions might play in that process; and yet others might be wondering how the many different aspects of faith communities' beliefs and practices might be able to relate to our complex societies in mutually beneficial ways, and how mediating institutions might be able to assist in this necessary task. Readers interested in the institutional aspects of our society and of the role that mediating institutions play will be particularly interested in Chap. 1 and in the case studies in Chaps. 2, 3, 4 and 5. Christians who want to understand how best to relate to large new housing and other developments, who want to know how the construction of mediating institutions might facilitate the building of such relationships, and who might be interested in a theological purpose for such relationship-building, will find the case studies in Chaps. 2, 3, 4 and 5 and then Chaps. 6 and 7 particularly relevant. Members of other faiths will also find those chapters helpful, but will need to make their own translations from the largely Christian character of Chaps. 6 and 7. While different readers will have different interests, and each reader will find some parts of the book of more interest than others, I hope that all of my readers will find food for thought in these pages, and the encouragement to create the many new mediating institutions that we are going to need.

Readers might value a brief outline of the book's structure: In Chap. 1 I discuss the institutional nature of both religion and society – which is what makes it so important that we create and maintain institutions that can mediate between the institutions of religion and society. The central chapters of the book, Chaps. 2, 3, 4 and 5, contain case studies: Chap. 2, studies of organisational mediating institutions that mediate between religion and workplaces; Chaps. 3 and 4, organisational mediating institutions in residential communities; and Chap. 5, both organisational and non-organisational mediating institutions that function across broader communities: across a borough, across London, or at national level. Chapters 2 and 3 draw case studies from the Thames Gateway (with comparisons from Germany and the USA); Chap. 4 looks further afield across South-east London, and again contains comparative material from elsewhere in Europe and from the US; and Chap. 5 studies mainly mediating institutions relevant to society as a whole.

Chapter 6 draws some conclusions, and in particular notes that as we have discussed mediating institutions we have often found buildings to be functioning in that capacity. The chapter concludes that creating and maintaining mediating institutions is an important task for the Church and for other faith communities. Chapter 7 is the most theological of the chapters. It suggests that the major reason for the Church establishing mediating institutions is to create signposts towards the coming City of God (defined as a community of peace and justice), and concludes that the more mediating institutions that we can construct and maintain, the more numerous and the more robust will be signposts towards the City of God, and the closer we shall be to turning our cities into something closer to the City of God.

1

Religion and Society as Institutional

Introduction

This introductory chapter provides some of the conceptual tools that we shall need if we are to study religious and other organisations and understand the kinds of relationships that we need to build between them.

The chapter will begin with definitions of 'institution' and 'organisation', will understand both religion and society as institutional realities, and will locate religious organisations in a sector of their own, and faith-based organisations as hybrids lying on the boundaries between the religious and other sectors. The chapter will then understand the relationship-building context as one of multiple secularisations and desecularisations in an urban world, and will introduce the Thames Gateway in which many of the case studies will be located.

© The Editor(s) (if applicable) and The Author(s) 2016
M. Torry, *Mediating Institutions*,
DOI 10.1057/978-1-349-94913-7_1

Institutions and Organisations

Some of the definitions that the *Oxford English Dictionary* gives of the word 'institution' are as follows:

- An established law, custom, usage, practice, organisation, or other element in the political or social life of a people; a regulative principle or convention subservient to the needs of an organised community or the general ends of civilisation [– the dictionary gives as examples the institutions of law, property, and slavery]
- An establishment, organisation, or association, instituted for the promotion of some object, esp. one of public or general utility, religious, charitable, educational, etc., e.g. a church, school, college, hospital, asylum, reformatory, mission, or the like; as a literary and philosophical institution, …
- Often occurring, like 'institute', in the designations of societies or associations for the advancement of literature, science, or art, of technical knowledge, or of special education.
- The name is often popularly applied to the building appropriated to the work of a benevolent or educational institution. (Oxford English Dictionary)

Among the definitions of 'organisation' in the same dictionary, the relevant one is as follows:

> An organised body of people with a particular purpose, as a business, government department, charity, etc. (Oxford English Dictionary)

This definition is similar to the second and third definitions of 'institution', and it overlaps with, but does not repeat, the first. This suggests that organisations form a subset of institutions. So, for instance, money is an institution, but it is not an organisation, whereas a trade union is both an institution and an organisation.

The agenda of this book is an institutional one, and not simply an organisational one. It *is* organisational, in the sense that much of the book will be about how religious and secular organisations relate to each other, and how we can facilitate improved relationships; but it is also about institutions such as marriage – institutions that are not organisations – and it asks how secular institutions and religious institutions relate to each other, how the religious and secular aspects of institutions that are both religious and secular might relate to each other, and how those relationships too might be able to be improved. In the case of non-organisational institutions – such as marriage – it might sometimes look as if we are trying to mediate between religious and secular aspects of the same institution. When this occurs we might find it useful to argue as if there were two separate institutions – religious marriage and secular marriage – that need to be reconciled. This will be legitimate if we recognise that we shall be using the 'two marriages' concept as a heuristic (educational) device, and that institutions such as marriage are inherently both religious and secular.

We shall also find ourselves using the word 'institution' in a third sense. As the Oxford English Dictionary suggests, 'institution' can refer to the building in which an organisation operates: and we shall sometimes find buildings functioning as mediating institutions.

We have already used the word 'institution' in three senses: in the sense of 'institutions, including organisations', in the sense of 'institutions that are not organisations', and in the sense of 'buildings in which organisations operate'. I will occasionally use the term 'non-organisational institution' for the second of these types of institution where confusion with an organisational institution might arise, but otherwise the reader will understand from the context whether 'institution' means 'institutions including organisations' or 'institutions that are not organisations'. If I use the word 'institution' to refer to a building then I shall be clear that it is a building about which I am writing.

Our agenda is therefore somewhat complex. We are asking how religious institutions and secular institutions relate to each other, and how we can facilitate such relationships; how the religious and secular aspects of institutions relate to each other, and how we can facilitate those relationships; and how religious organisations and secular organisations relate to each other, and how we can facilitate those relationships.

Religion as Institutional

Emil Durkheim defines religion as

> a unified system of beliefs and practices relative to sacred things, that is to say, things set apart and forbidden – beliefs and practices which unite into one single moral community called a Church all those who adhere to them. (Durkheim 1915: 47)

This is a definition couched in institutional terms. Durkheim follows it with an organisational definition by suggesting that a 'church' is essential to religion because religion is 'a collective thing' (Durkheim 1915: 47) which connects practices and ideas together 'to classify them and systematise them' (Durkheim 1915: 429). If Durkheim had been writing today then he might have written 'religious organisation' rather than 'church', but the point is the same: a religion is institutional, made up of organisations and systematised and categorised beliefs and practices (all of which are institutional realities according to the definitions of 'institution' at the beginning of this chapter). We might object that Durkheim was a sociologist, and so was likely to think like this, whereas individual religious experience can sometimes be more important for members of faith communities. However, the problem with inner experience is that it is difficult to study, and in particular difficult to compare with anyone else's religious experience in a systematic way (Bruce 1995: vii). This means that individual religious experience remains a private matter for the individual and of no social consequence – unless of course it issues in identifiable patterns of behaviour and language, at which point it becomes institutional.

We have arrived at a definition of religion that encompasses religious practices, expressed religious beliefs, and religious organisations. We can conclude that religion is its institutions.

Society as Institutional

In one sense Margaret Thatcher was right when in an interview for *Women's Own* in 1987 she said that there is no such thing as society. There is a living tapestry of men and women and people and the beauty of that tapestry and the quality of our lives will depend upon how much each of us is prepared to take responsibility for ourselves and each of us [is] prepared to turn round and help by our own efforts those who are unfortunate. (Thatcher 1987)

She might have put it better. She might have said that there is no such thing as a society that is not constituted by a 'living tapestry of men and women'. Then she would have been correct: but she would still not have captured the whole of what society is. Society *is* its many individual members: but it is also the institutions that it contains, such as money, the family, marriage, the law, the State, voluntary organisations, companies, guilds, trades unions, and, more broadly, customs, economic structures, and social structures. These are 'structures', ordered patterns of activity, which we influence just as much as they influence us. To take one example: the institution of the family (– a social institution to which Thatcher gave several honourable mentions in her interview for *Women's Own*). Our families shape us, and the ways in which we form families and behave in families slowly changes the institution of the family.

Durkheim wrote that

> when I fulfil my obligations as brother, husband, or citizen, when I execute my contracts, I perform duties which are defined externally to myself and my acts, in law and in custom. (Durkheim 1938:1)

Yes: and when I act as a brother, husband, or citizen, I influence the social structures to which those terms relate; and when I execute contracts I create or expunge money, and create or change organisational and personal relationships. Social facts change, and we change the social facts.

Among the more pervasive social institutions or structures are the kinds of authority types that Max Weber researched. For Weber, 'authority' means 'that a specific command will be obeyed' (Weber 1922: 4), whether from expediency or custom, because we recognise the legitimacy of the authority structure. Weber identified three types:

1. 'Classical', 'legal' or 'bureaucratic': 'Legal authority rests on enactment; its pure type is best represented by bureaucracy' (Weber 1922:

4). In relation to this type of authority, we obey a bureaucracy's rules, not the people who work for the bureaucracy. It is the system of rules that constitutes the institution, and the individuals out of which the bureaucracy is constructed are there to fulfil the roles demanded by the organisation: so here we have a broad institution, 'bureaucratic authority', within which particular organisations function as institutions.

2. 'Traditional': 'Traditional authority rests on the belief in the sacredness of the social order and its prerogatives as existing of yore. Patriarchal authority represents its pure type' (Weber 1922: 6). Offices are held at the pleasure of the lord. Feudalism is its developed form. (Weber 1922: 8)

3. 'Charismatic': Charismatic authority 'rests on the affectual and personal devotion of the followers to the lord and his gifts of grace (charisma)' (Weber 1922: 8). Prophets exercise this kind of authority. There are no rules, only devotion to the charismatic leader's mission. As the charismatic leader's authority wanes, the community develops rules to regulate its life. 'Routinisation' occurs, and a bureaucracy evolves. (Weber 1922: 10)

As with all other social institutions, none of these authority types is set in stone. They all change, and it is we ourselves who keep them in being, dispose of them, or change them. As Blumer puts it, institutions are

> subject to pressure as well as to reinforcement, to incipient dissatisfaction as well as to indifference; they may be challenged as well as affirmed, allowed to slip along without concern as well as subjected to infusions of new vigour …. A gratuitous acceptance of the concepts of norms, values, social rules and the like should not blind the social scientist to the fact that any one of them is subtended by a process of social interaction – a process that is necessary not only for their change but equally well for their retention in a fixed form. (Blumer 1969: 18)

This is true. However, when Blumer goes on to say that

> it is the social process in group life that creates and upholds the rules, not the rules that create and uphold group life, (Blumer 1969: 18)

he has left out half of the process. The social processes and the rules in group life constantly influence each other. It is not possible to separate individuals, social groups, and a society's institutions. They are locked together.

For our purposes, the conclusion to draw is that society is not just its individual members: it is also its institutions, some of which are organisations. Where these institutions are not religious – that is, where the main purpose of an organisation is not gathering for worship, or where an institution is not firmly attached to a faith community or a religious tradition – then I shall call them 'secular'. There is also of course a sense in which religious organisations and other religious institutions are 'secular', because they belong to a secular society (by which I mean a society largely shaped by secular practices, thoughtforms, and institutions): but nevertheless, we shall find the distinction between religious institutions and secular institutions useful, because it identifies organisations or institutions as either secular or religious, enabling us to discuss relationships between religious institutions and non-religious institutions, and between religious organisations and non-religious organisations.

Organisations in Sectors

We can categorise organisations into different sectors (Torry 2014b: 50–70). An organisation that creates services and products for customers, and in the process makes a profit that is then distributed to its owners, will be in the private sector; an organisation that provides services to a population, and is governed by a State or other governmental institution, will be in the public sector; and an organisation governed by a group of individuals who come together voluntarily to provide for the needs of a particular group in society, and who do not extract a profit from the organisation, will be in the voluntary sector (Billis 1993: 234; Salamon and Anheier 1993: 537; Kendall and Knapp 1995: 68). Organisations are complex, and often relate closely to each other, so the boundaries between the different sectors will be fluid, and there will be numerous 'hybrid' organisations that could legitimately be located in more than one sector (Billis 2010). For instance, a voluntary organisation might be largely funded by a local authority, and might work in a field heavily regulated by central government. We probably ought to locate such an organisation on the boundary between the voluntary and public sectors. A healthcare provider might be private, in the sense of being a privately owned company or a private partnership – as with General Practices in the UK – but they might be fully funded and heavily regulated by central government. Such organisations ought to be located on the boundary between the public and the private sectors. The trading arm of a development charity makes a profit and then distributes it to the charity, which locates the organisation on the boundary between the voluntary and private sectors. And perhaps a non-profit organisation providing public services and distributing a high proportion of its turnover to its management in the form of high salaries should be located where all three of the sectors meet. The boundaries between the sectors might be both fluid and contested, but the categorisation is sufficiently robust to be useful.

However, the categorisation raises an obvious question: Do religious organisations belong in the voluntary sector or in their own 'faith sector'? The answer is probably 'yes to both'. Religious organisations do of course share many of the characteristics of voluntary organisations: but there are also significant differences. A voluntary sector organisation's source of authority will generally be internal, in the form of a board of trustees. At the heart of a religious organisation is the activity of worship, and although the organisation will have a governing body of some kind, the source of authority lies in a deity structurally external to the organisation. To this ultimate source of authority every subsidiary authority structure, and every member, will be subject, at least to some extent, so not only might there be multiple subsidiary sources of authority, but every member will be able to appeal directly to the organisation's ultimate source of authority. The organisation is therefore constituted by authoritative members rather than by trustees, staff, and volunteers. If there are staff members or volunteers undertaking some of the work of the religious organisation, then they will be subject to the authority of every subsidiary authority structure and to the authority of every member, creating a somewhat complex situation when congregation members become staff members or volunteers. So there might be connections between religious organisations and voluntary organisations, and it might be legitimate to count religious organisations as belonging in some ways to a religious subgroup of voluntary organisations: but there are so many differences between religious organisations and other kinds of organisation that it is probably best to locate religious organisations in their own 'faith' or 'religious' sector (Chapman 2009; Torry 2005, 2012, 2014a, b).

We have already found 'hybrid' organisations located on the boundaries between sectors, so there might also be hybrid organisations lying on the boundaries between the religious and other sectors (Torry 2005: 117–22; Rochester and Torry 2010; Torry 2014a: 19–20). These are 'faith-based organisations'. A faith-based organisation is one of which the main purpose is not religious (so it is not a congregation) but that is closely connected with a religious organisation or tradition. A faith school might be structurally connected to its local parish church through its board of governors, and its curriculum might be regulated by a religious organisation: but it might also be funded and regulated by central or local government. It is a faith-based organisation lying on the boundary between the public and religious sectors. On the boundary between the religious and private sectors we might find a religious publisher with religious functionaries on its board of directors; and on the boundary between the voluntary and religious sectors we might find a community centre with a management committee made up of elected members of user groups, elected members of the local community, and members of a congregation's governing body. Where the public, voluntary and religious sectors meet we might locate faith schools; where the private, public and religious sectors meet we might find a religious broadcasting company; and where the private, voluntary and religious sectors meet we might locate a charity shop that distributes its profits to a faith-based development charity. We might struggle to find a hybrid organisation located where all four sectors meet. Perhaps a charity shop that distributes profits to a faith school.

The categorisation that we have developed still leaves some gaps, of course. Christian mission organisations such as the Church Mission Society and the London City Mission, and such organisations as workplace chaplaincies, are not congregations, and their main purpose is not worship, but their purpose is mission and is therefore arguably religious. Perhaps a separate category of mission organisations is required.

And then we find that in the UK the Salvation Army and the Church Army do not have worship as their main purpose, but that they evangelise and undertake social service activities. Either these organisations need to be in a category of their own or we need to think of them as unique organisations, each of which contains a variety of functions that would normally belong in a variety of different sectors (Torry 2014b: 70–73).

The importance of correctly locating religious organisations in their own category, and of locating faith-based organisations on the boundaries between the religious sector and other sectors, is that it enables us to think clearly about the requirements for relationships between different kinds of organisations. The fact that religious organisations are not simply voluntary organisations, even if they share some of their characteristics, means that public sector organisations cannot relate effectively to religious organisations if they regard them as voluntary organisations. (Twenty years ago Lewisham Council located religious organisations in the 'leisure' sector. We can understand how this might have occurred, but it could never have led to appropriate relationships. Relocation to the 'voluntary' sector was marginally more appropriate, but still not conducive to understanding or to appropriate relationships.)

Only if religious organisations understand different kinds of organisations as existing in different sectors will the difficulty of communication and of relationship-building be appreciated and will appropriate effort be put into creating the necessary channels for communication and relationship-building; and only if organisations in other sectors understand that religious organisations are located in a sector of their own will they understand how difficult it might be to understand and to relate to religious organisations. What is required is tailor-made relationships, not relationships taken off the 'voluntary organisations' peg.

Secularisations

As well as understanding where religious organisations need to be located, we also need to understand the social context in which they and other religious institutions now find themselves.

Religion matters, and not just to religious people. Nations, and groups within nations, are defined by religion; conflicts between and within nations are often driven by religion; and around the world, for millions of communities, and for individuals and households within those communities, religion defines their worldview, their life projects, their daily behaviour, and their relationships with each other, with wider society, and with the global community. There cannot be much that matters more than religion.

In some parts of the world it might look as if religion matters less than it did. Whatever is or is not happening in the rest of the world, Europe has experienced secularisation (Davie 2002). There are many ways of understanding this process. Is it about the history of ideas, a distancing of scientific and religious discourses from each other, or a change in the way in which we understand ourselves (Bruce 1992; Martin 1969, 1978; Chadwick 1975; Taylor 2007)? Or is it a distancing from religious symbols and practice (Brown 2001)? Or is it a diverse process, different in different places (Martin 2005)? It is all of these. Secularisation in Western Europe, and increasingly in other parts of the world, is not a single social process, but is rather a set of interlocking and mutually reinforcing processes, and so should probably be referred to in the plural as 'secularisations' as well as in the singular as 'secularisation'.

There are at least eight different but overlapping varieties of secularisation:

1. *The secularisation of ideas*: The way we think no longer has religious ideas at its heart, and often has no connection with them at all.
2. *Cultural secularisation*: Religious symbols and ideas no longer control our culture, whether that culture be working class, middle class, music, literature, drama, or the visual arts. References to religious ideas are increasingly ironic.
3. *Desacralisation*: Many of us no longer experience a sense of the sacred, of something transcendent: and if we do then we keep it to ourselves and it does not affect other areas of our lives.
4. *Practical secularisation*: Lots of people do not go to church, or get their children baptised, or get married in church. The number of funeral

services conducted by the Church of England fell from 200,000 per annum to 160,000 per annum between 2004 and 2013 (Church of England 2014, Table 37). If someone does go to church then everyone thinks of it as a voluntary activity like any other.

5. *State secularisation*: In the UK, if a mayor decides to have a chaplain then that is up to them. Nobody expects them to, or wonders why they do not have one. Prayers before local authority council meetings are now a contentious issue (Department for Communities and Local Authorities 2012; Mason 2014).

6. *Institutional secularisation*: In the UK, state schools no longer automatically ask the local curate to lead assemblies, as they once did. Hospitals have chaplains for all sorts of good reasons, but it is no longer because we think a hospital to be incomplete without one. There used to be deep connections between religious organisations and other institutions. No longer.

7. *Religious secularisation*: Religious organisations are now so influenced by other types of organisation that they are less religious than they used to be. Social events can be as important to a church's members as the holding of services, and if a new management method arrives from the denomination's head office then people moan about the time that it might take rather than ask whether it compromises the religious nature of the congregation.

8. *Secularisation of individual beliefs*: This kind of secularisation occurs when someone no longer believes that there is a God. (Torry 2010: 1–2)

These different secularisations will function differently in different countries, and how they appear in the UK might not be how they appear elsewhere: but they will all be found in some form or other in European and many other countries. The most visible type of secularisation will generally be 'practical secularisation', and particularly the decline in the numbers of people attending religious worship (Torry 2014a: ix; Hirschle 2010; Crockett and Voas 2006; Presser and Chaves 2007; Iannaccone and Everton 2004; Olson and Beckworth 2011): but the picture is a mixed one, particularly in cities that have experienced significant levels of immigration. Take Greenwich in South East London as an example. Here some of the congregations of the historic Christian denominations have declined, but some have increased, largely due to African Christian immigration; and all of the historic denominations are still represented. A large black-led Pentecostal congregation has for fifteen years occupied what was once a cinema in the centre of Woolwich, and another similar congregation now occupies the old cinema opposite. At the Woolwich Mosque, Friday prayers on major festivals can spill into the car park and sometimes into the road, and a sizeable extension will soon be open. Where numbers attending worship have declined, it might be more because lifestyles are changing than because of a loss of active members. Fortnightly attendance at Christian worship might now be more common than weekly attendance, so congregations look as if they are smaller even though there are just as many active members.

Institutional Secularisation and Desecularisation

The diverse patterns of practical secularisation and practical desecularisation might be the most visible aspects of a complex process, both in Greenwich and elsewhere: but the secularisation with which this book will be most closely concerned is that of 'institutional secularisation'. This

> entails basic social processes in which major societal institutions are differentiated from each other and no longer represent the same values or work together to provide an overall coherence to social life. (Bell 1997: 198)

In some countries, such as France, where the French revolution gave birth to a *laicité* that fractured most previous relationships between religion and other social institutions, institutional secularisation goes back a long way. In other countries the process has been more gradual, and has accelerated during the past fifty years, so that now there are few structural connections between religious organisations and other kinds of organisation. In particular, representative personnel of the different kinds of organisations no longer relate to each other as a matter of course, but only through shared interests and personal friendships (Torry 2005: 46–55; Torry 2010: 13–15; Martin 1978; Davie 1994).

This process is organisational. Institutional secularisation occurs as organisational connections change and organisations' personnel increasingly live in different conceptual and organisational worlds. Take, for example, educational organisations in the UK. Until the nineteenth century the churches were major providers of schools, but then the State began to take more seriously its responsibility for education, and local authorities began to build schools to serve the large conurbations within which church resources were never going to be adequate to provide education for the growing population of children. Faith schools remain an important part of the educational landscape in the UK, but that landscape is now more chaotic, and religious organisations, along with parents who want faith schools for their children, participate in a political process in which there is no longer an assumption that faith schools have an automatic place. So, for instance, an oversubscribed newly created 'academy' school with a designated religious character has to accept 50 per cent of pupils who are not of its designated faith (Department for Education 2014: 16). The relationship between religious organisations and State educational organisations is now sometimes described as a 'battle' (De la Bedoyere 2015; Institute of Ideas 2014).

But education is not simply an organisational reality. It is also institutional in a wider sense. Education contains such institutions as school assemblies, curricula, codes of practice, training methods, and the teaching profession. A relationship between religious doctrine and practice and a State school's religious education curriculum is a relationship between two institutions, even though it is not a relationship between two organisations. Institutional secularisation here is ubiquitous. To take one example: Fifty years ago in the UK it was still normal for state schools to sing hymns at daily morning assembly. Now it is not. In State schools, the institutions of morning assembly and of hymn-singing have parted company; and school assemblies and the Church's clergy have largely parted company as well.

A further example of institutional secularisation can be found in the changing relationships between the churches and industrial organisations in the UK. During the 1950s a large team of chaplains drawn from a variety of denominations provided pastoral care in numerous industrial premises in South London. Company employees in large numbers attended residential conferences and other meetings organised by the South London Industrial Mission (SLIM); and every year a 'harvest thanksgiving' service, at which company representatives presented examples of their work, packed Southwark Cathedral. Both industrial companies and the churches gave financial support to SLIM, and the denominations allocated paid posts that SLIM then filled and supervised. By the end of the 1990s it had become almost impossible to establish new chaplaincies in companies, and the denominations had withdrawn all of their posts. SLIM no longer exists (Torry 2010).

But having said all that, institutional desecularisation is in many contexts as significant a process as institutional secularisation. In many communities, congregations of a variety of faith communities now relate more closely to other institutions than they have for many years, and particularly to local authorities, which increasingly regard religious organisations as partners in the provision of individual and social welfare services (Dinham and Lowndes 2009) and as essential partners in the resolution of social crises (Torry 2014a: x; Berger 1999: 3; Davie 2002; Grant et al. 2003; Martin 2005; Wuthnow 2009). It might be true that many people's religion might now be more fluid, commercialised, and noninstitutional (Ward 2009: 132), that congregations are on average smaller, that fewer infants are baptised, that fewer people marry in church, that fewer families choose religious funeral services, that fewer Sikhs and Hindus attend the Gurdwara or Mandir regularly, and that a smaller proportion of Muslims attend the Mosque every Friday: but voluntary chaplaincy activity in Greenwich and elsewhere has seen an increase during the past fifteen years; the churches' engagement with the London Olympic and Paralympic Games in 2012 was substantial; and across the UK numerous church members and members of other faiths donate large numbers of voluntary hours to foodbanks, and many of those foodbanks are organised by individual congregations or by congregations working together. Institutional and practical secularisations are not necessarily correlated. Institutional desecularisation can occur in a context of practical secularisation, and institutional secularisation can occur in a context of such examples of practical desecularisation as growing congregations that absorb their members' time and energy in evangelism and congregation-focused activity.

Why Build Relationships?

Does any of this matter? Does it matter whether there are relationships between religious organisations and other kinds of organisations? – between religious institutions and the other institutions of civil society? – and between the religious aspects of institutions and the secular aspects of the same institutions?

Yes, it does.

There is not a single society that does not face challenges: climate change, ageing populations, water, food, and energy shortages, and in too many cases war, disease, and hunger. It must be more effective for organisations of different kinds to work together to solve these problems – and at least to co-ordinate what they do – than for organisations in different sectors to work in isolation. If organisations co-operate then resources can be more efficiently deployed, knowledge can be shared, and different tasks can be more appropriately allocated to the organisations best suited to carrying them out. When religious and other organisations do not work together then organisations in the voluntary, public and private sectors cease to understand religious organisations, society is less well served, and religious organisations find themselves isolated and unable to relate to the contexts to which they need to relate if they are to fulfil their own missions to serve and to evangelise.

In complex societies that contain a wide variety of institutions, for religious and secular institutions to work well together can only be good for communities, households, and individuals. Communities benefit when the elected or designated leaders of faith community congregations work closely with the police, the local authority, and other organisations and institutions, particularly when community crises occur, but also in the absence of crisis. Conversely, when religious and other institutions are not working well together, 'opportunities for encounter, mutual understanding and trust ... are lost' (Furbey 2009: 38), people and communities can get damaged, and religious organisations can get damaged too. Take a high profile current example: the religious and secular aspects of marriage are not working well together at the moment, and individuals, families and communities are suffering as a result.

A vitally important institution is language. Where members of faith communities – and particularly office-holders in religious organisations – do not understand the language used by other members of society, and by organisations in other sectors; and where any members of society – and particularly office-holders in private, public or voluntary sector organisations – do not understand the language used by religious people or organisations, then miscommunication can occur, to the detriment of all involved, and to the detriment of projects that organisations in religious and other sectors might be undertaking together (Baker 2009b). Religious literacy in civil society organisations, and civil society literacy in religious organisations, are primary requirements if religious and other organisations are to work together for the benefit of society. A peaceful community requires that people know, understand, and respect each other, and in particular that there is sufficient communication to enable the community to avoid conflict. If religious and other organisations are working well together, and if religious and other institutions relate to each other well, then mutual understanding will be enhanced and multi faith societies will be more likely to be peaceful ones. If conflict does emerge between different ethno-religious groups, then the resolution of the crisis will be a lot easier to achieve if religious and other organisations work well together, if different institutions – such as professions – are working well together, and if sufficient language is shared between all of the parties. It *is* possible to put together the necessary relationships during a crisis, but it will always be easier to create the required active relationships if good relationships already exist between religious and other organisations and between religious and other institutions.

In a society in which a variety of secularisations and desecularisations are occurring at the same time, it might be tempting to avoid the difficult task of bridging the gaps between organisations in different sectors and between religious and other institutions. A shifting and complex context can create anxiety, and can lead religious organisations and individuals to concentrate on their own agendas, and other civil society organisations and institutions to get on with the many other tasks demanding their attention. This would be a mistake. In a shifting and complex context it is even more important to create good relationships between the different sectors. It will never be energy wasted.

Internal and External Aspects of Organisations

The position that we have reached is this: Society is made up of individuals, but it is also constituted by institutions, among which are organisations. Similarly, religion is a matter of individual commitment, but it is also institutional and organisational. Our times are characterised by a variety of secularisations, among which is institutional secularisation: the distancing of religious and secular organisations from each other, and the distancing of religious and secular institutions from each other. So educational organisations and other institutions have become less religious, and at the same time educational and specifically religious organisations have become more distant from each other. This means that in the educational world, relationships between educational institutions and religious institutions have largely disintegrated, and faith-based educational organisations have shifted in a secular direction.

We shall find it helpful if we keep these different processes separate. Where educational organisations are faith-based organisations and they have wandered further towards the secular end of a religious/secular spectrum, then an institutional secularisation has occurred. We shall be returning to the question of faith-based organisations later in the book. A separate but often connected process is the distancing of specifically religious organisations from other kinds of organisations (which we are here calling 'secular' in order to distinguish them from religious organisations). Some of those secular organisations will be faith-based organisations, located somewhere on a spectrum between the religious and the secular. So here we have two very different processes: one is occurring within an organisation, and the other is a change in relationships between organisations.

A complicating factor is that these processes will often be connected. A faith-based voluntary organisation that builds stronger links with secular public sector organisations, and that loosens its connections with the religious organisation that gave birth to it, will be experiencing two different processes: relationships will be changing, and those changing relationships will cause the character and structure of the faith-based organisation to become more like those of the public sector organisations to which it is now relating more strongly, and less like those of the religious organisation from which it is distancing itself (DiMaggio and Powell 1983: 156).

There will always be a question as to which way causality is operating. Are an organisation's internal changes bringing about changing relationships with other organisations, or are changing relationships generating internal changes? In most cases the process is probably circular – and, in any case, there is always a question as to whether an organisation should be understood as purely its internal relationships, or whether it should be understood as constituted by both internal and external relationships.

However we view this complex situation, the agenda of this book is clear: it is primarily about the relationships *between* organisations – which is why a decision has been taken to designate organisations as 'religious' or 'secular', which means that for the purposes of this book faith-based organisations are often included in the 'secular' category.

Relationships Within and Between Institutions

Take authority structures. A political party might experience all three of Weber's authority types (Weber 1922: 4–10). Party leaders will often be where they are because they can exhibit charismatic authority; dynasties, where they occur, represent a traditional authority type; and any long-term complex organisation will need bureaucratic or legal authority to play a significant role if it is to survive in the longer term. Similarly, the typical religious organisation, a congregation, might exhibit all three types. A church council might function bureaucratically; a variety of individuals – such as worship leaders or choir masters – might exercise charismatic authority (in Weber's sense); and the clergy might exercise all three authority types. But there is also a unique religious authority type, because the primary authority structure for any religious organisation will be external to the organisation, whereas authority structures in secular organisations will be internal (provided we understand 'internal' to include electorates in the case of public sector organisations) (Torry 2005: 146–7, 177).

So in relation to authority types, religious institutions and secular institutions are different. Religious institutions recognise an external authority, whereas secular institutions do not. But there are also shared authority types, and in these cases we have to ask about the religious and secular aspects of those shared types. So, for instance, charismatic authority in a religious organisation might contain aspects of the *charisma*, the specifically spiritual gifts, listed by St. Paul in his first letter to the Corinthians (1 Corinthians 12:4–11), whereas this element will be absent in secular organisations; in religious organisations traditional authority will ultimately be understood as deriving from an external divine source, whereas in secular organisations traditional authority will have tribal or family roots; and in secular organisations bureaucratic authority will be perceived as entirely legitimate, whereas in religious organisations it will be experienced as less legitimate and at best as an unfortunate necessity (Torry 2005: 139, 2014a: 120, 184–5).

An institution that will always be both religious and secular is marriage. Marriage might be experienced as either religious or secular, but the institution itself will always be both. The reason for this lies in marriage's roots in societies that were intrinsically religious – and so while such modern inventions as civil partnerships might be properly secular, marriage never can be; and because civil partnerships and same-sex marriage relate closely to marriage, these too can take on religious aspects. We therefore have to ask about the relationship between religious and secular *aspects* of marriage, rather than about relationships between secular marriage and religious marriage.

Mediating Institutions

This book studies the relationships between religious and secular organisations, and asks how they might be strengthened; it asks about the relationships between religious and secular institutions, and how they might be strengthened; and it asks about the relationships between the religious and secular aspects of institutions, and how they might be strengthened, too. It is only interested in the internal secularisation or desecularisation of faith-based organisations where that relates to the main agenda of the book.

The thesis of this book is that 'mediating institutions' can facilitate the kinds of relationships that we need between religious organisations and secular organisations, between religious institutions and secular institutions, and between the religious and secular aspects of institutions. By 'mediating institution' I mean an institution that mediates: so a mediating institution might be an institution that mediates between a religious non-organisational institution and a secular non-organisational institution; or between the religious and secular aspects of an institution that is both religious and secular; or between a religious organisation and a secular organisation: or a mediating institution might be a non-organisational institution that mediates between a religious organisation and a secular organisation (with 'secular' here meaning 'non-religious', and as including faith-based organisations). This suggests that the category of mediating institutions will contain a subcategory of mediating organisations.

Where the mediating institution is an organisation it will contain individual members, so it will relate to religious and secular organisations in several different ways. Individuals in the mediating organisation will relate to individuals in religious organisations and to individuals in secular organisations (and the same individual might belong to two or three of these organisations, so the relating might be as much internal to an individual as between individuals); groups within the different organisations will relate to each other; and the organisational and social structures of the organisations will relate to each other. Non-organisational institutions are not composed of individuals, but they do relate to other institutions through individuals. So a religious authority structure will relate to a secular authority structures within a single individual, and a mediating institution might relate to both the religious and the secular institutions within that same individual: or individuals who relate to different authority structures might relate to each other and to a mediating institution. The secular and religious aspects of marriage will relate to each other – and perhaps collide with each other – in the experience of individual couples; a mediating institution might relate to both aspects of marriage within the experience of the couple; and individuals who relate to the different religious and secular aspects of marriage might relate to each other and to a mediating institution.

A mediating institution might be a 'law, custom, usage, practice, organisation, or … a regulative principle or convention' (Oxford English Dictionary), and so might be a one-off meeting, a series of meetings, a set of rules or guidelines, an authority structure, a practical method – in fact, anything that can be defined as an institution. Mediating institutions will therefore be of different kinds, and will be highly diverse; and each mediating institution might function in a variety of different ways: but always the mediating institution will *mediate*: between organisations, or between non-organisational institutions, or between different aspects of the same institution – and it will mediate between the religious and the secular: between religious organisations and secular organisations, between religious institutions and secular institutions, and between the religious and secular aspects of institutions that are both secular and religious. Fig. 1.1 offers a diagrammatic explanation of the role of mediating institutions.

Religion and Religions

So far I have written in mainly general terms: about the organisations and institutions of religion, about the organisations and institutions of society, about organisational sectors, about secularisation and desecularisation, and about the importance of relationships between organisations and institutions in the religious sector and organisations and institutions in other sectors. However, in order to discuss how such relationships might be created or enhanced, I shall spend most of this book studying particular organisations and institutions in particular places.

Most of the organisations that I shall study will be Christian ones, but there will also be a few organisations of other faiths, and some multi faith organisations. The bias towards Christian organisations is partly because I have known and worked with more Christian organisations than other kinds, and partly because several of the case studies resulted from research that related specifically to the Christian Church.

Fig. 1.1. Mediating institutions

In one sense there is no such thing as religion: there are only religions. The 'unified system of beliefs and practices' (Durkheim 1915: 47) that constitute a religion will be particular to that religion. Different religions might share a number of characteristics, such as the practice of prayer, the reading of sacred texts, and gathering for worship: but at the heart of every religion there is a radical uniqueness – and in most cases the theological foundations of different religions will differ radically, whereas peripheral matters can look quite similar. Take, for instance, the reading of sacred texts. Both Christians and Muslims read books regarded as sacred in some way: the Bible and the Qur'an. However, their statuses are utterly different. For Muslims, the Qur'an is God's chosen means of revelation to us, and Muhammad is the channel through which God gave the Qur'an (Suras 15: 9; 40: 1). For Christians, Jesus Christ is 'the Word made flesh' (John 1: 14), the primary revelation of God, and the Bible is a witness to him. The order of priority is different, and it is the order of priority that matters.

Because a religion's theology to some extent shapes the character of the religion's organisations and institutions, the different religions' radically different theologies will mean that their organisations will behave in very different ways, even if superficially there might be similarities. Therefore conclusions that we might draw from the study of Christian organisations cannot necessarily be applied to Hindu organisations, and vice versa.

We shall return to this issue later in the book, but in the meantime it is worth saying that none of this is a barrier to people of different faiths working together for the common good. Indeed, clarity about the differences between our religions can make it possible for individuals and organisations of different faiths to work out where they can legitimately work together and where they cannot; and such clarity can propel individuals and organisations from across the spectrum of any particular religion to commit themselves to working with people of other faiths, and then to do that.

But having said all of that, we can still agree with Emil Durkheim that a religion is

> a unified system of beliefs and practices relative to sacred things, that is to say, things set apart and forbidden – beliefs and practices which unite into one single moral community called a Church all those who adhere to them. (Durkheim 1915: 47)

This means that religions do share some characteristics that can be described in highly general terms, and therefore that in this sense there is such a thing as 'religion'. So throughout this book, where I use 'religion' as a generic descriptor, I am referring to a set of communities, in each of which people unite around sets of (relatively) unified beliefs and practices. Wherever the theological roots of religions, or the particular beliefs and practices of a particular religion, are in view, I shall use the names of particular religions – Islam, the Christian Faith, Judaism, etc. – rather than the generic 'religion'.

An Urban World

It is almost certainly true that 'the twenty-first century will be the urban age' (Katz et al. 2007: 476): but Harvey Cox's prediction that 'the rise of urban civilisation' would be accompanied by 'the collapse of traditional religion' (Cox 1968: 15) does not appear to have been quite so accurate. The urban world has not turned out as secular as he might have expected, but there is no denying the fact that urbanisation has been one of the main hallmarks of our era. 54 per cent of the world's population now lives in cities (United Nations News Centre 2014), cities are increasingly diverse, or 'hybrid', in terms of their ethnic and cultural characteristics (Baker 2009a), and, perhaps just as significantly, the character of life outside cities is now taking on many of the characteristics of urban living, particularly in relation to consumption and shopping patterns. Because both cities and religion are increasingly significant social facts, Graham Ward is correct to suggest that

> the sites where this world is highly focussed are our cities, particularly our global cities. It is, then, the confrontation between the ecclesial body and the secular city to which contemporary Christian thinkers need to return, and return continually. (Ward 2009: 204)

The case studies contained in this book are all taken from the urban world because that is the world that I know best, and because many of the case studies are based on research that the Church Commissioners asked me to carry out in the Thames Gateway: a diverse area of new urban developments. The main reason for concentrating on this particular area is because a major challenge facing the Church is how to relate to new housing developments, so to study how the Church is relating to a particular regeneration area might be helpful. A further reason for concentrating on evolving urban areas is that if we are to study organisations and institutions in today's world then it might be useful to study them in places of intense diversity. Rarely will we find greater diversity that in the particular urban world of the Thames Gateway, with its residential communities, commerce, industry, financial institutions, educational and health service organisations, entertainment and retail complexes, communication hubs, and much more. Rural areas contain some of these, but with nothing like the same diversity, and certainly never such a diversity all in the same place. The only institutions that we find in rural areas and not in urban ones are large agricultural and conservation organisations (– and I say 'large' advisedly, because city farms, ecology parks, and nature reserves are now normal aspects of urban areas). The Thames Gateway is therefore an ideal place in which to study the need for mediating organisations, and the roles that they might fulfil.

The Thames Gateway

The Thames Gateway extends from Deptford to the Isle of Sheppey along the south bank of the Thames, and from Canary Wharf to Southend along the north bank. It contains existing towns, marshland, and former industrial sites; and the channel tunnel rail link runs across it, with stations at Stratford and Ebbsfleet, providing a rapid connection to the Continent and to central London (and perhaps eventually to the North). Changing names are symptoms of a changing urban world. Instead of the Isle of Dogs, we now hear 'Canary Wharf' and 'Docklands'. Old residential and workplace locations – Canning Town, Limehouse, and Poplar – have turned into names for Docklands Light Railway stations. 'Woolwich Arsenal', as it is still known to residents of Woolwich and to local bodies such as Greenwich Council, is always referred to by its developer as 'Royal Arsenal Riverside'. What is now referred to as 'Greenwich

Peninsula' was known as 'Greenwich Marshes' until the Millennium
Dome was planned in 1996 and 'North Greenwich' tube station opened
in 1999 – fomenting a continuing battle over the name of the place,
and occasional attempts to persuade Transport for London to rename
the tube station 'Greenwich Peninsula'. The naming of places remains
entirely in the hands of local authorities, and they have no obligation to
consult.

'The Thames Gateway' is itself a name designed to define a physical
space as an opportunity for new built environment: but there the unity
of the construction activity ends. Perhaps the Thames Gateway can best
be understood as a branding exercise backed by various stakeholders in
the private and public sectors. The process of garnering community support for the Gateway had barely begun before the financial crisis in 2008
caused the primary stakeholders to apply the funding brakes: but now
that the construction industry is recovering from the recession, cranes
are reappearing from Docklands to Tilbury and from Greenwich to
Ebbsfleet, and 'the Thames Gateway' might again look as if it means
something. Ever since the Deputy Prime Minister John Prescott coined
the term, a plethora of different local authorities and partnership bodies have fulfilled a bewildering array of functions, and construction has
been by an uncoordinated patchwork of different developers. In just one
development, the Greenwich Peninsula, a masterplan published in 2002
determined the general layout of the development and the general sizes
and shapes of the buildings, but commercial and political pressures and
individual designers' interests have determined precisely what has been
built. So whereas the masterplan envisaged mixed tenure (owner occupation, shared equity, and social housing) throughout the development,
we are now seeing the residential blocks with the best views turned over
entirely to owner occupation.

So what will it be like when it's all finished? Take the area from
Greenwich to Northfleet along the southern bank of the Thames: The
Greenwich Peninsula (a huge diverse development of office blocks, entertainment district, and residential property), the Woolwich Arsenal (residential property), West Thamesmead (residential property), Dartford
marshes (residential property), Bluewater (a shopping centre, though
they call it a 'destination'), and the Eastern Quarry (more residential

property). This is probably a fair representation of what's intended for the whole of the Thames Gateway: a string of disconnected housing developments interspersed with out-of-town shopping centres. What is not envisaged is genuine new towns.

So is the Thames Gateway part of London? – that is, is it within an existing city? Or is it an 'exurbia' or an 'edge city' (Green 2008: 10–11)) – that is, a city in its own right? In the light of the above, probably the former, if it is anything at all, and is not simply commercially-driven discrete housing developments. Perhaps it is best to see it as two strings of diverse exurbias.

Lewis Mumford describes the development of cities through history, from providing security, to exchange, industry, and now the metropolis. Mumford's fears are understandable:

> Each historic civilisation … begins with a living urban core, the polis, and ends in a common graveyard of dust and bones, a necropolis, or city of the dead: fire-scorched ruins, shattered buildings, empty workshops, heaps of meaningful refuse, the population massacred or driven into slavery. (Mumford 1961: 54)

We don't envisage that for the Thames Gateway, at least, not yet, but strong possibilities are that it will become a soulless residential desert, or that it will end up under water if the Thames Estuary doesn't get the flood defences that it will soon need. For Mumford, the tightly-packed medieval city is the ideal city, with trade, housing, manufacture, government, services, religion, and everything else, all within walking distance. Above all, he seeks a sense of place: that is, that the residents of the city should know that they *are somewhere*. Residents on the Greenwich Peninsula are not even sure of the name of the place in which they live.

A personal note: I grew up in Dartford. It was a place. It had homes, schools, hospitals, and lots of shops in the town centre: a green-grocer's (I was at school with the proprietor's son), a butcher, bakers, the Co-op, Kerr's for school uniforms, and so on. Rarely was a shop unoccupied. It was still like that in 1998. In 1999 Bluewater opened five miles from Dartford. As its website says: 'Bluewater has successfully combined retail and leisure to offer a day out destination. Bluewater's average guest spends around 3 hours at Bluewater, and 98 percent of guests surveyed in exit polls say their visit is highly enjoyable.' Bluewater is a successful temple to consumerism. It even has texts carved into the stone. Sadly, this 'destination' has killed Dartford town centre; and the hospital, too, has gone out of town. There is little sense of place there now. At least it *was* once a place. There is a danger that the housing developments along the Thames Gateway won't ever be places which they could stop being.

As you will see when you read about the Greenwich Peninsula in some of the case studies, there is a possibility that at least this will become a place. The Greenwich Millennium Village now has a Square with a row of shops; there is a health centre; and there are now two primary schools, and secondary provision will be opening soon. There is as yet no community centre, but at least there is a nursery, and the same space can be used for community activities. At the end of the Peninsula is The O2, there are lots of buses, there are two parks, and there are workplaces: restaurants, shops, and office blocks. There are retail parks which feel as if they belong because they're walkable. In spite of the size of some of the new blocks of flats being built, the Peninsula has a human scale, and if Transport for London were to change the name of the tube station then residents would know that they live at 'Greenwich Peninsula': they would live in a *place*. As the number of residents grows from 2000 to 30,000, everyone involved will have to work hard to create community: but at least it should be possible to do so. I am more concerned about some of the other rather more monochrome developments along the Thames Gateway. Will they experience the 'mixity' of the city? (Green 2010: 7).

The Thames Gateway has huge potential, but that potential will only be met if the Gateway takes on the character of a city, either as a city in its own right, or as part of London. This will require planning to be extracted from the patchwork of authorities currently involved and given to the Department for Communities and Local Authorities: and this will need to be done soon. It will also need a minister inspired to create a genuine cityscape that learns from the world's greatest cities, and who at the same time can ensure that the Gateway becomes a patchwork of human-scale neighbourhoods – as great world cities such as London in fact are – each with its own character, and each clearly belonging to the whole.

One of the roles of faith communities is to say some of these things, and a useful indication of whether the Gateway is becoming city-like will be the character of religion in the Gateway. Will there be diversity, ecumenical relationships, inter faith relationships, groups, federations, and civic engagement? Will there be religious buildings in neighbourhoods, and religious buildings at the hubs that the Gateway will need to contain? And will there be significant religious architecture? (Think of Croydon in South London: it has all of this, so it could act as a model of a city within a city.) If none of this occurs then it will be a signal that the Gateway is not becoming a city or a part of the city.

It will not be easy. A major study of the city in the twenty-first century completely ignored the role of religion in the modern city, and even the contribution of religious buildings to the modern cityscape did not feature, either in the text or in the illustrations (Burdett and Sudjic 2007). A combination of academic and policymaking disinterest, masterplans that make no room for religious buildings, commercial interests that require every square metre to be saleable, and an increasingly secular and multi faith society, has provided the faith communities with one of their most difficult challenges, as well as with a significant opportunity. Take, for instance, the Greenwich Peninsula masterplan. When it was published there was no space allocated on the Peninsula for religious buildings, in a community that will one day contain 30,000 residents, 30,000 workers every day, and 30,000 visitors most days. Omissions such as this are both symptomatic and causal of secularisation: but, as in Greenwich, they can galvanise faith communities to work together, and to work with the developer and the borough council, to find solutions to a situation that everyone can identify as a problem. The result on the Greenwich Peninsula has been a mediating institution: an ongoing multi faith project within which the faith communities can continue to work together to serve the growing community on the Peninsula, and through which faith communities and other institutions can relate to each other.

It will take a bewildering variety of organisations and individuals to cooperate if the Thames Gateway is to become a signpost towards the Kingdom of God that I shall discuss at the end of this book. Significant to the process will be the role that religious organisations and institutions fulfil; and particularly significant will be the mediating institutions that this book is all about.

The Different Sectors of Urban Life

The urban world is highly interconnected: there are multiple personal and structural connections between residential areas and workplaces, and between government, educational, healthcare, and cultural institutions. To split them up the different aspects of urban society will always be rather artificial: but in order to give some structure to the discussion of mediating institutions, the next four chapters tackle various aspects of society. Chapter 2 will be about workplaces; Chaps. 3 and 4 about residential areas; and Chap. 5 about some of the institutions of civil society: and each chapter will ask how mediating institutions are facilitating relationships between religious institutions and the kinds of institutions that the chapter is about.

Bibliography

Baker, Christopher. 2009a. *The hybrid church in the city: Third space thinking*, 2nd ed. London: SCM Press.

———. 2009b. Blurred encounters? Religious literacy, spiritual capital and language. In *Faith in the public realm: Controversies, policies and practices*, ed. Dinham Adam, Furbey Robert, and Lowndes Vivien, 105–122. Bristol: Policy Press.

Bell, Catherine. 1997. *Ritual: Perspectives and dimensions*. New York and Oxford: Oxford University Press.

Berger, Peter L. 1999. *The desecularization of the world*. Grand Rapids: Eerdmans.

Billis, David. 1993. *Organising public and voluntary agencies*. London: Routledge.

———. 2010. *Hybrid organizations and the third sector: Challenges for practice, theory and policy*. Basingstoke: Palgrave Macmillan.

Blumer, Herbert. 1969. *Symbolic interactionism*. Englewood Cliffs, New Jersey: Prentice Hall.

Brown, Callum G. 2001. *The death of Christian Britain*. London: Routledge.

Bruce, Stephen (ed.). 1992. *Religion and modernization: Sociologists and historians debate the secularization thesis*. Oxford: Clarendon Press.

———. 1995. *Religion in modern Britain*. Oxford: Oxford University Press.

Burdett, Ricky, and Deyan Sudjic (eds.). 2007. *The endless city*. London: Phaidon Press.

Chadwick, Owen. 1975. *The secularization of the European mind in the nineteenth century*. Cambridge: Cambridge University Press.

Chapman, Rachael. 2009. Faith and the voluntary sector in urban governance: Distinctive yet similar? In *Faith in the public realm: Controversies, policies and practices*, ed. Adam Dinham, Robert Furbey, and Vivien Lowndes, 203–222. Bristol: Policy Press.

Church of England, Lord Green Steering Group. 2014. Talent management for future leaders and leadership development for bishops and deans: A new approach. www.churchofengland.org/media/2130591/report.pdf. Accessed 18 Dec 2015.

Cox, Harvey. 1968. *The secular city*. Harmondsworth: Penguin (first published by the Macmillan Company, New York, in 1965).

Crockett, Alasdair, and David Voas. 2006. Generations of decline: Religious change in 20th century Britain. *Journal for the Scientific Study of Religion* 45(4): 567–584.

Davie, Grace. 1994. *Religion in Britain since 1945: Believing without belonging*. Oxford: Blackwell.

———. 2002. *Europe: The exceptional case: Parameters of faith in the modern world*. London: Darton, Longman and Todd.

De la Bedoyere, Quentin. 2015. The plot to eradicate faith schools. *Catholic Herald*, 30th July 2015. www.catholicherald.co.uk/issues/july-31-2015/the-plot-to-eradicate-faith-schools/. Accessed 18 Dec 2015.

Department for Communities and Local Government. 2012. Eric Pickles gives councils back the freedom to pray. www.gov.uk/government/news/eric-pickles-gives-councils-back-the-freedom-to-pray--2. Accessed 18 Dec 2015.

Department for Education. 2014. *School admissions code*. London: Department for Education. www.gov.uk/government/publications/school-admissions-code--2. Accessed 18 Dec 2015.

DiMaggio, Paul, and W. Powell. 1983. The iron cage revisited: Conformity and diversity in organisational fields. *American Sociological Review* 48: 147–160.

Dinham, Adam, and Vivien Lowndes. 2009. Faith and the public realm. In *Faith in the public realm: Controversies, policies and practices*, ed. Adam Dinham, Robert Furbey, and Vivien Lowndes, 1–19. Bristol: Policy Press.

Durkheim, Emile. 1915. *The elementary forms of the religious life*. London: George Allen and Unwin.

———. 1938. *The rules of sociological method*. Chicago: University of Chicago Press.

Furbey, Robert. 2009. Controversies of "public faith". In *Faith in the public realm: Controversies, policies and practices*, ed. Adam Dinham, Robert Furbey, and Vivien Lowndes, 21–40. Bristol: Policy Press.

Grant, Don, Kathleen M. O'Neil, and Laura S. Stephens. 2003. Neosecularization and craft versus professional religious authority in a nonreligious organization. *Journal for the Scientific Study of Religion* 42(3): 479–487.

Green, Laurie. 2008. Postcards from utopia. In *Building utopia? Seeking the authentic Church for new communities*, ed. Laurie Green and Christopher R. Baker, 1–21. London: SPCK.

———. 2010. "I can't go there!" The urban vocation. In *Crossover city: Resources for urban mission and transformation*, ed. Andrew Davey, 2–13. London: Mowbray.

Hirschle, Jochen. 2010. From religious to consumption-related routine activities? Analyzing Ireland's economic boom and the decline in church attendance. *Journal for the Scientific Study of Religion* 49(4): 673–687.

Iannaccone, Laurence R., and Sean F. Everton. 2004. Never on sunny days: Lessons from weekly attendance counts. *Journal for the Scientific Study of Religion* 43(2): 197–207.

Institute of Ideas. 2014. Keeping the faith schools? In *Battle of ideas*. London: Institute of Ideas. www.battleofideas.org.uk/2014/session_detail/8990. Accessed 18 Dec 2015.

Katz, Bruce, Andy Altman, and Julie Wagner. 2007. An agenda for the Urban Age. In *The endless city*, ed. Ricky Burdett and Deyan Sudjic, 474–481. London: Phaidon Press.

Kendall, Jeremy, and Martin Knapp. 1995. A loose and baggy monster: Boundaries, definitions and typologies. In *An introduction to the voluntary sector*, ed. Justin Davis Smith, Colin Rochester, and Rodney Hedley, 65–94. London: Routledge.

Martin, David. 1969. *The religious and the secular*. London: Routledge and Kegan Paul.

———. 1978. *A general theory of secularization*. Oxford: Blackwell.

———. 2005. *On secularisation: Towards a revised general theory*. Aldershot: Ashgate.

Mason, Rowena. 2014. Councils to be allowed to hold prayers at meetings under new bill. *The Guardian*, 18 December 2014. www.theguardian.com/society/2014/dec/18/local-councils-pray-meetings-bill. Accessed 18 Dec 2015.

Mumford, Lewis. 1961. *The city in history: It's origins, its transformations, and its prospects*. London: Secker and Warburg.

Olson, Paul J., and David Beckworth. 2011. Religious change and stability: Seasonality in church attendance from the 1940s to the 2000s. *Journal for the Scientific Study of Religion* 50(2): 388–396.

Presser, Stanley, and Mark Chaves. 2007. Is religious service attendance declining? *Journal for the Scientific Study of Religion* 46(3): 417–423.

Rochester, Colin, and Malcolm Torry. 2010. Faith-based organizations and hybridity: A special case? In *Hybrid organizations and the third sector: Challenges for practice, theory and policy*, ed. David Billis, 114–133. Basingstoke: Palgrave Macmillan.

Salamon, Lester M., and Helmut K. Anheier. 1993. Measuring the non-profit sector cross-nationally: A comparative methodology. *VOLUNTAS: International Journal of Voluntary and Nonprofit Organizations* 4(4): 530–554.

Taylor, Charles. 2007. *A secular age*. Cambridge: The Belknap Press of Harvard University Press.

Thatcher, Margaret. 1987. Interview for *Women's own*, London: Margaret Thatcher Foundation. www.margaretthatcher.org/document/106689. Accessed 3 Ded 2015.

Torry, Malcolm. 2005. *Managing God's business: Religious and faith-based organizations and their management*. Aldershot: Ashgate.

———. 2010. *Bridgebuilders: Workplace chaplaincy—A history*. Norwich: Canterbury Press.

———. 2012. Is there a faith sector? *Voluntary Sector Review* 3(1): 111–117.

———. 2014a. *Managing religion: The management of Christian religious and faith-based organizations*: vol 1, 'Internal relationships', Basingstoke: Palgrave Macmillan.

———. 2014b. *Managing religion: The management of Christian religious and faith-based organizations*: vol 2, 'External relationships', Basingstoke: Palgrave Macmillan.

United Nations News Centre. 2014. *More than half of world's population now living in urban areas*. United Nations News Centre: UN survey finds. www.un.org/apps/news/story.asp?NewsID=48240#. Accessed 18 Dec 2015.

Ward, Graham. 2009. *The politics of discipleship: Becoming postmaterial citizens*. London: SCM Press.

Weber, Max. 1922. The three types of legitimate rule, pp. 6–15 in Etzioni, Amitai and Lehman, E. (eds) (1980) *A sociological reader on complex organisations*, 3rd ed, Austin: Holt, Reinhart and Winston.

Wuthnow, Robert. 2009. *Boundless faith: The global outreach of American churches*. Berkeley: University of California Press.

2

Mediating Institutions Between Religion and the Workplace

Introduction

Workplace chaplaincy has been a sustained institutional approach to the relationship between religion and a secular world. In this chapter I shall tell some of the story of workplace chaplaincy in the UK, and then offer accounts of recent institutional engagement in the Thames Gateway and elsewhere, before drawing some conclusions.

Workplace Chaplaincy in the UK

During the First World War, the chaplains who lived and often died among the soldiers in the trenches discovered just how deep the gulf was between the Church and British working men. An important institutional response was ordination training open to men without university education (Church of England 1918: 54, 83, 161; Reiss 2013: 76–92).

During the Second World War, in Scotland (Ross 1997), in England, and on the Continent after the Normandy landings, the clergy of the main denominations were active in pastoral care: providing liturgy,

© The Editor(s) (if applicable) and The Author(s) 2016
M. Torry, *Mediating Institutions*,
DOI 10.1057/978-1-349-94913-7_2

spiritual counsel, and whatever needed doing. In South London, Cuthbert Bardsley, the Church of England Rector of Woolwich, regularly visited workers in the air raid shelters at Siemens Brothers, a large engineering company. After the war, a growing loose network of chaplains visiting the industries along the South Bank of the Thames became the South London Industrial Mission (SLIM). Lunchtime services at the Cathedral would attract congregations of two hundred; study groups were held in works canteens; lectures were held after work; and weekend conferences provided opportunities for fellowship and education. In such events, and particularly in the annual industrial harvest thanksgiving service in Southwark Cathedral, SLIM was an organisation mediating between religious and secular organisations. The purpose of all of this activity was to 'bring the Christian Faith into close relation with the workaday world' (Cuttell 1962: 60): it was 'reconciliation', between the two institutions of Christian Faith and the working world, as well as between institutions within the working world such as trades unions and managements. A further mediating institution was language. After the Second World War the whole country was engaged in 'reconstruction', and both the Cathedral and SLIM hitched their mediating activities to this word with which both religious and secular organisations could identify.

By the 1980s regular meetings and conferences for working men and women had largely ceased, but until the 1990s chaplains continued to visit the declining number of industrial premises in South London. By the turn of the millennium it had become difficult to negotiate chaplaincies, the denominations had removed posts and funding, and the South London Industrial Mission ceased to function. For fifty years SLIM had created a bridge between the Christian Faith and the Church on one side, and working men and women, and industrial and other institutions, on the other. SLIM's closure was a result of the churches becoming more interested in themselves than in the institutions of the society within which they operated, and industrial and other private and public sector organisations ceasing to see the point of an institutional connection with the churches or with their representative personnel. Institutional secularisation had increased, and the mediating institution that for half a century had attempted to tackle it had not possessed the autonomy necessary to enable it to continue in the face of increasing indifference in religious and secular institutions.

The picture was similar elsewhere in the UK. Take, for instance, Sheffield. Ted Wickham, who had worked in industry before ordination, spent much of the Second World War visiting a large arms manufacturing company in Staffordshire. After the war, Leslie Hunter, Bishop of Sheffield, invited him to Sheffield. Wickham and a growing team of chaplains visited the large steelworks around the city, joined in informal gatherings of workers at break times, and organised their own discussion meetings. In both South London and in Sheffield the chaplains would seek out individuals – often trade union shop stewards – to co-ordinate group meetings and to disseminate information. The aim was institutional: to 'influence the influences' (Wickham 1964: 19). Even the visiting of individuals on the factory floor was done with an institutional intent: 'to create a web of relationships' (Wickham 1957: 245).

There were a number of significant differences between the South London and Sheffield experiences of industrial mission. In South London there were few large companies, and most of the companies that chaplains visited were small businesses. In Sheffield it was all large steel mills and engineering companies. In South London, most of the chaplains were also parish priests, whereas in Sheffield a large team of full-time chaplains was created. In South London an important aim was to retain deep relationships with local congregations, because one of the purposes was to relate the Church to the world of work. In Sheffield, chaplains would sometimes hold congregations and their clergy in contempt. This was no way to mediate between the Church and industry as institutions, and was one of the roots of the crisis that occurred during the early 1970s when a new Senior Chaplain imposed a more Church-centred theology on the Mission. Chaplains who disagreed with the new approach either left or were dismissed. The new Bishop of Sheffield supported the Senior Chaplain. Between them they had yanked the Mission towards the Church and away from the industrial world with which the chaplains had been attempting to identify.

Renamed the South Yorkshire Workplace Chaplaincy, workplace chaplaincy continues in and around Sheffield. The purpose of the chaplaincy is now

1. The promotion of spiritual hospitality within the whole work/learning community.

2. The provision of confidential pastoral/spiritual support to all individuals.
3. To contribute to various programmes and events which promote spiritual hospitality and the understanding and valuing of cultural diversity and differing religious/spiritual/beliefs/values.
4. The promotion of good relations and well-being in the work/learning community.
5. An independent caring and professional perspective on the religious and multi-cultural issues associated with your organisation and the life of the community within it. (South Yorkshire Workplace Chaplaincy 2015)

Chaplains are provided to companies on the basis of service level agreements. No longer is the bridging of a gulf between secular and religious institutions an aim, as it was at the beginning.

During the First World War, the Church of England and other churches in the UK had come to understand the gulf between the Church and the Christian Faith on the one hand, and working class people and industrial organisations on the other; and during and after the Second World War a large number of industrial missions were established to function as mediating institutions. Most of these institutions have either closed or their missions have drifted from bridging the gulfs between secular and religious institutions to serving individual needs and the internal dynamics of secular organisations. But as the rest of this chapter will show, a new wave of mediating institutions has now come into being to take up the original vision.

The Greenwich Peninsula in the Twenty-First Century

The Greenwich Peninsula is East of the centre of London and is surrounded by a river deep enough for large ships, so it is no surprise that it boasts a history of industry that required bulky raw materials, manufactured bulky items, or made smells which those West of the Peninsula did not wish to experience. At various times a soap works, a food refinery, a power station, engineering companies, an undersea cables manufacturer, and aggregates yards have been located there, and, until the advent of natural gas, Europe's largest gasworks was to be found at the northern end of the Peninsula. In the middle of the Peninsula were playing fields and social clubs belonging to some of the industrial concerns; and nearer to the river there were allotments.

By the 1990s, the Peninsula to the East of the Blackwall Tunnel approach road was mostly polluted and derelict. The gas works had gone, as had the power station and the engineering companies. All that was left was a yacht club, the Pilot Inn, a row of cottages, and, to the South, some aggregates yards. To the West of the approach road were more aggregates yards (useful for the many construction projects along the Thames Gateway), the food refinery, and the cable manufacturer, which now concentrates on signal boosters and related equipment rather than on the cables themselves. Where the tunnel approach road now is, and to the South of where the gas works had once stood, there used to be a residential community occupying houses built by the gas works and by other industrial concerns to house their own workers. Next to the approach road the community's school still stands: a large three-storey building, now used as a museum store; and next to that is a small engineering company, on land once occupied by the parish church, St. Andrew's, built by the gas company for its employees.

The first sign of new life was the battle for a tube station. The docks north of the river were long closed, and during the early 1980s the Government had recognised their potential as a site for new office development to relieve pressure on the crowded City of London. The boroughs involved had done nothing, so the Government established an Urban Development Corporation to take over planning powers from local authorities. The practical problem was that there was no transport link to central London, or to anywhere else. The Jubilee Line extension was therefore planned to link central London, Canary Wharf, and Stratford (already planned to be a future transport hub). The new line was to link Waterloo, London Bridge, the East London Line (at Canada Water), Canary Wharf, and Stratford. No stations were planned for Southwark, Bermondsey, or the Greenwich Peninsula, even though the line would pass immediately below all three. The plans looked like evidence for an intense and irrational prejudice against South London among transport planners. Southwark Council and Simon Hughes MP mounted a successful campaign for stations at Southwark and Bermondsey (arguing that regeneration of both communities required better public transport links), and Greenwich Council mounted an equally vigorous campaign for a station on the Greenwich Peninsula, successfully arguing that this huge tract of land would never be developed without adequate public transport being provided. (The most recent example of transport planners' prejudice against South London was the plan to take the new Crossrail line underneath Woolwich without building a station there. A station is now to be built, but only because sufficient private funding has been secured from the developers of the Woolwich Arsenal site).

Because there was to be a station opening on the Greenwich Peninsula, Greenwich was able to bid for the Millennium Exhibition being planned to celebrate the turn of the Millennium. Many of us thought that Birmingham might be a better place for the exhibition, because of its more central location, and because Birmingham already possessed good transport links: but Greenwich won the competition (London bias among policy-makers?), and in 1996 it was announced that a Millennium Dome would be built on the Greenwich Peninsula to house the Millennium Exhibition. When the Labour Party won the General Election in 1997, the Government affirmed its commitment to the exhibition. Strangely, Michael Heseltine, the Conservative minister originally in charge of the project, had kept the exhibition in-house. The new Labour Government had not yet learnt to contract out public services, and so maintained this position. It is remarkable that such a massive and innovative building, containing a complex exhibition, all organised by a civil servant, Jennie Page, opened on time. (Don't believe all that you might have read in the press about the cost of the project. The land had to be decontaminated, new roads had to be built, and all of the mains services had to be laid to the site. Somebody was going to have to pay for all of that one day if the Peninsula was ever to be developed. It just happened to be the Millennium Experience Company that had to pay for much of it so that the Millennium Exhibition could open at the beginning of 2000). Just as remarkable – given the way in which the Jubilee Line extension was held to ransom by electricians – was the opening of North Greenwich Station in 1999, in time for the exhibition.

The Millennium Exhibition was superb. The predicted number of visitors did not materialise, and a few of the exhibition zones left rather a lot to be desired, but most of the exhibition was imaginative and contained cutting edge technology. Numerous visitors came back four or five times, and the exhibition achieved the highest number of visitors for any visitor attraction in the UK that year. It also obtained the highest visitor approval rating. Admission was incredibly cheap considering that the ticket price included the exhibition zones, a new Blackadder film, and the superb central acrobatic show.

It is with the Millennium Exhibition that the modern story of the faith communities' involvement on the Peninsula begins. I was licensed to serve in the Parish of East Greenwich in February 1996 on the day on which it was announced that the Millennium Exhibition was to be held in the parish. Greenwich has for many years had a functioning set of Ecumenical Borough Deans. Each denomination appoints one, and they meet regularly so that the churches in the borough can work together to relate to the civic authorities, and particularly to the local authority, the health services, and the Metropolitan Police. When the Millennium Exhibition was announced, the Borough Deans established a quarterly forum to enable churches to share information about activity during the millennium year. This was to ensure that two churches would not be doing different things at the same time in the same place, and that what could best be done together would be done together. (The Parish of East Greenwich gave birth to the Greenwich Passion Play, with a cast of 800 in Greenwich Park on Good Friday 2000, but the event involved people from all over the borough of Greenwich and beyond because the forum enabled regular communication to occur). The forum established subgroups, and one of these was on chaplaincy for the Millennium Exhibition. There was a general understanding (partly mediated by the Lambeth Group, chaired by the Archbishop's Chaplain, and containing representatives of a variety of faiths) that because the turn of the Millennium was a celebration of the two thousandth anniversary of Jesus' birth (give or take three or four years), the religious content of the exhibition should be multi faith but with a significant Christian element. So the Faith Zone had two elements: an exhibition of the ways in which the nine major world Faiths celebrate a variety of life events; and an exhibition on the history and current reality of the Christian Faith. Churches Together in England – England's churches' umbrella group – was already interested in facilitating a Christian chaplaincy; and our local group asked if Nicholas Rothon, already seconded by the Roman Catholic Church to the Churches' Millennium Office, could be asked to co-ordinate the Chaplaincy. Churches Together in England agreed.

The twenty-strong volunteer chaplaincy contained Christians of a variety of denominations, and it was a pleasure to belong to such a committed and pastorally skilled group of people. Whenever the Exhibition was open there were two chaplains present. We led Christian prayers both morning and afternoon in the Prayer Space that we managed for the people of any faith to use, either as individuals, or as groups to celebrate particular faiths' festivals. (Because the Millennium Dome was paid for with National Lottery money, Muslims built their own small Mosque outside the Dome, although individual Muslims sometimes visited the Prayer Space. The chaplains had a good relationship with the visiting Imam). Some chaplains preferred to locate themselves in the Prayer Space so that they could welcome people who came in; some preferred to wander the Dome, meeting staff and visitors; and some of us spent many hours in the staff canteen, meeting members of staff during their breaks.

At the end of 2000 the exhibition closed, John Prescott, the Deputy Prime Minister, came to thank the staff and the chaplains treated Nicholas Rothon to lunch and a gift. We agreed with the Millennium Experience Company that I would remain as a chaplain to the security guards and maintenance team at the Dome, so I watched the zones and buildings inside the Dome dismantled, watched everything from exhibition zones to saucepans auctioned off, and one day looked across the floor of the Dome and saw simply an empty space. For four years I visited the handful of workers still working at the Dome, and read press reports of the Government's unsuccessful attempts to find a new use for the building. Finally English Partnerships, which was by then the landowner, recognised that only a scheme that involved most of the Peninsula was going to work, because only such a scheme would encourage the kind of major investment that both the Dome and the huge amount of empty land would require. A masterplan competition was held, and in the Autumn of 2002 the winner was announced: Meridian Delta Ltd.

(MDL) (now Greenwich Peninsula Regeneration Ltd.: GPRL): a consortium of LendLease, an Australian multinational construction company, and Quintain Estates, which owns land on the Western side of the Peninsula. An additional partner was Anschutz Entertainment Group (AEG), which is what it says it is: an entertainment empire wholly owned by Philip Anschutz. The deal was that AEG would develop the Dome as a major entertainment venue, and build a hotel next to it, and that the consortium would develop a ring of office blocks around the Dome and the rest of the land as a residential community of 10,000 homes on the rest of the land.

When it is finished this development will contain a transport hub, the world's most successful arena and its associated entertainment district, hotels, large office blocks (containing enough space to fill two and a half Canary Wharf towers), Ravensbourne College (a relocated highly successful design and media higher education college), and enough housing for a new town when added to the existing Greenwich Millennium Village at the southern end of the Peninsula.

The first we saw of the plans for most of the Peninsula was when the winning masterplan was published. I phoned MDL, and after being passed from one person to another, I found myself talking to Susie Wilson, appointed to manage the developer's relationship with the surrounding community. I suggested to her that in a community of over 20,000 there might be some who wished to practice their religion, and that there might be religious organisations that wished to serve the new community, yet the masterplan had allowed not a single square inch for religious buildings. We agreed to meet, and found that we had a mutual friend, Malcolm Cooper, the industrial chaplain at Bluewater, the new shopping centre outside Dartford. LendLease had recently built Bluewater, and Susie had fulfilled there a similar function to the one that she was now undertaking on the Peninsula. We fixed a meeting in March 2003 to which came representatives of the borough's multi faith forum, the Ecumenical Borough Deans, Stephen Pallett from Greenwich Council, and Susie. It was the most creative half hour meeting that I have ever attended. The faith communities promised to work together in the new community, and to provide a chaplaincy service to every institution and at every stage of the development; and MDL and Greenwich

Council promised a building, and a temporary building from which the faith communities could serve the new community if the permanent building was delayed. A steering group was appointed from among the faith community representatives at the meeting, and I was appointed Site Chaplain.

We established the Greenwich Peninsula Chaplaincy as a charitable trust, and when in 2005 construction of the huge arena and surrounding restaurants and bars began inside the Dome (renamed The O2), we provided a team of three chaplains for the construction workers, and quickly recruited another five to create a team of eight, so that we could ensure that for part of every working day there would be a chaplain on the site. The construction company, Sir Robert McAlpine, welcomed the chaplains' presence, and Greenwich Local Labour and Business (GLLaB: the employment and training agency established by Greenwich Council to ensure that as many construction jobs went to local people as possible) provided us with health and safety training. Ongoing training for chaplains has twice been provided by Greenwich Community College working with the chaplaincy to create an accredited course on chaplaincy skills and community development. These training relationships constitute interesting mediating institutions in their own right, lying as they do between religious organisations (the faith communities to which chaplains belong) and the secular training organisations.

At the height of the construction project there were two thousand construction workers inside the Dome working on a complex and often innovative project. The twenty thousand seat arena had to be built without the use of cranes, so when the four and a half thousand ton steel roof was built it had to be constructed on the ground, jacked up, and twisted onto a ring of concrete towers built to very fine tolerances by a process of continuous pouring as the wooden shuttering was slowly jacked up. We quickly learnt important facts about the construction industry, and particularly that nationalities had their specialities: Indian gangs poured concrete, the Scottish and Irish dug holes in the ground, Turks laid paving stones, Romanians constructed scaffolding, and other Eastern Europeans did pretty well everything else.

A major difference from the previous Dome chaplaincy team was that now there were Muslim and Sikh members of the team as well as

Christians: but there was still the same diversity of approach, with some chaplains preferring to wander the site, some to visit the site offices, some to spend hours in the canteens, and some to do a bit of everything.

The arena was already taking shape inside the Dome when the Government decided that there were to be several major new casinos, and one massive 'regional' one. AEG wanted a huge casino inside The O2, and Greenwich bid for a licence. The chaplaincy held a consultation among the faith communities of Greenwich, and wrote a paper that explained the differing views that the different faiths held on gambling (most against, some Christian churches ambivalent, and the Roman Catholic Church in favour), but which also explained that the consensus was that East Greenwich had problems enough, and that a regional casino would increase the opportunities for problem gambling, and would result in more damaged families. (I had asked what kind of casino was envisaged, to discover that most of it would be rows of slot machines.) We promised to support workers and punters if a casino was built, but the message of our paper was consistently negative towards the idea. It was therefore something of a surprise to be told that the Government's Casino Advisory Panel website contained a paper purporting to be from us and saying that we approved of a casino, and particularly of the employment that it would bring into the borough. I wrote an email to the Borough Council and to AEG, and received an apology from the latter – and early the following morning a phone call from the BBC told me that someone had leaked our emails and that they were all over the press.[1] I had four television news film crews through the vicarage door that day. Some of the press coverage was quite intelligent, comparing our own position paper with the paper on the Casino Advisory Panel website.

The furore died down, and I was invited to attend the public hearing on Greenwich's bid for the casino. Strangely, I was seated with the borough council's delegation. Opposite us were the seats for objectors, including a seat for the Salvation Army, which rather unfortunately remained empty. I made the obvious point that if there were to be a casino in The O2 then no Muslim, Hindu, Sikh, or Pentecostal Christian would wish to work there, thus making a diverse workforce unlikely; and that members of

---

[1] http://news.sky.com/story/450818/new-row-over-casino-dome

these communities, and more generally families with children, would be unlikely to visit the venue.

The regional casino was awarded to Manchester, which made us somewhat sorry for Manchester: but then the Archbishop of Canterbury told the House of Lords that he could not see how the words 'regeneration' and 'casino' connected with each other, the House of Lords established a committee to look into the issue, and when Gordon Brown became Prime Minister his 'moral compass' took casinos off the agenda. To everyone's credit the chaplaincy remained friends with AEG and with Greenwich Council. The space in The O2 intended for the casino remains empty. The O2 is a magnificent entertainment venue, with the world's most successful arena (on a variety of criteria), a diverse workforce, and a diverse visitor profile.

The Greenwich Peninsula Chaplaincy recruited some more chaplains, and when The O2 opened, the Entertainment District Manager, Malcolm Tilsed, helped us to negotiate chaplaincy arrangements with each of the restaurants and bars in Entertainment Avenue, the internal street running round the interior of The O2. We established four pairs of chaplains, one pair for each day from Monday to Thursday, with each pair being allocated its own group of restaurants and bars to visit; and we also appointed chaplains to visit nightclub staff, first of all in the smaller Inc Club, and subsequently in the massive Matter nightclub. The chaplaincy's work then expanded elsewhere. With the South London Industrial Mission's demise, my own longstanding chaplaincy work at the food refinery came under the auspices of the Greenwich Peninsula Chaplaincy; and we established a team of chaplains for ASDA, in the retail park to the South-east of the Peninsula. In 2009 the Borough Commander asked us to provide chaplains for Plumstead Police Station, so we created a team of four (a Hindu, a Sikh, a Muslim, and myself). Throughout, we have provided chaplains for construction sites on the Peninsula, first of all in the Greenwich Millennium Village, then for Bovis LendLease as Ravensbourne College and the Transport for London offices were built just south of The O2, then at the site where the first high-rise residential block was being built, and subsequently on other sites.

This is all old-fashioned workplace chaplaincy – chaplains visiting workplaces, to listen to workers, and to respond to their spiritual and other needs: but it is also quite diverse. At the food refinery, some of the employees had worked on the site for thirty years by the time the plant closed, so a chaplain visiting for thirteen years could get to know quite a lot of people quite well. Restaurant staff working in The O2 might only be there for a week or two before moving to another branch of the chain, or to another job. Construction sites are somewhere between the two: a small group of workers will be on the site from the beginning of the project to its completion two years later: but most of the workers will work on the site for a week or two before moving to another project.

The approach is a mixture of pastoral care and institutional engagement. Availability is exercised through being there: through walking around construction sites, the college, The O2, and police stations (but not when the office doors are shut); or by sitting in staff canteens and joining in conversations if that appears to be welcome. Availability invites conversations in which chaplains listen to the concerns of the workers that they are spending time with. This is a task that takes patience and sensitivity, and sometimes it leads from listening to individuals' concerns to engagement with the organisations in which they are working, or with some other institution, such as a trade union. Sometimes it is the chaplain who finds themselves pursuing an issue, gently and privately, through the communication channels of an organisation; and sometimes, at a quarterly chaplains' and welcomers' meeting, the Co-ordinating Chaplain will hear chaplains express concerns about a company or a situation, and will decide to investigate the issue and then to communicate with managers or others who either have – or ought to have – an interest in the issue.

Following agreement at the meeting in March 2003 to a permanent building for the faith communities to use together, and to a temporary building if that were to be delayed, it became clear at the beginning of the 2008 recession that the building of the high-rise blocks along the eastern edge of the Peninsula was going to be a slow business. The trigger date for the temporary building (related to the building of the first residential block) was then reached, so in July 2010 three lorries delivered three sections of a large portakabin to a site close to North Greenwich Station; and by September 2010 the building was ready and was officially opened by the Mayor of Greenwich. In 2013 the building was expanded in the process of moving it to a new site next to the cable car station.

As soon as we knew that the temporary Prayer Space would be delivered, we recruited a team of volunteer welcomers to staff the building for three hours a day so that individuals could use it for prayer and reflection, for a conversation with a welcomer, or just for some peace and quiet. Most of the building's visitors are people working or studying in the institutions at the northern end of the Peninsula: The O2, Greenwich Borough Council, the shops, Transport for London, construction sites, and Ravensbourne College. The welcomers also welcome individual faith communities that use the Prayer Space for their own events on the basis of agreements with the Greenwich Peninsula Chaplaincy Steering Group. Baha'i, Muslim and Christian groups have all used the building in this way. Above all, the Prayer Space is *there*. From being a place with no religious buildings, the Peninsula is now a place in which a clearly religious building is one of the early arrivals. The building enables faith communities and the chaplaincy to serve the religious and other needs of people living in, working in, and visiting the Peninsula, and enables individuals and faith communities to express and nurture their religious commitments.

There are some significant differences between the Greenwich Peninsula Chaplaincy and the industrial missions of the last century. First of all, the Greenwich Peninsula Chaplaincy is composed entirely of volunteers, including the Co-ordinating Chaplain. This means that few financial resources are needed, and the organisation is not vulnerable to closure by funders. It can suffer from reductions in available voluntary labour, of course, but an occasional reduction in voluntary labour can always be repaired by a recruitment drive, whereas an organisation that closes because it can no longer afford paid staff is difficult to revive. Secondly, the Greenwich Peninsula Chaplaincy is multi faith. Some of the more traditional industrial missions have now branded themselves as workplace chaplaincies and claim to be multi faith, but there are none that I know of that are genuinely multi faith in the sense in which the Greenwich Peninsula Chaplaincy (GPC) is. The GPC has a constitution that privileges no particular faith community, and it has no structural links with any particular faith communities. It issues contracts to faith communities for the use of the Prayer Space, but those contracts are entirely under the control of the GPC's trustees, and the contracts leave the trustees entirely in charge of the chaplains' team and of everything that happens in the Prayer Space. Any of the posts, including that of Co-ordinating Chaplain, can be occupied by members of any faith community. When in 2014 I ceased to be Co-ordinating Chaplain, the trustees appointed my Muslim colleague to co-ordinate the team of chaplains. The genuinely multi faith character of the GPC means that it is easier to negotiate chaplaincies than it would be for a chaplaincy structurally connected to a particular faith community; and it means that no individual faith community can close down the chaplaincy. What has emerged on the Greenwich Peninsula is therefore a mediating institution that is potentially more robust than alternative kinds of workplace chaplaincies, and one that is mediating in a second sense, in that it can mediate between the institutions of different faith communities as well as between religious and secular institutions.

The involvement of a variety of faith communities is not simply theoretical. Since 2003, the Greenwich Islamic Centre (the Woolwich Mosque) has provided a trustee and a particularly hard working chaplain who visits The O2, Ravensbourne College, a police station, and construction sites. Muslim Friday Prayers are held in the Prayer Space. Sikh Temples in Greenwich have provided five chaplains at various times, and also a trustee. The Hindu Temple has provided welcomers and chaplains. The Local Spiritual Assembly of Baha'is has provided two successive trustees and has used the Prayer Space for its meetings. Bromley Synagogue has provided a trustee. The Methodist and United Reformed Churches have between them provided three chaplains and a trustee, and for some time used the Prayer Space for a fellowship group on Thursday mornings. The Roman Catholic Church has provided a trustee and a chaplain. The Salvation Army has provided a chaplain. Evangelical Free Churches have provided a trustee who for over ten years has been chair of the board of trustees. The Church of England has provided trustees (including the treasurer) and several chaplains, including quite a number from the Parish of East Greenwich.

The reason that members of very different faith communities can work together so happily is that the chaplaincy has established some firm rules that nobody is allowed to break. Everything that everyone can agree to do together in good conscience is done together: so the different faiths work together to manage the workplace chaplains' team, the Prayer Space, a team of welcomers, events, newsletters, a website, training courses, and an intercessions request book in the Prayer Space: but the different faith communities never worship or pray together, and each one only offers education or instruction in their own faith. Prayers at noon on weekdays are Christian; prayers at 1.15 p.m. on Fridays are Muslim. Worship on Sundays is Christian. Also helpful are the guidelines to which chaplains and welcomers are expected to adhere. Chaplains and welcomers are welcome to use the resources of their own faiths to meet individuals' spiritual and other needs, and if asked about their own faiths they can offer explanations; but no chaplain or welcomer can of their own volition try to persuade someone else of the virtue or truth of their own faith. There are fine lines here, but the chaplains and welcomers have become expert at navigating them.

The Greenwich Peninsula, with The O2, the college, construction sites, offices occupied by Greenwich Borough Council and Transport for London, a transport hub at North Greenwich Station, and growing residential communities, is in many ways a microcosm of the world in which we now live; and the Greenwich Peninsula Chaplaincy is the kind of mediating institution that we shall need in every community of institutions if relationships between faith communities and the organisations and other institutions of civil society are to be constructive. In the highly secular world of such institutions as entertainment organisations, higher education colleges, retail parks, construction sites, and police stations, religious organisations are unlikely to be able to form structural relationships with such secular organisations, both because of the gap between secular and religious presuppositions and language, and because no modern secular organisation that employs staff from a variety of ethno-religious communities will want to be seen to be favouring one faith community over others. A workplace chaplaincy with clear rules and guidelines, offering something to organisations and their personnel that might be useful to them – and offering it on a genuinely multi faith basis – is the kind of mediating organisation that might enable a genuine relationship to occur between the secular organisations within which its chaplains work, and the religious organisations from which those chaplains come, and to which the chaplaincy relates in a variety of different ways – through its board of trustees, its advisory council, the events it holds, and countless personal relationships. The relationships between chaplains, their faith communities, and the many people among whom they work, form a web of personal relationships that can constitute a deep relationship between secular and religious organisations and their personnel, thus generating institutional relationships between institutions. Greenwich Council and Anschutz Entertainment Group were able to regard the Greenwich Peninsula Chaplaincy as a legitimate conversation partner in relation to its application for a major casino because the Chaplaincy could represent the views of the borough's faith communities, and because at a variety of different levels, from the personal to the organisational, it already had good relationships with all of the parties involved.

It is difficult to see how any of this could have been achieved if we had not established the Greenwich Peninsula Chaplaincy as a mediating institution.

Bluewater

North Kent, being on the North Downs, was once a major cement manufacturing area. (When I grew up in Dartford, the cement works to the east used to spread their dust across the town when the wind was from that direction). Left over from that era are the chalk quarries scattered across North Kent. One of these, now known as Eastern Quarry, is being turned into a housing development. Next door is the quarry that is now home to Bluewater: a 'destination' containing shops (including John Lewis, Marks & Spencer, and House of Fraser), restaurants, and a cinema. Families go there for the day; and at weekends and on bank holidays, at around 10 a.m., the queues for the A2 Bluewater exit can stretch a mile or more.

Malcolm Cooper, a Methodist minister, worked for Kent Workplace Mission. When LendLease started to build Bluewater he became the chaplain to the construction site, and when the centre opened he recruited a team of Christian clergy and laypeople from a variety of denominations to be volunteer chaplains to the various shops and restaurants. This became a very stable team, and Malcolm's many years at Bluewater gave him a deep knowledge of the centre as a whole, of its management, and of the many different venues located there.

As well as pastoral care, Malcolm's and the team's long involvement meant that they could find themselves involved in issues facing Bluewater and its workers. A particularly interesting one was Boxing Day opening. At first, no shops opened on Boxing Day. Then some shops wanted to open, even though their workers had no wish to work on Boxing Day. Some of the shops opened, but John Lewis did not. Then John Lewis, fearful for its market share, followed the others. Where regulation is lacking, commercial competition will always compromise workers' rights.

Malcolm Cooper retired in 2011, and in 2012 Ray Borrett was appointed jointly by Bluewater and Kent Workplace Mission (which also manages industrial, police, transport, careworker, local authority, and some other retail chaplaincies). The brief was to develop the chaplaincy in a more multi faith direction, so there is now an Imam appointed by the Muslim Chaplains' Association (which is branching out beyond its prison chaplaincy focus), and there is also a Rabbi who visits regularly. Most of the visiting work continues to be undertaken by the sixteen volunteer Christian chaplains.

Ray is employed by Kent Workplace Mission, but is also a member of Bluewater's senior management team; and while such dual accountability might potentially cause conflicts of interest, its virtue is that it institutionalises the mediating function of the Bluewater chaplaincy as a whole, and of Ray's chaplaincy role in particular. When Malcolm Cooper arrived as chaplain of the construction site, the money for the post came from the Methodist Church: but now, even though Ray is employed and paid by Kent Workplace Mission, most of the money comes from Bluewater. Whether companies should be paying for their chaplains has for many years been a live issue in the workplace chaplaincy movement (Torry 2010: 88, 171–2). In the case of Bluewater, the financial arrangements cohere with the overall institutional arrangements, so they make sense, and arguably contribute to the chaplain's and the chaplaincy's role as a mediating institution between a secular retail destination and the faith communities to which the chaplaincy relates. In such a context, critical comment on Bluewater's policies and practices will inevitably be in private (one to one, or in closed meetings such as the store managers' forum), but the fact that Kent Workplace Mission and the Methodist Church are represented alongside Bluewater's management on a chaplaincy steering board ensures a continuing level of autonomy for the chaplaincy that balances the lack of autonomy implied by Ray's membership of Bluewater's senior management team.

In order to be a mediating institution, a chaplaincy needs to relate as closely to religious organisations as it does to the managements and institutions of secular organisations. The Bluewater chaplaincy relates directly to the congregations from which its volunteer chaplains are drawn (– many of the chaplains are local ministers); it relates to the churches at regional level through Kent Workplace Mission; it is actively supported by the umbrella body Churches Together, Ebbsfleet; and Ray preaches in local churches as often as he can. In a context in which a chaplaincy's autonomy is constantly at risk of being compromised by payment by the industry visited and by management arrangements, deep connections with faith communities at a variety of levels are essential.

As well as the pastoral care of workers, and sometimes of customers, the chaplaincy is now structurally involved in Bluewater's staff wellbeing strategy, in its major incident plan, and in its mental health first aid network. The chaplaincy co-ordinates Bluewater's team of counsellors, and it hosts the community forum through which Bluewater relates to the local area. In relation to each of these activities, and in relation to the package as a whole, the chaplaincy functions as a mediating institution.

Another important task of the chaplaincy is to manage 'The Place of Quiet', a welcoming space available to staff and customers of any faith or none. Around the walls of the circular space visitors will find alcoves containing objects and sacred texts relating to a variety of faiths, and there are ablutions facilities for Muslims, Hindus and others to use. There is also a space for conversation with a chaplain.

Essential to the Bluewater chaplaincy's role as a mediating institution is the employment of a full-time chaplain. In purely practical terms, the management of a large team of volunteer chaplains and of a prayer room is made a lot easier by the presence of a full-time co-ordinator, and communication between the chaplaincy and the many organisations within Bluewater is made easier by there being a single and constantly available communication channel: but perhaps even more important, the full-time chaplain becomes a mediating institution in his own right in ways that volunteer chaplains who give a few hours a week cannot. This aspect of the full-time chaplain's role is enhanced by the particular institutional arrangements at Bluewater.

In relation to the Bluewater chaplaincy's multi faith aspect, the journey has begun. There are now relationships with recognised personnel from three faith communities, and with the institutions of more than one faith. Ray chairs the North Kent Council for Interfaith Relations, which supports the chaplaincy. However, Kent Workplace Mission remains a Christian organisation, so the chaplaincy remains institutionally Christian. This means that while the chaplaincy can be a mediating institution between the Christian Faith and Bluewater, it struggles to relate Bluewater to faith communities in general. To my knowledge, no chaplaincy has yet managed to make the journey from a 'host and hosted' model (in which a particular faith community makes space for other faith communities to join in) to a 'level playing field' model (in which no faith community has a privileged role). Bluewater might therefore have to live with a partially completed journey, which of course it might be perfectly willing to do.

The Bluewater chaplaincy acts as a highly effective mediating institution between Bluewater and religion (with religion represented more by the Christian Faith and its organisations and personnel than by other faith communities and their organisations and personnel). The recipe for this success includes a team of committed volunteer chaplains, a full-time chaplain, and institutional arrangements that tie the chaplain and the chaplaincy bloth to Bluewater and to North Kent's religious organisations.

Stratford City, the Athletes' Village, and the Olympic Park

The two places most clearly signed from Stratford Station are the Olympic Park and Stratford's Westfield Shopping Centre: a place a bit like Bluewater, except that it easier to get there by train than by car. The Stratford Westfield also has a 'rest and faith space', 'InSpiration'. Like Bluewater's 'Place of Quiet', this is managed by a Christian organisation, 'Inspire': a charitable company, the first charitable object of which is 'the advancement of the Christian religion'. The Rev'd Christiana Asinugo is half-time Vicar of St. Matthew's, Stratford, and half-time chaplain of Westfield, and she and a variety of groups and churches (and particularly St. John's, Stratford) organise Christian events in the 'rest and faith space', and manage a team of twenty volunteer chaplains. Multi faith relationships are also similar to those at Bluewater: an Imam visits the shopping centre and attends 'Inspire' meetings, but there is no structural connection with a Muslim organisation. The difference from Bluewater is that the Westfield chaplaincy is not embedded in Westfield as an organisation in the same way as the Bluewater chaplaincy is: and, in particular, Christiana is paid by the Diocese of Chelmsford, and not by Westfield. The Westfield chaplaincy is a mediating institution facilitating relationships between Westfield and the Christian Church – and the Church of England in particular.

The Westfield chaplaincy is by no means the only mediating institution in Stratford, so Stratford is the case study that I have found most difficult to allocate to a chapter. Either I had to break it up and locate different parts of it in the 'workplaces' and 'residential areas' chapters, or I had to keep it together in one of them, which is what I have chosen to do.

The Athletes' Village is an important part of the Olympic and Paralympic Games legacy. The athletes' accommodation is being turned into a whole new community, and two new twenty-one storey tower blocks are being built. The new community has its own new postal district: London E20. All of it is in the parish of St. Paul's, Stratford, which initially signposted new residents to nearby faith communities, but is now facilitating religious activity in the Village itself. Here the mediating institution is the Rev'd Annie McTighe, a pioneer minister attached to St. Paul's, who has already worked with the local health centre and residents' association to create a parents' and toddlers' group, and has established a monthly worship event in a restaurant. St. Paul's has also given birth to a temporary café that will be open for four months while the new community waits for a commercial café to open.

Annie combines her work in the Athletes' Village with being chaplain to the Olympic Park, and so is a mediating institution in another element of the Olympic and Paralympic legacy: and she fulfils the same function at Stratford International Station. The Vicar of St. Paul's, Stratford, the Rev'd Jeremy Fraser, who arrived from the Greenwich Peninsula in 2013, is a governor of the school that serves the Athletes' Village, and represents the school as a trustee of 'East Village', a charitable company that employs a £1m endowment from the Village development company to provide community facilities for the growing population of the Village. As well as chairing the Village's Safer Neighbourhood Committee, Annie is also a trustee of East Village, representing the Village's residents. The fact that both Jeremy and Annie have been appointed by secular organisations to a secular board of trustees, and that they cannot escape from their roles as representatives of a faith community, and will therefore be seen by other members of the board of trustees as representatives of the Church, means that they function as mediating institutions in this context, too.

The picture that is emerging is of mediating institutions constituted by individual members of the Church of England's clergy. Another piece of that picture is Carol Richards, who is Town Centre Chaplain to Stratford (under the auspices of the Essex Churches Council for Industry and Commerce: a Christian workplace chaplaincy organisation). Since 2007 Carol has chaired the Town Centre Forum where retailers and the managements of a variety of venues get together with representatives from the police and the borough council to communicate about joint activities and concerns. Carol is not a member of the clergy, but is commissioned for her role by St. John's Church in Stratford and by a Christian workplace chaplaincy organisation.

These personal mediating institutions are, of course, institutional (although not organisational), because it is their institutional connections that enables them to facilitate relationships between the religious and the secular. Stratford also benefits from organisational mediating institutions. 'Inspire' we have already mentioned. 'Faith in Schools' is a Christian organisation that offers volunteers to teach religious education in schools, and it also organises educational activities in church buildings for school classes to visit before the major Christian festivals. 'Transform Newham' is a charity that makes grants for mission activity (– for instance, for a youth worker at St. Paul's, Stratford), and so functions as a facilitator of mediating institutions.

During our account of the faith communities' relationships with new developments in Stratford – with Westfield, the Olympic Park, the town centre, and the Athletes' Village development – we have encountered rather a bewildering assortment of mediating institutions standing between religious and secular institutions. There isn't necessarily anything wrong with this, but where a multiplicity of mediating institutions emerges, some additional tasks need to be fulfilled. The complexity needs to be communicated to faith communities so that everyone knows which mediating institution is doing what; communication is needed with developers, local authorities, and other civil society institutions, so that they know to which mediating institutions they should relate; and the different mediating institutions might need an additional institution to mediate between them (– a function fulfilled for Christian mediating institutions by 'Churches Together, Stratford': an informal monthly meeting of representatives of churches). This is all very different from the simplicity of the situation on the Greenwich Peninsula, where a single mediating institution provides a single communication hub, automatically generating a clarity that, in contrast, faith communities and civil society organisations in Stratford have to work hard to create. A further difference is that in Stratford the mediating institutions are purely Christian. This means that other faith communities will be less related to those areas of the life of secular society where Christian mediating institutions are providing the links between religious and secular institutions.

This complex situation will continue to evolve. 'Olympicopolis' is now under construction in the Olympic Park: a new Victoria and Albert Museum, London College of Fashion campuses, a six hundred seat theatre, a choreography school for Sadler's Wells, and an outpost of the Smithsonian Institution. Creative digital companies are moving into buildings in the Olympic Park; and Transport for London and the Financial Conduct Authority are relocating offices into the new office buildings in Stratford. Even more new homes are planned around the area of the Olympic Park and in the centre of Stratford. In recognition of Stratford's importance to London's economy, Transport for London is reallocating all of the Stratford railway stations from Zone 3 to Zone 2 (Spittles 2015).

Most of the mediating institutions in Stratford are organised by the Church of England. It is therefore a problem that the huge Olympics development – encompassing the Athletes' Village and the Olympic Park – is in more than one parish; and even more of a problem that it is in four boroughs, two dioceses, two Episcopal areas, two archdeaconries, and four deaneries. Most of the Olympics stadia are in the Diocese of Chelmsford, but some of the buildings and some of the new developments are in the Diocese of London. Before and during the Olympic and Paralympic Games, both the Diocese of Chelmsford's and the Diocese of London's websites talked about the Olympics as if they were only in their territories. Duncan Green was either the Church of England's Olympics co-ordinator, or an appointee by the Dioceses of London, Chelmsford, and Southwark, or a secondee from the Diocese of Chelmsford, with no reference to anywhere else, depending on which website you read. Carol Richards, Annie McTighe, and others, have done what they can to share information across boundaries, but it might be preferable to move a few boundaries so that the entire development ends up in one borough: perhaps Newham, where much of it is. It might also be a good idea for Newham to develop a functioning Borough Deans network and a functioning inter faith forum, and, perhaps even more important, a multi faith umbrella mediating institution for all of the post-Olympic developments. A lot of good mediation between the faith communities and the complex institutions and populations of Stratford is already happening. A little more co-ordination could make it all a lot more effective.

Canary Wharf

The docks at the northern end of the Isle of Dogs on the north bank of the Thames were never going to survive in the new containerised world. (Tilbury survived rather than thrived because of trade union intransigence and management incompetence in the face of changing technology, and the subsequent migration of Europe's container hub to Rotterdam).

Plans came and went, and when a new conservative government came to power in 1979 it formed the London Docklands Development Corporation, took planning control away from the local authority, and in 1987 appointed the construction company Olympia and York to build office developments. Canary Wharf was born, and the same company (under different company names) has been in charge of creating and managing the development throughout. For many years there was just 1 Canada

Square, the square office block with a pyramid on top, largely because public transport links were so inadequate. The first part of the Docklands Light Railway had opened in 1987, ready for the tower's opening in 1988, but for ten years that was all there was. In 1999 the Jubilee Line extension linked Canary Wharf to central London and beyond, and a large collection of towers is now anchored among the old docks. The development as a whole covers 97 acres, and there are 15 million square feet of office and retail space. The defunct docks have been refurbished, and around them have grown blocks of expensive flats and lively retail and entertainment areas. From being something of a commercial anxiety in its early days, Canary Wharf is rapidly becoming a significant extension of the capital's financial centre. It weathered the recent recession relatively unscathed.

The Church's relationship with Canary Wharf got off to a bad start. The development area was in two parishes: St. Anne's, Limehouse, and the Parish of Poplar; and it borders the parish of Christ Church, Isle of Dogs. When the development was announced, local clergy led a procession round the island, with a coffin at its head. Local people's feelings were understandable, and it was also understandable for the churches to be clearly on the side of the existing residential community. Because planning control had been removed from local authorities to an unaccountable quango, local people really did have no say in what was going to be happening on their doorstep – a common experience in the Thames Gateway (Fox 2008a: 38) – and they quite correctly foresaw that the place in which they lived was about to be radically transformed (Hamnett 2003: 241–5). But that is as far as the parishes' relationship with the development went. As building began, there was little contact between the three parishes, or between any of the parishes and the new development. Things are now a little different. St. Anne's, with help from St. Helen's, Bishopsgate, runs a church in a barge moored at West India Quay. Martin Seeley, then Vicar of Christ Church, Isle of Dogs, persuaded the owners of Canary Wharf to provide a shop space in the development free of rent for use as a prayer room. This is still managed by the Canary Wharf Estate, and there is a users' group that organises the timetable of faith community events. All Saints remains the parish church of Poplar.

In 2004, the Bishop of London appointed a chaplain for Canary Wharf, Fiona Stewart-Darling. She now works with a Roman Catholic priest, an Imam, a Rabbi, and two volunteers who visit retail units; and the chaplaincy team is now the 'Canary Wharf Multifaith Chaplaincy'. As on the Greenwich Peninsula, members of different faiths do not pray together, and shared silence before meetings represents the fact that they stand together on the religious side of the religious/secular divide, and that their theologies are radically different. The team works together, meets together regularly, trains together (for instance, in business ethics and in listening skills), and is involved with various companies' major incident planning,

Chaplaincy in retail areas is similar to chaplaincy in other retail developments, such as Bluewater; and when Fiona can find time for construction site chaplaincy she wanders the construction sites in the same way as any other construction site chaplain would. But Canary Wharf is mainly financial and commercial companies, and because they have to be strict about security, access to offices has to be negotiated and is normally by invitation only. This makes business community chaplaincy a somewhat specialist activity.

The Canary Wharf Multifaith Chaplaincy service is inevitably fairly niche in the way that it operates in its unique context, although it shares some similarities with other models of workplace chaplaincy. Its task is to work in partnership with the companies to facilitate relationships between faith, ethics, values, and changing workplace culture; to help people of faith to understand and relate their faith to their work; and to respond to spiritual and pastoral needs. Individual conversations, seminars, visits by groups of interested parties (normally faith groups), discussion groups, religious services, emailed presentations, and a website presence, are just some of the varied activities undertaken by the chaplaincy team. One of the Muslim Chaplain's tasks is to teach Muslims how to prepare for the sermon which is delivered during Friday prayers.

During the past few years redundancy has been on most companies' agendas, and although the chaplain might not relate directly to those whose posts have already been declared redundant, there is often contact with workers anxious about the possibility, with employees who are suffering from 'survivors' guilt', or with senior managers who have had to decide which roles to make redundant and who want to ensure that the process is carried out in the most humane way possible. When someone dies at work, or while on sick leave, both individuals and the company are bereaved, and the chaplain has a role to play; and when a tragedy hits an office of a Canary Wharf company based in another country, again the chaplain has a role to play. Following the terrorist acts in Paris in November 2015, café and restaurant staff were feeling particularly vulnerable, so additional work was required in their context. As with any chaplaincy, conversations can be about anything and everything, and although the chaplain's task is not to proselytise, but is rather to be available for conversation with the employees they meet, it is often the employee who will bring the conversation round to God, or to other faith issues, and will then steer the conversation around their own agenda.

During the working week there are about 110,000 employees on the estate. Approximately Twenty five per cent of these come from the six nearest London boroughs. The remaining seventy-five per cent might commute daily from around London or further afield: from the South Coast, Cambridge, Grantham, Bristol, Winchester, or Leicester; weekly from such places as Devon, Leeds, or Edinburgh; and others internationally. Those on a fast track graduate scheme might be from anywhere in the world, and might be working at Canary Wharf for only a short period of time. Such a complex community, diverse in terms of nationality, culture, ethnicity, and faith, provides a unique context for a unique chaplaincy. Sometimes putting a Canary Wharf employee in touch with someone at the 'home' end of their commuter line can provide the right context for both pastoral care and thinking through issues at work. There are no clear boundaries here. Pastoral activity can happen in amongst conversation about normal business activity – for example, a conversation about a company mission statement, or about policies on corporate responsibility; and prophetic structured engagement with companies over ethics and culture can sometimes be a way into pastoral opportunities.

Sustainability for chaplaincy teams can be a problem. Teams composed entirely of volunteers are subject to fluctuations in the availability of voluntary labour, and chaplaincies that rely on full-time chaplains are at least as vulnerable, because even if they are originally funded by a faith community, they will often be expected to generate their own funding as time goes by. It then becomes important to be able to say what chaplains are doing for the institutions to which they relate. Fiona is employed full-time, the Muslim Chaplain (an Imam) and the Jewish Chaplain (an orthodox Rabbi) are part-time, and a part-time office manager is also employed. Salary and other costs are now met by the service charge paid to the Canary Wharf Estate by companies working in Canary Wharf. The one exception is that Fiona's accommodation is still partly funded by the Diocese of London: an attempt by the Diocese to maintain a partnership within a multi faith chaplaincy that is mainly accountable to a secular company, and to ensure that there is a future Anglican presence should the current Anglican chaplain leave.

From a situation in which the only relationship between the Church and the Canary Wharf development was one of antagonism, there is now a diversity of constructive engagement: a workplace chaplaincy, a prayer room, and a congregation meeting in a barge. The Church is doing what it can. But which of these are mediating institutions? The multi faith chaplaincy team certainly is. Fiona is licensed to All Hallows by the Tower, and she preaches throughout the Diocese of London; and the other team members each have their own religious accountability: so the individual members of the team are intimately connected to their own faith communities as well as to Canary Wharf's secular institutions. The team as an organisation, by being visibly present and by doing the things that it does, enables religion and the secular to relate to each other. The chaplaincy and its chaplains are the human face of their faith communities to the business world, and the human face of the business world to their faith communities. The chaplaincy will soon be a charitable limited company with trustees from the Diocese of London, Canary Wharf Group (the estate owners), and the business community (through a steering group composed of senior executives of global companies). It will therefore be something of a hybrid between a 'host and hosted' multi faith chaplaincy and a 'level playing field' one. This is probably appropriate to the situation.

The prayer room also functions to some extent as a mediating institution, as it is a visible religious statement in a secular place. As a sort of building, the barge fulfils a similar function. However, the purpose of both the prayer room and the congregation on the barge is to facilitate personal religious belief and practice, rather than to enable relationships to develop between religious organisations and secular organisations, or between religious traditions and a secular financial and commercial world. In this respect, Canary Wharf Multifaith Chaplaincy is the primary mediating institution in Canary Wharf.

The Gossner Mission: The Church Relating to Industry in Mainz-Kastel After the Second World War

The Gossner Mission was founded by John Gossner in 1836, its first activities were to send missionaries to Australia and to found a hospital in Berlin, it continues to work internationally (currently in India, Nepal, Zambia, and Germany), and from the beginning it has seen its work as the dual task of evangelism and seeking justice for poor and marginalised members of society.

Of particular interest to us here is the Mission's work in Germany after the Second World War. During the war its Berlin headquarters hosted meetings of leaders of the Confessing Church – that part of the Church that resisted co-option by National Socialism – and for as long as it could it continued to welcome Christians of Jewish background. Soon after the war ended it turned its attention to the relationship between Christian Faith and an industrial society.

Horst Symanowski fought in the German army, but after being seriously wounded he joined the Mission's staff in 1943. He worked in East Prussia, and then, following the Russian occupation of the territory in 1945, he moved west to train teachers of religion for Berlin's schools. In 1948 he returned to East Germany to assist in the rebuilding of farms and villages; and then a year later he returned to West Germany to start a mission centre in Mainz-Kastel. As Symanowski put it, he had exchanged the 'cold, clear atheist air' for the 'Christian fog' along the Rhine.

In order to get to know industrial workers he worked in manual jobs for six months of each year between 1950 and 1954, and for the intervening periods he organised the building of a centre in which to base his growing workplace ministry. He recruited five hundred young people from all over the world to stay in Mainz-Katel for short periods to help with the building work. When it was finished, the centre had enough accommodation for a hundred residents: a mixture of university students, apprentices, and young industrial workers with nowhere else to live. Gossner Haus also hosted gatherings of industrial workers. Some of their discussions started off from the agenda which the workers brought with them from their workplaces, and some set off from biblical texts: but always the content of the discussion was drawn from the lives of the working men themselves (– on the whole it was men). To cater for shift workers, some of the discussions started at 11 p.m. and continued until 2 a.m.. Gossner Sundays once every six weeks included a common meal, more discussion, prayers, and occasionally the sacraments of baptism and the Eucharist – a sharing of bread and wine that merged into the shared meal.

Alongside its relationship with the industrial world of Mainz-Kastel, Gossner Haus worked hard at its relationship with the Church. From 1954, Symanowski organised month-long work camps for ministers, and from 1956 substantial six month courses, each one attended by up to a dozen ministers. The aim was to immerse ministers, and particularly young ones, in the radical estrangement of industrial workers from the Church, and to enable the ministers to discover God at work in the industrial world.

Symanowski's aim, in both the industry-directed activity and the church-directed activity, was to transform institutions – both industrial and ecclesiastical institutions. So through his listening to discussions among working men he would discover the characteristics of their workplaces that were dehumanising them, and these issues would then form the agenda for gatherings that contained both managers and workers. Some of the themes tackled in this way were automation, shift patterns, and trust in industrial relations. This was *gesellschaftliche Diakonie*: service in or of institutions.

In Symanowski's time, Gossner Haus was functioning as a mediating institution, mediating a relationship between the Church as institutional and the industrial world as institutional, between men working in industry and the Church's personnel, and between the Christian Faith and a secular industrial worldview. Gossner Haus still pursues this agenda, although now more with unemployed people than with people working in industry, and now in partnership with other organisations rather than on its own.

Symanowski himself was also functioning as a mediating institution by creating relationships between the Christian Faith and a secular industrial worldview, between the Church's ministers and men working in industry, and between the Church and industrial institutions. When we take Symanowski's work as a whole, including his paid employment in industry, during which he was alongside industry's workers and listening to them, we can see that he functioned as a mediator in two different ways: first of all as a minister working alongside other men in industry, in much the same way as the French and British worker priests, who worked in industry in order to serve its workers and to find God at work there (Perrin 1965; Erlander 1991; Mantle 2000; Torry 2010: 71–5); and subsequently as a pastor to working men, enabling them to connect the Christian Faith to their daily lives in the workplace. Neither approach is that of the workplace chaplain, so we have here a different approach to the individual minister being a mediating institution, and in the Gossner Mission a different institutional approach to workplace chaplaincy.

The United States of America: Interfaith Worker Justice – And Citizens UK

As Interfaith Worker Justice says about itself: it organises in order to mobilise people of faith

> in support of economic justice and worker rights at the local, state and national levels;

it educates, by preparing

> interfaith resources and materials to help inspire and inform people on worker and economic justice issues. Congregations across the nation rely on IWJ to provide worship and educational resources for both special and everyday events that draw people into the movement for worker justice;

and it advocates for workers' rights,

> working with partners and allies to influence the national conversation on
> … wage theft, jobs, paid sick days and workplace standards, and protecting
> the right of workers to stick together in Labor Unions. But we are also at
> work, with and through our affiliates, to pass pro-worker legislation at the
> local and state level.

What it wants to see is a nation in which workers can experience

> wages, health care, and pensions that allow workers to raise families and
> retire with dignity, safe working conditions, and protection under labor
> law – regardless of immigration status – and an end to the practice of pit-
> ting immigrant and U.S.-born workers against one another;

it wants to see workers able to

> organise and bargain collectively to improve wages, benefits, and condi-
> tions without harassment, intimidation, or retaliation.

It wants to see a

> fair and just participation in a global economy that promotes the welfare of
> both domestic and foreign workers.

The movement registers as 'worker justice congregations' those congregations of any faith that advocate for justice for workers and for good jobs,
that are good employers themselves, and that support ethical businesses.
Interfaith Worker Justice counts as an 'ethical businesses' are businesses
that

> pay workers above the norm, because they believe that workers' pay should
> lift them out of poverty and they want to retain valuable employees. …;
> provide some benefits and are seeking to add more; encourage workers to
> have a voice in the workplace; offer training and opportunities for advance-
> ment of workers; [and] hire and promote a diverse workforce.

A network of 'Worker Centers' enables low-wage workers to organise in their own localities. The Centers are led by workers, develop their own 'worker leaders', and are facilitated by 'interfaith worker advocates'. The network of Worker Centers serves sixteen thousand workers a year, enabling them to work together to obtain justice in the workplace. Eighty per cent of those workers have experienced 'wage theft', which is where

> employers pay less than the minimum wage; refuse overtime pay; force workers to work off the clock; hold back final paychecks; misclassify employees as independent contractors; steal tips; and fail to pay workers at all.

Interfaith Worker Justice holds national days of action on the issue, publishes educational material, holds educational events, encourages congregations to pray, and advocates for legislation at state level.

Interfaith Worker Justice has seventy local affiliated organisations. In Chicago the affiliated organisation goes under the name 'Arise'. It

> partners with immigrants and leaders from the religious, government, legal, labor, and academic communities to end workplace abuse. Arise Chicago has passed City and County Ordinances to prevent wage theft, helping Chicago to become a city where business ethics and families can thrive.

The Arise Chicago Worker Center provides worker-led training for workers; publishes a workers' rights manual; trains workers' leaders; and organises workers so that they can fight for their rights in their workplaces. A particular focus is domestic workers, who are often isolated from each other, and are therefore in particular need of the kind of support that the Workers' Center can offer.

As with the national network, Arise works closely with congregations. Over the Labor Day weekend it provides a hundred speakers for services, it keeps a list of clergy who actively support workers' rights, and it encourages congregation members to join picket lines. A significant recent campaign, in which a number of congregations have been involved, has been the campaign for a higher minimum wage in Illinois (– in the USA, states can set their own minimum wages at levels higher than that of the national minimum wage).

Interfaith Worker Justice and its local affiliates stand in the community organising tradition associated with Sam Alinsky (Alinsky 1971) and Arnie Graf (Graf 2015), and represented in the UK by Citizens UK (Citizens UK 2015). Citizens UK's best known and perhaps most effective campaign is for a Living Wage pegged at levels that would allow every family to have an income equal to the Minimum Income Standards published by the Joseph Rowntree Foundation. Numerous companies, borough councils, and other employers, have now agreed to be Living Wage Employers. (The Chancellor of the Exchequer's July 2015 theft of the 'Living Wage' terminology for his so-called 'National Living Wage' – which is not a Living Wage in the normal definition of the term – might have seriously damaged the campaign. Was that his intention?) Both faith communities and trades unions support Citizens UK in much the same way as faith communities, trades unions, and workers work together in Interfaith Worker Justice and in Arise.

Interfaith Worker Justice, Arise, and Citizen's UK, function as mediating institutions, enabling faith communities to relate to a variety of other organisations; enabling their members to relate to the members of a variety of organisations, and to individuals who do not belong to anything apart from the local Worker Center; and enabling faith communities to relate to the issues facing workers in their workplaces. In this process, the religion remains religion, and the secular remains secular. This is what makes mediation possible. What holds the different players together is the problems that they are trying to tackle, and the better kind of society that they all want to see. It would be a lot more difficult for the congregations involved to tackle the complex issues that so many workers face if each congregation was trying to do that on its own. Interfaith Worker Justice, Arise, and Citizens UK, enable congregations, trades unions, and numerous organisations and individuals, to work together to ensure that the campaigns have some effect. In the midst of the campaigns, the education, the prayer, and much else, faith communities relate to significant workplaces issues, and workers and workers' organisations relate to faith communities. Genuine two-way relationships happen.

Conclusions: Mediating Institutions Between Religion and the Secular Workplace

In relation to industry and commerce, the Church has generally done what it can: and it has often done it by creating mediating institutions. The South London Industrial Mission was a charitable company, managed by a Board of Directors; the South Yorkshire Workplace Chaplaincy is a charitable company; and the Greenwich Peninsula Chaplaincy is a charitable trust. At Bluewater and Canary Wharf the organisational arrangements are somewhat more fluid, but the postholders remain accountable to their own faith community organisations, to faith-based organisations with wider briefs, and to the companies in which they work. At Bluewater and Canary Wharf the chaplaincies are best described as voluntary associations: identifiable groups with names, purposes, membership criteria, and rudimentary rules about how to make decisions (Billis 1993: 160–63), although Canary Wharf is now heading in a more organised direction. Stratford is an interesting case of a loose association of organisations. The Gossner Mission, Interfaith Worker Justice, Arise, and Citizens UK, are organisational responses to the need for relationships between the religious and the secular.

In each of the places that we have studied there is an organisation of some kind that can relate to the faith communities and to the companies working in those places, and that can relate to individuals within faith communities and to individuals within the companies among which they work. These are all mediating institutions, and without them it is doubtful whether it would be possible to relate faith community organisations to secular companies, or individuals in those companies to individuals in faith communities – except, of course, where members of faith communities work in those companies.

Given the importance of these mediating institutions, it would be to the benefit of the faith communities and of the secular organisations to which they relate to ensure their adequate resourcing, and, just as importantly, their autonomy. Without autonomy, a mediating institution cannot mediate, and therefore falls out of the category of mediating institutions. Of course, no mediating institution will be entirely autonomous

in relation to faith community organisations or to the secular organisations to which it relates. Access to secular organisations and their personnel implies a loss of autonomy, and legitimacy among faith community
organisations requires a certain amount of loss of autonomy. A workplace
chaplain cannot make derogatory public statements about the companies
that they visit without risking rejection, and if a mediating institution
is to relate constructively to faith communities then their paid staff and
volunteers will mostly need to belong to faith communities and to be
in good standing within them. So the question arises as to how, given
such constraints, the maximum possible autonomy can be assured. The
obvious answer is to ensure that the mediating organisation has a constitution that contains no structural connections with faith community
organisations or with secular organisations. The best way to achieve this
is a charitable trust with a self-perpetuating board of trustees. The board
will be wise to ensure representation of a wide diversity of faith commitments among its members, but the constitution will need to ensure
that no faith community organisations have rights of appointment. It
will also be important that the constitution favours no particular faith
community, and that the chaplaincy forms no contracts with secular or
religious organisations on terms dictated by those organisations. The only
organisation discussed in this chapter that fulfils all of these requirements
is the Greenwich Peninsula Chaplaincy. Organisations with constitutions
that mention the Christian Faith or Christian churches, but not other
faiths and other religious organisations, cannot fulfil the criteria; and
although associations might potentially fulfil them in practice, there is
never any guarantee that they will do so. Constitutions that give rights to
particular religious organisations or to their postholders will immediately
compromise the association's autonomy; and a participant paid by a company served by the association will similarly compromise the association's
autonomy.

But as we have recognised, organisations do not constitute the entire
category of institutions: and in the context of relationships between secular and religious organisations, and of relationships between individuals
working in those organisations, each individual chaplain, and chaplaincy itself, functions as a mediating institution, quite apart from the
chaplaincy organisations to which chaplains are accountable. Wherever

there is an individual recognised as a chaplain – as a pastoral figure some-how related to a religious tradition – then new relationships can emerge between the religious and secular organisations to which the chaplain relates, and between individuals within the two kinds of organisation. This is one of the reasons for the trend in congregations and parishes appointing chaplains in faith schools. The chaplain functions both as a pastor to which individuals can turn, and as a mediator between the con-gregation and the school. So in the absence of a functioning chaplaincy organisation, a second best approach is religious organisations appoint-ing chaplains to secular organisations, with those chaplains relating to associations of chaplains, both for their own support, and to provide the basis for the development of an autonomous chaplaincy organisa-tion. This is how most chaplaincy organisations have started out. Bishop Leslie Hunter appointed Ted Wickham in Sheffield, Cuthbert Bardsley appointed Colin Cuttell in South London, and the Bishop of London appointed Fiona Stewart-Darling in Canary Wharf. The exception is the Greenwich Peninsula, where a meeting between faith community repre-sentatives and representatives of the borough council and the developer appointed the author as the first chaplain, and also appointed a steering group that would become the Greenwich Peninsula Chaplaincy's board of trustees.

To conclude: autonomous workplace chaplaincy organisations can be effective mediating institutions; individual chaplains can be mediating institutions; and chaplaincy as an activity can be counted as a highly effective mediating institution.

Bibliography

Alinsky, Saul. 1971. *Rules for radicals: A pragmatic primer for realistic radicals.* New York: Random House.

Billis, David. 1993. *Organising public and voluntary agencies.* London: Routledge.

Church of England, 1918. *Christianity and industrial problems, being the report of the archbishop's fifth committee of inquiry.* London: SPCK.

Citizens UK. 2015. www.citizensuk.org/what_we_do. Accessed 26 Nov 2015.

Cuttell, Colin. 1962. *Ministry without portfolio.* London: Toc H.

Erlander, Lillemor. 1991. *Faith in the world of work: On the theology of work as lived by the French worker-priests and British industrial mission.* Uppsala: Uppsala University.

Fox, Michael. 2008a. The receiving community. In *Building utopia? Seeking the authentic Church for new communities,* ed. Laurie Green and Christopher R. Baker, 23–39. London: SPCK.

Graf, Arnie. 2015. Community organising and blue labour. In *Blue labour: Forging a new politics,* ed. Ian Geary and Adria Pabst, 71–83. London: I.B. Taurus.

Hamnett, Chris. 2003. *Unequal city: London in the global arena.* London: Routledge.

Mantle, John. 2000. *Britain's first worker-priests.* London: SCM Press.

Perrin, Henri. 1965. *Priest and worker: The autobiography of Henri Perrin* (translated and with an introduction by Bernard Wall). London: Macmillan.

Reiss, Robert. 2013. *The testing of vocation: 100 years of ministry selection in the Church of England.* London: Church House Publishing.

Ross, Donald M. 1997. *God It's Monday.* Edinburgh: St. Andrew's Press for the Scottish Churches Industrial Mission.

South Yorkshire Workplace Chaplaincy. 2015. www.sywc.org.uk. Accessed 18 Dec 2015.

Spittles, David. 2015. The new world in Zone 2: Olympicopolis. *Evening Standard,* 18 November 2015, pp. H&P 6–7.

Torry, Malcolm. 2010. *Bridgebuilders: Workplace chaplaincy—A history.* Norwich: Canterbury Press.

Wickham, E.R. 1957. *Church and people in an industrial city.* London: Lutterworth Press.

——— 1964. *Encounter with modern society.* London: Lutterworth Press.

3

Mediating Institutions in Residential Communities in the Thames Gateway

Introduction

Residential areas are composed of individuals, families, households, and institutions, and some of those institutions are organisations. For instance, a residential area might contain such organisations as residents' associations, political organisations, schools (which we shall deal with in Chap. 5), shops, and residential management companies, and might also be served by such other institutions as regular refuse collection, planning regulations, and parking rules. Faith communities are constituted by their individual members, by organisations – the stereotypical religious organisation being a congregation – and by such institutions as funerals, social events, and clergy.

Religion and a residential area will relate to each other within any religious individual who lives there, and also whenever a member of a faith community relates to someone else: whether to a member of the same congregation, to someone belonging to the same faith community, to a member of another faith community, or to someone who does not belong to a faith community. The residential area and religion will also relate to each other when the institutions of residential areas relate to religious

© The Editor(s) (if applicable) and The Author(s) 2016
M. Torry, *Mediating Institutions*,
DOI 10.1057/978-1-349-94913-7_3

institutions: so when a residents' association and a congregation work together on a project, or members of the clergy relate to local councillors. Congregations exercise 'quiet care' (Harris 1998: 156) across personal relationships within the congregation, or through semi-organised congregational activities; and they will sometimes work alone or with other congregations to create faith-based organisations that will then relate to the congregation and to other local organisations.

In this chapter we shall study a variety of organisations and other institutions in a number of different residential areas in the Thames Gateway. As in the previous chapter, we shall be particularly interested in the institutional relationships that exist between faith communities and residential areas, and we shall of course be asking about the existence and the character of mediating institutions.

Thamesmead

My father was a local government officer working for the Greater London Council (GLC), and when I was a child – I must have been about ten – he took my brother and me to a rather windswept place and showed us a massive building site. He and his colleagues were proud of Thamesmead, and rightly so. It was a substantial improvement on the homes that many of the tenants who would move there were coming from. There was a sense of optimism, of making things better. It was the 1960s.

The site was difficult geologically, so the plans drawn up in 1962 for the Erith end of the site were for clusters of dwellings on concrete decks four metres above ground level and constructed on deep concrete piles. By 1965, additional land to the west had been made available by the Ministry of Defence, and preparation of the land began by constructing lakes and canals to channel the marshland's water to the river. Then in went the piles (including piled foundations for the drains), the concrete decks, and homes for a new town of 60,000 people: a mixture of high rise blocks and low rise houses, maisonettes, and flats. The ground floor was for the cars, largely because of the danger of flooding. 1968 saw the first tenants moving in, and most of what we knew as Thamesmead until the turn of the millennium was completed by 1974.

Thamesmead was built by the GLC, so the fact that it straddled two boroughs, Bexley and Greenwich, was not too much of an issue. However, when Margaret Thatcher abolished the GLC and gave responsibility for its housing stock to the London boroughs, the borough boundary through the middle of Thamesmead did become an issue, as it meant that no borough council was taking responsibility for the community. In 1982, in an attempt to circumvent the problem, Thamesmead Town Ltd. (TTL) was established to manage the town as a whole. In 1998 the decision was taken to break up TTL into three different organisations: Tilfen Land (land holdings), Gallions Housing (a registered social landlord, which was given responsibility for the social housing stock in the original central Thamesmead development), and Trust Thamesmead: an expansion of an existing charity, charged with community development, and responsible for some community buildings. This structure was established in 2000. The pendulum has now swung again, and Tilfen Land, Gallions Housing, and Trust Thamesmead, have been taken over by Peabody in preparation for the regeneration of South Thamesmead.

The Thamesmead Community Association (TCA) had been established in 1969, early in the life of the development, to provide the infrastructure for white working class culture – because it mainly was white working class families that were moving into the new Thamesmead; and in 1976 the TCA set up the original Trust Thamesmead. This rather paternalistic but well-loved Trust ran social (drinking) clubs, gyms, an employment project, and boxing clubs; and, taking its cue from the community response to a child drowned in one of the many canals running across Thamesmead, Trust Thamesmead applied for funding and built a leisure centre.

A merger with the remaining functions of Thamesmead Town in 1998 did not go smoothly. The old Trust Thamesmead had a community organisation ethos, whereas Thamesmead Town had been established by the GLC and had adopted its bureaucratic methods. The last straw for many residents was when the new Chief Executive sacked Mary Chambers, 'Lady Thamesmead', a longstanding servant of the community.

In 2004 Mick Hayes was appointed Chief Executive of the post-2000 Trust Thamesmead. He found that the organisation was in effect the umbrella for around one hundred local organisations. These had all been set up with community support, but there were no longer the resources to sustain so many of them. A facilities manager and a human resources manager were hired, premises were rationalised, a social enterprise facilitator was employed, and Trust Thamesmead now focuses on developing around twenty community organisations a year, and assisting them with training, infrastructure, and fundraising skills, so that they can become accredited, accountable, self-supporting, and sustainable. A particular success was Thamesmead Gym, with its own management committee, which has improved the building and opened the organisation to women. Gym membership soon rose to four hundred.

Land to the west of the original development had lain empty until it became attractive to private developers during the early 1990s and registered social landlords had money for building social housing. The land was not expensive because transport connections are not exactly brilliant (– a situation that will change markedly when Crossrail comes to Abbey Wood Station in 2018), so low density housing was possible; and a mixture of townhouses and low-rise flats has been marketed as 'Broadwater', 'Gallions Reach' and so on, rather than as 'Thamesmead'. (The cheapness of the land, particularly of the land next to Belmarsh Prison, means that two additional prisons are now being built there.) So now in West Thamesmead we find housing, schools, and a village hall, along with a couple of rows of retail units of the corner shop and takeaway variety. While some of the new developments, such as the one to the west of Belmarsh prison, are becoming successful established communities, others, such as some of the new blocks of flats, were largely bought by absentee landlords who took the rent and did not pay their mortgages. This was the subject of a television exposé, and led to flats being repossessed, to empty flats, and to owner occupiers being unable to sell their properties.[1]

A major and positive factor in Thamesmead's recent history is that during the past fifteen years parts of Thamesmead have seen a large number of people of West African origin moving in. School results have improved, and local churches resound with large and exuberant West African congregations.

---

[1] www.ft.com/cms/s/0/41524d5c-91ac-11dd-b5cd-0000779fd18c.html

The Abbey Wood Estate, to the south of Thamesmead, was itself relatively new when Thamesmead was built. It had a small modern parish church: but this small church building and its priest were clearly not going to be sufficient for the pastoral care of the huge new community of Thamesmead to the north. It was the 1960s, Thamesmead was a new community, and the Church was doing new things, so clergy were appointed and buildings were planned. The clergy who moved into Thamesmead lived in council housing, and initially held services in the community club room. They saw their role as community developers as much as religious functionaries. The first church building was the Baptist Centre, then came the Church of the Cross (funded by the Church of England and other denominations), and then, in 1977, St. Paul's Ecumenical Centre (again jointly funded, this time with the Roman Catholic Church participating).

Winds of change were blowing through the Church as well as through wider society, and many in the Roman Catholic Church were looking forward to change. In 1964 the Second Vatican Council approved the document *Unitatis Redintegratio*:

> Today, in many parts of the world, under the inspiring grace of the Holy Spirit, many efforts are being made in prayer, word and action to attain that fullness of unity which Jesus Christ desires. The Sacred Council exhorts all the Catholic faithful to recognise the signs of the times and to take an active and intelligent part in the work of ecumenism. (Roman Catholic Church 1964)

The Roman Catholic Archbishop of Southwark and the Church of England's Bishop of Southwark decided on an experiment: a church building at the heart of Thamesmead that their two churches would use together. They hoped that the Second Vatican Council and negotiations between different denominations would engender sufficient change to enable the different denominations in England to unite into a single national church so that the Thamesmead experiment would soon represent the norm. Where better to represent the united Church of the future than the new community of Thamesmead? St. Paul's Church building was designed so that worshippers enter along a corridor with moveable glass panels on both sides. On the left is space for a congregation made up of members of the Church of England, the Methodist Church, and the United Reformed Church; and the Roman Catholic congregation uses the space to the right. There is an altar at the end of each space, and the altars face each other. When the experiment started, most Sundays saw the two congregations worshipping separately, with the joint congregation to the left served by ministers of the different participating churches and using a variety of liturgies; and the congregation to the right served by a Roman Catholic priest using the Roman Catholic liturgy. On one Sunday a month the screens opened, the altars were placed side by side, and the service was Roman Catholic, but with two ministers, so that when it came to the communion the congregation divided to allow people to receive communion from their own denomination's minister. Both St. Paul's and the Church of the Cross had joint congregations made up of Church of England, Methodist, and United Reformed Church members. (I use the term 'United Reformed Church' here, but for the earlier part of the period under review there were Congregationalists and Presbyterians. They came together as the United Reformed Church in 1972). Ministers rotated between the St. Paul's joint congregation and the Church of the Cross joint congregation; and the liturgies rotated between Church of England liturgy and Methodist and United Reformed Church liturgies, depending on who was presiding. The constitution and financing of the St. Paul's building was complex, to say the least, as was the institutional structure of the united congregation. The St. Paul's building was owned by Thamesmead Christian Community Ltd., which in turn is jointly owned by the four participating denominations. The two congregations are represented on the company's board.

The times were unrealistically optimistic, and, perhaps one should say, were an era with little appreciation of human sin or institutional intransigence. The Second Vatican Council appeared to promise radical change, all over the world Roman Catholic liturgy changed from Latin to the vernacular – and then the momentum stopped. The Roman Catholic Church changed little, the pontificate of John Paul II functioned largely as if the Second Vatican Council had never happened, and the other denominations did not come together into a single organisation. Talks between the Church of England and the Methodist Church failed to achieve organic unity, and in 1982 the Church of England rejected a proposed covenant with the Methodist and United Reformed Churches. Thamesmead was left holding together a complex experiment for over forty years: an experiment that required huge amounts of internal communication and constant negotiation to keep going, draining clergy, officers, and congregation members of energy, and leaving little energy to spare for other sorts of ministry and mission.

By 1986 two generations of pioneering Church of England Team Rectors in Thamesmead had moved on (Jim Thompson to be Bishop of Stepney, and Keith Pound to be the Chaplain General of Prisons), and Chris Byers was appointed to be Team Rector. His was the kind of ministry that the situation needed: pastoral, and community-oriented. When a black teenager, Ronan Adams, was killed, Chris established 'Rainbow Days' to enable Thamesmead's diverse community to celebrate itself. By 1998 Chris had been instrumental in establishing the new Trust Thamesmead, and was near to retirement. New housing was starting to take off in West Thamesmead, so a second full-time priest was appointed to do some work there. He soon left to become a hospital chaplain. It had not been easy to know what to do in a completely new community without clergy housing and without a church building. And then, because Chris Byers would be retiring in two years' time, and because anyone applying for the post of Team Vicar in West Thamesmead would not know who the next Team Rector would be, the post proved difficult to fill.

(This is an ongoing problem with team ministries. Team Vicars and Team Rectors are both of incumbent status, but one is Team Rector and the others are Team Vicars: that is, there is also a hierarchical relationship. This structural ambiguity can cause considerable problems in working relationships. If candidates for a Team Vicar post know how the current Team Rector plays this relationship – either as a Vicar/Curate relationship, or as an autonomous colleagues relationship – then they can decide whether that is a relationship that they can work with. If it is clear that the current Team Rector will soon be retiring then candidates will not know how the new Team Rector will treat the working relationship. It is difficult enough finding a good field of candidates for urban Team Vicar posts. Suburban or country town incumbency posts, where the priest is *the* Vicar of the parish, can look much more attractive. The added complexity of a Team Rector about to leave can make it impossible to get the right people to apply for Team Vicar posts).

Chris vacated the Team Rector's post and the Diocese of Southwark provided him with a post that enabled him to oversee the transition from the old Trust Thamesmead to the new one: but then it proved difficult to find anyone willing to be Team Rector of Thamesmead. Chris eventually retired, and the new Team Rector, Barry Thorley, reflected the modern face of Thamesmead in being mixed race as well as British born. He quickly tired of juggling the complications of joint services, and the congregation had tired of never knowing who would be presiding on Sunday morning and which liturgy they would be using. After a consultation exercise, decisions were taken to abandon the monthly joint services with the Roman Catholic congregation; to locate the Church of England minister at St. Paul's, and a Methodist or United Reformed Church minister at the Church of the Cross; to hold a Church of England service every Sunday at St. Paul's, and a United Reformed Church or Methodist Church service at the Church of the Cross; and to retain joint membership of the different denominations in the two joint congregations. This consultation exercise did not touch the structural or governance problems of St. Paul's Church – there is still no clear answer to the question: 'Who pays to mend the roof?' – but it did reduce considerably the complexity of ministry and worship. The St. Paul's congregation grew, and everyone had more time and energy for mission and pastoral care.

By this time large numbers of black Africans were moving into Thamesmead, and the churchgoers among them were attracted to St. Paul's as well as to the more Pentecostal black-led churches such as the New Wine Church in Woolwich, to the Baptist Church meeting in a building managed by Trust Thamesmead, and to the many house churches in Thamesmead. The St. Paul's congregation's leadership became more racially diverse, the liturgy diversified to include African music and drumming, and the diverse congregation came to reflect the diverse community of Thamesmead. There is no contradiction between growing the congregation (through making the worship space more welcoming, providing a junior church and a young people's group, and putting on an inviting and participative liturgy) and serving the community (Enoch-Onchere and Boxall 2007). Meeting the spiritual needs of a community is at the heart of serving it; a sizeable congregation welcoming families for the baptism of their children can be more welcoming than a struggling small one; and maintaining a larger congregation can provide the time and energy for a deeper relationship between the congregation and the community around it.

When Chris Byers vacated his post, Colin Buchanan, Bishop of Woolwich, used a discretionary post to appoint Chris Beales to undertake some consultancy work in Thamesmead and to organise some Millennium celebrations. Beales had been an industrial chaplain, had been employed at Church House on industrial and economic affairs, and had worked for the Inner Cities Religious Council (a Government-financed forum of faith communities with an interest in urban regeneration), and he was looking for a new challenge. He had little parochial experience. He facilitated some interesting activity in Thamesmead, and particularly a locally-run festival. He also improved relationships between the churches working in Thamesmead, and gave birth to the Christian Community Partnership, which initially organised Millennium celebrations and then continued with a variety of other jointly-managed community activities.

Chris Beales' report was useful at the time, and it is still useful to anyone trying to understand the evolution of the Church in Thamesmead. His audit made a modest number of proposals, which boiled down to a) getting relevant training for church volunteers and b) encouraging churches to do together those things where doing them separately does not add value, namely fundraising, publications, communications, and media relationships. The Thamesmead churches agreed on a joint publication, The Channel, and Trust Thamesmead took up the challenge of supporting volunteers in Thamesmead to get relevant training to sustain their organisations (not necessarily faith-based organisations, of course). Chris Beales' challenge still sounds loud and clear today: 'Even the more willing and open [church] members have not easily found an effective way to turn aspiration into action. We must develop mechanisms for serious and sustained engagement. We are supposed to be people of faith...' (Beales 2001: 30)

What Chris Beales did not do was look carefully at the longer term spiritual needs of West Thamesmead. A vicarage was planned, but there was nothing in the report about land being required for a church building. West Thamesmead, because it contains a substantial amount of affordable family-sized housing, is becoming a place where families are settling down. Traditional church activity is therefore appropriate. The earlier in the building of a new development land is obtained, the easier it is to obtain a suitable plot and to ensure the necessary permissions; and in West Thamesmead, unlike in some tightly-masterplanned developments, land was available. An opportunity was missed.

In 2005, Simon Boxall arrived as Team Vicar in West Thamesmead. He and his wife Rachel, having spent many years with the South American Missionary Society in Brazil, were attracted by the missionary opportunities offered by the new development. They used their vicarage as fully as possible for the work of the Church, although one of the problems is that, being in a residential development, the vicarage is not zoned for religious or educational use, and there has to remain something rather unofficial about the activity. There is of course no problem with holding church meetings in private homes: the problem arises when regular events are advertised as open to the public. Church meetings did occur in the vicarage: for worship, prayer, and study. There was high-quality, all-age 'Messy Church', as well as a regular afternoon Sunday School; Rachel started the Open Gateway Craft Club committee to co-ordinate three successful groups for scrapbooking, card-making, and sewing; and barbecues were held in the vicarage garden. Local people attended, including some who also belonged to St. Paul's Church, and some who were not traditional churchgoers at all. This was a 'ministry of presence' (Fox and Hutson 2008: 137), but a rather draining one, because although Simon and Rachel were embedded in their community, they were not members of an identifiable congregation that was embedded in it.

Simon and Rachel moved on, and there was a predictable hiatus in the activity. The Sunday service survived for a while in the vicarage, and then closed. The weekday Bible study lasted a bit longer, but then that closed as well. While there is something very New Testament about meetings in people's homes, if continuity of activity is required then a dedicated space is essential. The Open Gateway Church, as the gatherings in the vicarage were called, explored possibilities in the local school, and also made occasional use of a not very well-sited community hall, but the activity gravitated back to the vicarage. It was the nearest thing there was to a religious building. During the vacancy in the post the parish has negotiated the use of a school hall, so that when a United Reformed Church minister moves into West Thamesmead in 2016 a congregation can meet. It is hoped that a group from St. Paul's will form the kernel of the new congregation, which will meet on Sunday afternoons, partly so that the core group can continue to belong to St. Paul's. This will enable the congregation's and the minister's work to be mediating in character because it will be forming relationships between a religious organisation and a secular society. A new possibility on the congregation's agenda is a community café: because West Thamesmead needs one.

The Church of England, and particularly its clergy, played a significant community-building role during the early years of the new Thamesmead community, especially in relation to institution-building and community development. More than typical was Patrick Forbes, who was one of the first members of the clergy team in Thamesmead. He started the community newspaper, *Insight* (eventually replaced by the *Thamesmead Times*), and then Thamesmead's long-running community radio station, *Insound*, which became *Radio Thamesmead*, and then *Millennium Radio*. It was Forbes who gave birth to the original Trust Thamesmead. Eventually the balance tipped somewhat towards mission as congregation-building: but still Thamesmead's clergy expect, and are expected, to involve themselves in the whole of the life of the community. The current Team Rector, Patrick Eggleston, as well as doing all of the things that we would expect of a member of the clergy – pastoral care, leading worship, and involvement with the church school and with other schools in the community – also engages with Trust Thamesmead, with other local organisations, and with plans for Thamesmead's future developments. This is a welcome balance between attention to religious organisations and attention to the wider community. Members of the St. Paul's united congregation are also becoming increasingly involved in social initiatives such as a health and wellbeing project: Thamesmead Health Champions, which promotes and organises courses about healthy lifestyles. Patrick is on the project's steering group. Churches in Thamesmead and in the surrounding area work together to provide a Christians Against Poverty debt advice centre, and St. Paul's is now planning to host money workshops for the local community. The pattern is a common one: Patrick does the organising, and congregation members join in. Ecumenical activity continues as well. The churches work together to create a choir for the event at which the Christmas lights are turned on; and they work together to run the debt centre and to support the Thamesmead branch of the Greenwich Foodbank. All of these activities function as mediating institutions, and together they form a strong bond between the evolving Christian community and the fast-changing community of Thamesmead, and they help to make Thamesmead into the exciting place that it still is.

We have encountered a variety of different mediating institutions as we have explored Thamesmead and some of its organisations. Until the Church of the Cross became in practice a Free Church, and St. Paul's a Church of England congregation alongside a Roman Catholic one, joint services mediated between the Free Churches and the Church of England, and between the joint Free Church and Church of England congregation and the Roman Catholic Church. An interesting question is whether, in the end, the services acted as mediating institutions or reminders of irreconcilable ecclesiastical positions. Management structures, that might at one time have mediated between the different congregations, and between different denominational allegiances, had become drains on energy and enthusiasm, rather than useful mediating institutions. Given the right management structure, the St. Paul's church building could still be an important mediating institution; and the clergy can certainly be that whenever they and their congregations serve the Thamesmead community together. The Church of the Cross is now served by a Church of England minister, as is St. Paul's. They both still have ecumenical congregations, so within each congregation mediation between different denominations occurs: but no longer is there an ecumenical team of clergy, meaning that mediation between the different denominations as institutions is less likely to occur.

Between religious organisations and the various secular Thamesmead organisations we constantly find the clergy. In particular, the Church of England acted quickly to appoint clergy as Thamesmead was tenanted. Members of the clergy rapidly formed strong relationships with secular institutions, and helped to found some of them. The clergy remained well-engaged with Thamesmead's secular institutions, and Chris Byers in particular stood in a long tradition of mediating clergy. But the clergy were not the only mediating institution. Rainbow Days, millennium celebrations, and other local events and festivals in which the clergy have been involved, have been important mediating institutions between the churches and Thamesmead's secular institutions.

When we study relationships between religious individuals and the residential community as a whole, again we find the clergy functioning as a mediating institution. We also find music functioning in this way. The African drumming that Barry Thorley introduced into the Church's liturgy functioned as an effective mediator between the Church as an institution and Thamesmead's growing West African population.

Throughout this case study we have made frequent mention of church buildings: the positive and negative aspects of the design and management of St. Paul's; the Church of the Cross; William Temple Church in Abbey Wood; and the lack of a church building in West Thamesmead. As in many communities, the church buildings in Thamesmead host a variety of activities: at St. Paul's an after school club and young people's activities; at the Church of the Cross a playgroup, a summer holiday club for children, and regular young people's activities; and at William Temple Church 'Neutral Ground', a project that enables children whose parents live apart to spend time with the parent they don't live with in a supervised environment (Neutral Ground 2015).

It was a correct decision to locate a member of the clergy in the new development of West Thamesmead, and to provide them with adequate accommodation. Perhaps less sensible was doing this before ensuring that a publicly accessible congregation could meet on a regular basis. In order for a member of the clergy, and the events that they might organise, to mediate between a congregation and other institutions in a new community, there has to be a congregation. Without one, the religious end of the mediation process doesn't exist. St. Paul's Church as an organisation does not appear to have asked itself whether it might have provided from within itself a small congregation that could be located in West Thamesmead so that straight away there would be a religious organisation that could relate to the wider community through the mediating work of its clergy and other members. An existing congregation not only forms the essential religious organisational end of the relationship with the wider community and its institutions, but it also facilitates the social and institutional relationships required to build a larger congregation.

In Thamesmead we find things that we shall go on finding: that church buildings function as mediating institutions, and that the Church's clergy, as well as belonging to the congregation, are also important mediators in their own right between the congregation and wider society. In a period in which we increasingly expect every member of a congregation to be active in outreach, and the clergy to be congregational facilitators, this might not be a welcome message: but if it is true that the clergy are in practice effective mediators between the Church and the institutions and individuals of the wider society, then both they and their congregations need to regard that as a pivotal role to which the clergy need to apply a significant proportion of their time and energy.

The Beacon Project

In 2005 Bluewater had been open for six years, Ebbsfleet Station and the Ingris Park housing development at Greenhithe were being built, and the Thames Gateway plan for the area between Gravesend and Dartford included the Bridge Estate to be built by Taylor Wimpey and Dartford Council. The Methodist Church was working inter-denominationally on a number of projects, in particular with the Church of England on 'Fresh Expressions'. Graham Horsley, Evangelism and Church Planting Secretary for the Methodist Church, was keen to appoint someone and then see what happened: so Bart Woodhouse started work. The aim was to plant a church. Research was the first task: so Bart involved himself in Dartford Council's negotiations over the Section 106 agreement (the agreement that specifies the infrastructure and other contributions that the developer will make to the new community), and forged a good relationship with Jeremy Kite, the leader of Dartford Borough Council. Bart also secured the support of the Methodist Circuit to buy a house on the Bridge Estate as a base for his ministry. When he moved into the house with his wife Rachel and their three children in January 2008, the school had not yet opened, and they were among the first people to live on the estate. This gave them an opportunity to contribute to shaping the development's future. The Beacon Project had begun. An early step was to gather a group of six existing Christians who continued to attend other local churches. Initially only Bart and his family lived on the estate, but then two more of the core group moved in.

Early on, 'cell churches' gathered in Bart's and other people's homes for worship, prayer, fellowship, art evenings, Christian meditation, and other events. This was appropriate when there were few houses on the estate, all close to Bart's home, and, as at the beginning of any new housing development, making relationships is both essential and relatively easy. But by 2010 it was clear that the cell church approach was appealing mainly to the already committed, so monthly 'Celebrate' events in the school hall were organised. In 2013 this became a weekly Sunday morning service, with a congregation of about fifty: still informal, charismatic, and café-style in ethos, but now looking more like a traditional congregation, with the children going out for their own activities for part of the service. Relationship-building remains the primary evangelistic method, so newer congregation members tend to be friends of congregation members, and not necessarily from the estate: but more members are now coming from the estate, attracted by the Beacon project's numerous secular and faith-based activities.

From the beginning of the project, social events have been an important element of the strategy. Since 2009 the project has participated in the 'Big Lunch' co-ordinated by the Eden Project: an annual picnic to which everyone in the community is invited. Forty people came to the first Beacon Project Big Lunch. Now four hundred attend, and the event is like a large village fête.

The Beacon Project's activities can be located on a 'religious – secular' spectrum. The weekly Sunday morning service is a clearly religious event, as are continuing cell groups, an Alpha course for enquirers, prayer meetings, and gatherings for prayer for healing. At the secular end lie the Big Lunch and the weekly baby and toddler group (for which there is a high demand on this estate full of young adults having children). 'Messy Church', the child-centred craft-based events resourced by the Bible Reading Fellowship, lie around the middle of the spectrum. Special Christmas and Easter Messy Church events attract 150 people, most of them not involved in the Church in any other way. Also around the middle of the spectrum we find Bart's regular pastoral visiting of people living on the estate.

The most recent new project is a community coffee shop (Beacon Project 2016), which now provides the physical community hub that the estate lacked. The constitution of the community interest company that has been established to manage the café requires that a core group of the company's members should be members of the Methodist Church, and that the director (currently Bart) should also be a Methodist. This organisation and its activities also belongs between the religious and secular ends of the spectrum. The activity is secular, in the sense that it is a café for the whole community, and that there is no explicitly religious content: but the constitutional connections with the Methodist Church will ensure a continuing intimate connection with the religious end of the spectrum, and with the religious organisation, personnel, and activities of the Beacon Project.

By being actively involved in the estate's planning, with the institutions that relate to the estate, and with the estate itself as an early resident, Bart has been as much a mediating institution as the Beacon project as a whole. An early project was the Bridge Estate's Residents' Association, founded in 2008. Both residents and developers came to the first meeting, the association has a constitution and is managed by an elected committee, and it has forged links with local Police Community Support Officers, through whom a Bridge Estate Neighbourhood Watch scheme has been established. A website for residents, complete with live chat, is available. Through his early relationship with the Kent County Council, Bart was appointed a governor of the new primary school before it was built; and the Kent County Council link also resulted in membership of the steering group for the Learning and Community Campus now located on the estate.

The Beacon Church is now a church that does all of the things that churches do, so it is a congregation that needs to relate to the community in which it is set. It does this through the activities strung along the 'religious – secular' spectrum: the coffee shop, the Big Lunch, and the baby and toddler group. Bart Woodhouse is involved in the community both structurally and personally in such local institutions as the Temple Hill Community Development Trust, which runs a working lunch every six to eight weeks to which representatives of a variety of organisations are invited. Bart therefore functions as a mediating institution in his own right. He is not an ordained minister. In the context of the predominantly young demographic of the Bridge Estate, this does not appear to make any difference to the mediating function that he is able to fulfil.

Messy Church is an interesting institution. Elements of the events are explicitly religious, but other elements can be regarded as faith-based craft activities. The carers and children who attend will relate to the events in a wide variety of different ways, depending on their existing relationships to the Christian Faith and Christian organisations. Messy Church therefore functions as a self-enclosed mediation institution, containing within the one institution the religious, the secular, and the mediation between them. This might be one reason why Messy Church events tend to develop their own committed congregations with little overlap with other congregations, such as the Beacon project's Sunday morning congregation. Overlap does of course happen, but when it does it will often be via a familiar route: personal relationships between congregation members and interested non-members. Messy Church itself mediates less between an existing congregation and the secular activities and secular participants of the events, and more between the religious and secular elements of the events themselves.

The diverse bundle of institutions and activities that have developed on the Bridge Estate provide a useful model for a mediating package. Significantly there is nothing new here. Similar diversities of church activity can be found in other new developments on the edges of cities (Baker 2008: 111). The Beacon Project's religious activity is increasingly traditional. This is no surprise. What is significant is the way in which activities and institutions, and Bart himself, are strung along the full length of the 'religious – secular' spectrum, thus offering the best possible context for mediating activity.

The Greenwich Millennium Village

An early Thames Gateway project was the Greenwich Millennium Village, at the southern end of the Greenwich Peninsula. This was projected to contain a thousand new homes to house approximately three thousand people. Innovation was to be its major characteristic. It was to contain owner-occupied homes, social housing, and shared ownership property; it was to be as environmentally friendly as possible, both in the materials used to build the homes, and in its low energy use; and its design was highly distinctive. (The masterplan and some of the earlier blocks were designed by Ralph Erskine). It was a slow start, but John Prescott – Deputy Prime Minister, and an enthusiast for the Thames Gateway – got to hand over the first set of keys during 2000; and during the early 2000s several rows of townhouses, three larger blocks of flats ('apartments'), and some smaller blocks, were completed.

Not everything has gone to plan. The masterplan contained an 'Oval Square': blocks of flats in an oval shape at the northern end of the early phases, with shops on the ground floor. Instead, the straight lines continued to each of the corners, and a square was eventually created to the East of the bus lane and the road, with shops (again eventually) on the ground floor. Bizarrely, bus loudspeakers still announce arrival at 'Oval Square'. And there have been other changes, too. The Combined Heat and Power plant did not originally generate any power at all, although it has recently begun to do so; there is no community centre; it took fifteen years for a children's playground to arrive; and the development is not exactly tenure-blind, as it was intended to be. The innovative idea was that social housing, shared ownership property, and owner occupied homes, would be mixed up together, and that it would not be obvious which properties were of which tenure type. Things have not worked out like that. Moat Housing Association, the Registered Social Landlord, prefers to keep its properties together, as it is easier to manage properties served by the same staircases and lifts than properties scattered all over a development; when the consortium (lead developer Taylor Wimpey) built Becquerel Court and Farnsworth Court, two large blocks along West Parkside, they needed cashflow, and so built Becquerel Court as entirely owner-occupied properties and then put into Farnsworth Court the social housing that should have been in Becquerel Court. In the oldest section of the estate, on one side of the street there is a row of owner-occupied live-work units (with the 'work' unit routinely recruited as an extra living area), and, on the other side, social housing townhouses. The situation is designed for conflict.

An additional problem is that the Village is far from being tenure-blind visually. In some of the blocks it is unfortunately rather obvious which of the cores are wholly or predominantly social housing, because their lobbies do not have carpet on the floor and the other lobbies do. (Anti-social behaviour has been a problem. It is caused by people of different tenures, but most of the more generalised complaints relate to social housing tenants because their properties are grouped into identifiable staircases, whereas private sector tenants who cause problems are scattered throughout the Village.) The Village is not tenure blind in relation to services, either. Social housing tenancies forbid the keeping of pets, but owner-occupied leases do not. Some social housing tenants do keep pets, and Moat has sensibly decided to do nothing about it. In 2013 there was a threat to reduce the concierge parcel collection service for social housing tenants but not for owner-occupiers or private tenants: a threat sensibly withdrawn. The mixing of tenures remains a battle-ground because it has been half-hearted and compromised. The next time someone tries it, they need to do it properly. Only genuine tenure-mixing, with the same quality of housing and the same services for all tenure types, will be a true test of the concept.

Interestingly, a mile to the south of the Greenwich Millennium Village, in Westcombe Park, there is plenty of mixed tenure housing. During the 1950s and early 1960s, Greenwich Council (which then covered a smaller area than the current larger Greenwich borough) was different from some surrounding boroughs: it tended to buy houses and turn them into flats rather than knocking down houses and building high-rise blocks. There are one or two high-rise blocks, but a study of the skyline will reveal just how few there are in West Greenwich, East Greenwich, Westcombe Park, Blackheath, Kidbrooke, and Charlton. (The situation is very different further to the East, in what was once the borough of Woolwich.) The result is that, in Westcombe Park, a single row of houses can contain housing association flats, privately rented flats, privately rented houses, owner-occupied houses, and owner-occupied flats – and it is not always obvious which is which. This situation has now changed slightly, with some large houses having been expensively turned from flats into single large dwellings: but the area is still a lesson in how mixed tenure can work well. A possible conclusion here is that in those blocks in the Greenwich

Millennium Village in which there are currently no or very few social housing tenancies, Moat should buy flats that come onto the market.

One problem for which the developers are not to blame is that, because the Village is close to a Jubilee Line station, and only a few minutes from both Canary Wharf and central London, the properties are very lettable. The first shop to arrive in the square was an estate agent, and much of its business is the management of six month and one year leases of flats that owners have moved out of but have retained rather than sold. Early in the life of the Village the developer recognised that a growing problem was individuals and companies buying several flats each in order to let them out, so the company imposed a limit of two flats on any individual buyer: but no-one can control what happens when the original buyer moves out. An educated guess is that more than half of the properties in the Village are now let on short term leases. We lived in the Village for six years, at the start of which most people on our staircase were owner-occupiers. By the time we left, most the twelve units were let on short-term leases, and we were the second longest standing residents. Some of the flats changed hands three times while we were there, and some went through half a dozen tenancies. It is surely significant that a community of over a thousand dwellings struggles to elect a committee for a residents' association of which every resident is a member.

The Village was the brainchild of Alan Cherry, Chairman of Countryside Properties (UK) Ltd., which has built the development in a partnership with Taylor Wimpey. Sadly, Cherry died five years into the life of the Village. His company is now owned by the Copthorn Group, which is jointly owned by the Cherry family, the Bank of Scotland, and the Lloyds Banking Group. The next phases of the Village are now being built on land to the south. These were delayed by the recession, which hit Taylor Wimpey and other construction companies hard because they were left holding substantial stocks of land on which they had taken out loans but on which they could not afford to build. Another reason for the delay was that the most southerly part of the new development would have caused Cemex, owners of one of the aggregates yards, to break European rules on noise levels near to residential properties. Cemex went to the High Court, and won, leaving plans for the next phase in limbo. Ways of containing the problem have now been agreed, the masterplan has been redrawn, and new residents are now moving into the first new phase.

In case there is any doubt: Greenwich Millennium Village is a good place to live. There are two parks, public transport is frequent and plentiful, a walk by the river is around the corner, there is a row of shops containing a small supermarket, an estate agent, a dry cleaner, a chemist, and a spa and café, and outside the shops there is a village square which is increasingly busy when the weather is fine. And there are now schools and a health centre. One of the schools relocated from temporary buildings in East Greenwich, while the other is an extension of an existing Church of England school, and both have been judged 'outstanding' by Ofsted.[2]

When it's all finished, the Greenwich Millennium Village will still be a good place to live. It will be even better if there are plenty of properties with outside space that families with children can afford to buy, and if some way can be found to encourage genuine owner occupation. That may not be easy to achieve, but for a viable community to be created we need a sufficient number of people committed to the Village because they live in it *and* own property in it.

Tim Tabor writes in his study of the Greenwich Millennium Village:

The GMV successfully creates a pleasant, socio-economically inclusive neighbourhood with many positive environmentally sustainable features, yet it appears not to create as strong a community as its proponents suggest. This does not necessarily mean it has been poorly designed; instead, design can and probably has to at least a small degree helped facilitate and provide the opportunity for community – but to a much larger degree it has just created a pleasant place to live. [It is possible that the Village will develop as a community] in the future as it matures – as length of residence appears to be a major factor in determining the strength or level of community, so long as the number of people renting their homes on a short term basis does not increase. … Urban villages certainly create neighbourhoods conductive to community, but this is *no guarantee* that community will take root. Instead, there needs to be more emphasis on improving and helping the institutions and individuals that organise the community in addition to a recognition of the multiplicity of different community net-

---

[2] http://reports.ofsted.gov.uk/inspection-reports/find-inspection-report/provider/ELS/100111
http://reports.ofsted.gov.uk/inspection-reports/find-inspection-report/provider/ELS/100171

works and types of community that are not based on a single place or neighbourhood. … From an environmental perspective, urban villages can definitely play a positive role with regard to creating a built environment that conforms to high ecological standards and in encouraging positive environmental behaviours such as lower car use and recycling. Most importantly however, it must be acknowledged that building urban villages will not inevitably create community nor environmentally sustainable behaviours – there are more complex social, economic, political and demographic factors at play that must be addressed as well; and although parts of the urban village principles do look to address these, policy and implementation often concentrate too much on the built environment at the neglect of the social environment. (Tabor 2010: 60–61)

As in other similar developments, residents' commitments to the Village lie along a spectrum., between regarding the Village as their home for life, and regarding themselves as transient (Fox 2008b). How residents will shift along this spectrum as the Village matures is an interesting question. Will the dwellings in both the existing and the new phases be bought as investments and let on short-term leases (– or not lived in at all, which is what is happening to some of the high rise blocks to the north of the Village)? Will the new community being built to the north of the Village relate to the Greenwich Millennium Village? Across the residential community, can a way be found to prevent a few wealthy companies and individuals from accumulating large numbers of dwellings? Will the new blocks to the north and south of the Village be genuinely mixed-tenure and tenure-blind? A good sign is that some of the townhouse properties on the ground floors of the new blocks are social housing. A bad sign is that the developer and the borough council have agreed that the housing on the north-western tip of the Peninsula – with the nicest views up the river towards Westminster – will contain no affordable housing at all. Here financial considerations are making the decisions that will close off options for the maturing community on the Peninsula (Perumbalath 2008: 72). It is odd that if a developer wishes to change the colours of the balconies before a block of flats is built then a consultation exercise has to be carried out. For changing the entire ethos of a large part of a development no consultation is required.

  And will there be children and elderly people? Some of the new buildings to the south of the Village are low rise and suitable for families; and ground floor housing in the new blocks to the north is large enough for families, and the second floor of each of the three-storey dwellings looks out onto an internal courtyard: so the Peninsula community is hoping for families with children. A second primary school is now open, and after a number of false starts there will soon be secondary education provided by the primary school becoming an all through school.

A major issue facing the Village, which will eventually subsume all of these questions, is that eventually the Village will no longer be an identifiable 'village' at all: it will be just one part of a continuous development from The O2 to the edge of the aggregates yards south of the Peninsula (and surely those too will be turned over to housing as soon as all of the existing riverside developments are completed and sold). The Greenwich Peninsula will then be a single development containing The O2, hotels, office blocks, Ravensbourne College, schools, health centres, and 10,000 homes. It will need to be a town with a name if its residents are to have any chance of feeling that they 'live somewhere'.

It is no easy matter to build such a large and diverse community from scratch – 'community', not just buildings for a community to occupy. While the total number of housing units might be smaller than the number built in such new towns as Stevenage and Welwyn Garden City, the total package is more diverse, more dense, and altogether more challenging. The new towns were long enough in the building to enable community to evolve; and crucially they attracted large numbers of families with children, and enabled them to stay for the longer term, thus creating a bedrock of families with children on which a community can more easily be created. On the Greenwich Peninsula that particular factor will not be available to the same extent. New ways will have to be found to build community, and the faith communities will have to be part of the answer.

An Early Attempt to Establish a Congregation in the Greenwich Millennium Village

In Chap. 2 we came across St. Andrew's Church: the church built by the Gas Works management for its workers. During the 1960s, Peter Griffiths (the son of the Vicar of Christ Church), and Peter's wife, Jean, ran a declining Sunday School in the building. They were the building's last users. Services had ceased years before. The Sunday School closed, the building closed in 1965, it fell into disrepair, and it was finally demolished in 1984. The site was leased to O'Keeffe, the engineering company, and the proceeds were applied to the creation of Christ Church Forum.

The next part of the Peninsula's Christian story starts around the time of the demolition of St. Andrew's. Christ Church, East Greenwich, was still meeting in the large and crumbling Christ Church building. The parish's heyday had been a century before, when a large congregation and numerous parish organisations had given the parish a name for religious efficiency. But by the early 1980s its future was uncertain. We have already given an account of how the church building became Christ Church Forum, and how a new worship area was built on the end. Also significant to our story was the Rothbury Fellowship, a Congregational Church that met in Rothbury Hall, halfway up Blackwall Lane towards the Peninsula. Rothbury Hall had been built at the beginning of the twentieth century during a short period when it was believed that if congregations met in buildings designed to look like music halls then they would more easily attract new members. Rothbury Hall is still there – used by Emergency Exit Arts, which builds extravaganzas for carnivals and other large-scale artworks, and also runs a sideline in firework displays; and round the back is Stream Arts, another independent arts project. The exterior is crumbling but is still weirdly ornate, and the roof is topped with steeples on onions. Inside, the plaster gallery decorations can still be glimpsed through the bits and pieces of temporary artworks. By the early 1980s the Rothbury Fellowship was small and unable to maintain the building, so they sold it to Greenwich Council, which still owns it, and contributed the proceeds to the development project at Christ Church. Church Urban Fund money, parish trust funds, the sale of the parish's curacy house, the Rothbury Fellowship money, and various other grants, enabled the old Christ Church building to be developed as meeting rooms and offices, and the new worship space to be built on the end; and when Christ Church moved into the new worship area, the Rothbury Fellowship moved in too. Christ Church met at 9.30 a.m. every Sunday morning, and the Rothbury Fellowship at 11 a.m.

By 2001 the Rothbury Fellowship was a small congregation struggling to reach double figures. It was a joint Methodist and United Reformed

Church congregation; the minister was a Methodist, Chrissy Ross; and she and the Methodist and United Reformed Church authorities were finding it hard to justify continuing the post. But there was money available for 'new work', so to move the Rothbury Fellowship to the Peninsula and call it 'new work' looked like an attractive option. The United Reformed Church paid for a house in the new Greenwich Millennium Village, and the congregation left Christ Church and began to meet once a fortnight (not once a week) in the Millennium Primary School, first of all in the hall, and then in a smaller room. A few months later it closed, Chrissy Ross and her husband Ian Jackson moved out of the Village, and Chrissy left the Methodist Church's ministry.

Holy Trinity, Greenwich Peninsula

The Sunday congregation that now meets on the Peninsula belongs to the Parish of East Greenwich, and it has a story of its own to tell.

After the Rothbury Fellowship's attempt to start a church on the Peninsula, members of St. George's, Westcombe Park, sometimes wondered whether something ought to be done to serve the slowly growing community in the Greenwich Millennium Village. Mark and Alvin, two Church of England priests, moved into the Village, and began to relate to the parish; and when it was suggested that a Lent study group should be held in the Village, Alvin offered their flat, and after Easter the group continued to meet occasionally for prayer and discussion. Ben and Jules moved into the Village and brought their son Alfie to St. George's. Again, we wondered what we should be doing in the Village.

In 2007, the group decided that the Village should at least be able to celebrate Christmas. So we approached the Millennium Primary School's headteacher, Amanda Dennison, who welcomed the idea that one evening during the week before Christmas we should hold an all-age crib-building and then a carol service, and that we should advertise the events throughout the Village. Christmas Eve crib-buildings are a runaway success at St. George's, which now has to hold two of them; and the Christmas carol service is always well attended. We did not expect the same kind of numbers in the school hall, but at least these were events that we knew how to do, and we could do them without too much extra work.

We prepared the service booklets, had invitations printed, and then delivered the invitations to every letter box throughout the Village (– Alvin organised that for us: the ubiquitous entryphones mean that invitations can only be delivered by borrowing the universal key from the Village Manager). Members of Greenwich United Church (based in West Greenwich) and of St. George's came along to the events, as did a handful of people from the Village. But perhaps the most significant aspect of the exercise was that during a meeting with Amanda early in December 2007 to sort out some final details, she asked us whether we wanted to use the school hall for Sunday morning services. The black-led Pentecostal church that had used the hall on Sunday mornings was about to leave, and she wanted the next church to meet there to be one that would serve the Village. I was glad that I was not the only representative of the parish in the room. Also in the room was Julie Mason, one of the St. George's Churchwardens, and always responsible for the St. George's crib-building services, and the Rev'd Cynthia Finnerty, a non-stipendiary minister at St. George's, and for many years previously its organist. We looked at each other, and we said yes. Actually what we said was that we would have to ask the Parochial Church Council, but it was clearly more appropriate to say yes than to say no.

A few weeks later the Parochial Church Council (PCC) agreed that a small group from St. George's would be sent to the Peninsula to start a new congregation. This was commendably mission-minded and sacrificial of St. George's Church, which was willing to send some of their most experienced members, including myself, the Team Rector.

So again we distributed invitation cards, at a Sunday morning service in February 2008 St. George's commissioned us to go to start the new church, and the following Sunday morning we met in the school hall. We had recruited a student from Trinity College of Music to play the piano, we had prepared service booklets and taken necessary items in cardboard boxes, we had prepared to offer people tea and coffee after the service, and we held a Parish Communion service in the way that we knew how. In that sense there was nothing innovative about what we were doing. We had picked up a service from St. George's and held it in a school hall instead, in the same way in which churches were forming new congregations in new housing estates fifty years ago (Beeson 1963). Twenty people came: half a dozen of them from the Village. And from then on we met in the school hall every Sunday morning, with numbers hovering around fifteen, until there was a sudden drop when Village residents who had not been able to sell their flats found that they could, and in the space of a few months four couples left, two with their children.

It is this congregation, which the PCC agreed to call Holy Trinity, Greenwich Peninsula, that moved to the Prayer Space when it opened in September 2010, and subsequently moved to the school hall in the new church school on the Peninsula. The congregation is called 'Holy Trinity' because in the Peninsula's multi faith context, and particularly in the context of the multi faith Prayer Space, we all needed to be clear about the distinctive characteristics of our own faiths, and 'Holy Trinity' marks out the congregation as distinctively Christian.

Whether or not to move to the Prayer Space was a difficult decision to make. The Millennium Primary School is in the Village, whereas the Prayer Space is not; the Prayer Space is a building with a welcoming and religious purpose, whereas the school is a secular building with somewhat unwelcoming architecture; the Prayer Space has gatherings of other faiths in it and ought to have a Christian congregation worshipping in it on Sunday mornings – but that would mean that we were not worshipping in the only residential community on the Peninsula on Sunday mornings; the Prayer Space is cheaper to occupy than the school hall … . Prayer and discussion led to unanimous decisions by the Holy Trinity Church Council and the Parochial Church Council, and as soon as the Prayer Space was available the congregation moved into it. The later move to the new church school on the Peninsula was a move back towards the Village, but away from an identifiably religious building.

Holy Trinity has now been meeting for eight years, and is constituted as the church of the Greenwich Peninsula District of the Parish of East Greenwich – which means that it elects its own wardens and District Church Council to manage its affairs, and it elects representatives to the Parochial Church Council so that it can contribute to the life of the parish alongside Christ Church, East Greenwich, and St. George's, Westcombe Park.

Holy Trinity does all of the things that parish churches do. It holds services every Sunday; it celebrates the major festivals, and makes sure that its Christmas events are well advertised; and it holds discussion groups and social events.

With much help from members of St. George's and others, Holy Trinity held a highly professional passion play with a thirty-five-strong cast in the Village Square on the Tuesday of Holy Week 2011, and gathered a sizeable audience. A further passion play was held in the Square during Holy Week 2013. The rehearsals as well as the performances were held in the Square, attracting significant attention from Village residents. In Chap. 4 we shall be saying more about passion plays, but it needs to be said here that these events have been significant both for the Holy Trinity congregation and for the Village. They have been mediating institutions, standing between the congregation and the community in which it is set, enabling communication to happen and relationships to be built.

The many discussions held on Sunday afternoons in the café in the Village Square have been similar in intention. The congregation's move to the Prayer Space raised the question: How is the church to be publicly available to the Village now that people have to walk to the other end of the Peninsula on Sunday mornings? The answer was to occupy the only public space available: the café. Sunday afternoons are generally fairly quiet at the café, so the management warmed to the idea: and about once every six weeks a discussion was advertised around the Village. Sometimes the discussion was of a religious nature, and sometimes not: but always there was a connection with some aspect of life in the Village. Most of the discussions were led by Village residents, although occasionally we invited people to lead them if we thought that they might contribute in an interesting manner to a relevant debate. Like the passion plays, the café discussions were a mediating institution, enabling the Village to relate to the congregation, and enabling the congregation to relate to the Village (– to an institution, the café, and to the community as a whole, as well as to the individuals who attended).

In 2014 my wife Rebecca and I left the Greenwich Peninsula, but Holy Trinity of course continued, helped along by staff and officers of the wider parish. When we left, the congregation was still small, but there were more people from the Village attending than before the move to the Prayer Space. A new Vicar of Holy Trinity has arrived: the Rev'd Rob Ryan. The congregation is now meeting in the new school's school hall and is experimenting with a Sunday evening service time. Every Friday morning there is a gathering for prayer in the vicarage; on Wednesday evenings people gather for a meal and an opportunity to study together; and everyone is working out what other new things the situation now requires. It is already clear that among those new things will be the increasing centrality of new communications media. Holy Trinity has always had a website, but for those of us who did not grow up with the internet, a website feels like a poster that you read on a computer. To the generation that grew up with the internet – which means most of the people who live in the Village – a website is a dynamic communication tool, and is part of a package that includes Twitter, Facebook, and much else. To Rob Ryan all of this comes naturally. Those of us to which it does not need to recognise the importance of websites, Twitter accounts, Twitter feeds, Facebook pages, and all the rest, as essential mediating institutions: standing between the congregation and the wider community, and enabling communication to occur between them. Those of us to whom none of this feels inevitable need to hand over control of communications media to people to whom it does. Yes, posters on noticeboards, and Christmas cards delivered to every letterbox, still function as useful mediating institutions – but in the modern world they will never be enough.

Everything must be tested for its ability to be a mediating institution in its current context: which means that some things might need to change. It also means that some things might not change. In the park, just to the north of the Greenwich Millennium Village, there is a war memorial. This was rescued from the demolition of the gas works at the northern end of the Peninsula by one of the last staff members there, Kay Murch. She then got a job with English Partnerships, which took over the land from the Gas Board, and still she kept hold of the war memorial. When English Partnerships created the park just before the Millennium Exhibition opened, Kay managed to get the memorial erected at the southern end of it. She died soon after that, but she had achieved her goal.

When in October 2010 the Holy Trinity congregation moved to the Prayer Space, it had to ask itself what it should do on Remembrance Sunday. Both of the other churches in the parish mark the two minute silence, St. George's inside the church building, and Christ Church out on the pavement. Having a war memorial nearby provided an obvious opportunity: so for several years now, on Remembrance Sunday, the congregation has gathered at the war memorial for a traditional memorial event (sometimes preceded by a reading of First World War poetry). The words have been entirely traditional. There have always been Village residents present who do not normally attend Holy Trinity services: and a recent innovation has been to continue the event in the café rather than in the congregation's normal Sunday morning location, in an attempt to keep the Remembrance Sunday congregation together. Remembrance Sunday events are an important mediating institution up and down the country, and no less so on the Greenwich Peninsula. Sometimes nothing new is required.

A New Faith School on the Peninsula

The new school on the Peninsula is an extension of a church school in Woolwich. Because the UK Government wants to see more 'Free Schools' and 'academies' established, in order to centralise power and to deplete the influence of local authorities on education, it will no longer permit local authorities to build new schools: so local authorities now regularly build extensions of existing outstanding schools on new sites. If the new site is managed by the same board of governors and the same senior management team as the existing school, then it is the same school. North Greenwich is short of school places, so an extension of St. Mary Magdalene School in Woolwich is taking shape on a site just north of Millennium Primary School in order to provide a large new school that will take children all the way from reception to eighteen years old. The first couple of years in the primary age group are now on site, and in 2016 the first year of the secondary phase will occupy empty school buildings elsewhere before moving to the Peninsula when the new all through school has been built.

   In Chap. 5 you will find a detailed general discussion of whether faith schools can function as mediating institutions. Here I need to say how the new church school on the Peninsula is attempting to fulfil that role. First of all, the Holy Trinity congregation has moved into it, bringing the congregation nearer to the Greenwich Millennium Village: so the school building is a mediating institution in the sense that it enables the congregation to relate more easily to the residential community. (The downside of the move is that the congregation now relates less easily to the other faith communities that use the Prayer Space, and less easily to the institutions at the northern end of the Peninsula.) The school's senior management team and many of the teachers are Christians, and many of the governors are as well (including the current Team Rector of the Parish of East Greenwich, Margaret Cave, and other governors appointed by the parish's Parochial Church Council). The new Team Vicar on the Peninsula is chaplain to the new school as well as to a sister church school in East Greenwich. This occupation of roles by Christians enhances the school's relationship with religious organisations, giving it an opportunity to mediate between those organisations and the surrounding residential community. Clearly admissions criteria influence whether or not a faith school can be a mediating institution. Initially most of the places in the first years at the new school on the Peninsula are community places: that is, they are open to anyone who lives in the vicinity, with admission depending on distance from the school. Only a few places are 'foundation places', with admission based on religious affiliation. If this situation persists then there will be more chance of the new school functioning as a mediating institution. If too many of the places become foundation places, and it remains an excellent school, then the school might become an institution that alienates the community from religion, and thus the very opposite of a mediating institution.

There is no enmity between the new faith school and Millennium Primary School. Both are fully subscribed, both are outstanding schools, their headteachers get on well together (– if this were not the case then their close proximity might pose more of a problem), and the parish's clergy are still welcome visitors at the Millennium Primary School: but that does not mean that the arrival of a new faith school has not affected Millennium Primary School. Previous institutional connections between Millennium Primary School and the Holy Trinity congregation – the congregation meeting in the school hall, and the Vicar of Holy Trinity being a governor of the school – no longer apply; and the Millennium Primary School is now almost next-door to a faith school, which emphasises its non-religious character. This suggests that Millennium Primary

School cannot now function as a mediating institution. In Chap. 5 I make the general point that by attracting Christian teachers and congregational involvement, church schools deprive community schools of Christian teachers and congregational involvement, and thus contribute to the secularisation of society. The situation on the Greenwich Peninsula would appear to be a particularly clear example of this process.

Clergy Posts and Housing

When I arrived in the Parish of East Greenwich in 1996 there were two congregations, one at Christ Church and one at St. George's, and a single full-time post. The Millennium celebrations were about to arrive in the parish, and I was expected to contribute to those (– not only was I one of the chaplains at the Millennium Exhibition, but we were the parish that gave birth to the Greenwich Passion Play: of which more in Chap. 4). I asked for a second post and was given it. Christopher Morgan arrived as Team Vicar of Christ Church later in 1996. We had been told that when either of us left after 2000 we would not be replaced, because the original reason for the second post would no longer apply. The parish knew this and understood the reasoning. East Greenwich is a larger residential community than Westcombe Park, and the church school is in East Greenwich, so it was likely that the post to disappear would be the one at St. George's. The St. George's District Church Council therefore sponsored Cynthia Finnerty as an Ordained Local Minister, she completed the training course, and she was ordained to serve in the parish in preparation for the full-time post's disappearance. But then the major development on the Peninsula was announced, and the diocesan authorities agreed that the parish could retain two posts if one of them moved to the Peninsula. Plans were made for a new regulation vicarage to be built in the next phase of the Greenwich Millennium Village, but the recession caused that to be postponed, so when a suitable property for a temporary vicarage became available in the Village the Church Commissioners gave the money, the Diocesan Board of Finance bought the property, and my wife Rebecca and I moved into the fifth floor apartment in Becquerel Court.

It made a huge difference living on the Peninsula. I became a school governor, I got to know people, we could use our large living room (or rather, our large everything room, the flat being open plan) for parish and chaplaincy events, I could be a member of the residents' association (and a committee member and then its secretary), and I could be what a Church of England minister is meant to be: located in the community that I served. My successor on the Peninsula has found that after just a few weeks living in the midst of the community he is beginning to experience similar involvements. We tried to persuade the Methodist circuit that Jane Rice, a Methodist deacon appointed to work on the Peninsula, needed to live in the Greenwich Millennium Village rather than in the house in Charlton that they had bought to go with her post: but those responsible for such decisions did not see it like that. They thought that she was near enough. We said that she was not, because she was not on the Peninsula.

We have recounted above the Methodist and United Reformed Church attempt to found a church in the Greenwich Millennium Village. Greenwich United Church, in West Greenwich, to which some of the remaining members of the Rothbury Fellowship gravitated when their Peninsula congregation closed, worked alongside Holy Trinity on the basis of a local covenant. We involved each other in our activities, and held joint events (for instance, at Christmas). The covenant did not establish any additional institutions. It allowed for a representative of each church to attend the decision-making meeting of the other, and it required us to be clear about which events were to be organised jointly and which were to be events of a particular church to which members of the other would be invited. Above all, it required good communication. Greenwich United Church was responsible for the Cubs and Beavers that met in the Millennium Primary School for a few years. In 2014 Jane Rice left for Derby, and Martyn Coe, the minister of Greenwich United Church, for the Lake District. Greenwich United Church's involvement on the Peninsula ceased. Because Martyn's congregation was located in West Greenwich, and not on the Peninsula, neither he nor other members who gathered occasionally at the Prayer Space had been able to function as mediating institutions. The exception to this was Jane Rice, who became an honorary member of the Holy Trinity congregation. She could therefore function as a mediating institution, facilitating relationships between Holy Trinity and such institutions as the young mothers group.

In 2003 Christopher Morgan left East Greenwich for Norbury and was replaced by Derek Clacey; and when Derek retired in 2013 the diocesan authorities told us that we were to lose half a post. We negotiated for the retention of St. George's Vicarage, so that a house-for-duty post could be established at St. George's, where Cynthia Finnerty had been the vicar in practice if not in name since I had left for the Peninsula, and where continuity now had to be provided. The Team Rector's post moved to Christ Church, East Greenwich, and a full-time post has been put together for the Peninsula by including chaplaincy at the church school in East Greenwich and at the new church school on the Peninsula (along with its twin school in Woolwich).

All of this material about clergy movements might seem like mere detail compared with the mediating institutions discussed so far in relation to the Peninsula, both in Chap. 2 in relation to the faith communities' relationships with The O2, Ravensbourne College, construction sites, and ASDA, and in this chapter in relation to the Holy Trinity congregation's relationship with the Greenwich Millennium Village: but it is not. We have already recognised that the clergy are an important mediating institution that connects congregations with the communities in which they are set. It has been the provision of clergy posts and housing that has facilitated the relationship between Holy Trinity and the institutions and community of the Greenwich Millennium Village – of which more below. And it has been the provision of clergy posts and accommodation that has enabled the Greenwich Peninsula Chaplaincy to be so effective since its foundation in 2003. My own full-time post provided the freedom to give large amounts of time to workplace chaplaincy and to the management and staffing of the Prayer Space; other members of the parish's clergy – Derek Clacey, Cynthia Finnerty, and our curate, Jeremy Fraser – gave much time and energy to the work of the Chaplaincy (– Cynthia Finnerty still gives her time to these tasks); and members of clergy from neighbouring parishes have been chaplaincy trustees. Having a sufficient number of posts, and sufficient time available (in Cynthia's case entirely unpaid), has enabled the clergy of the parish to engage with secular organisations and their personnel in ways not open to those members of a congregation who need to earn a living: so in relation to this function, as well as in relation to the time and energy that they can give to residential communities and to other institutions, the clergy are irreplaceable mediating institutions. The Christian churches need to know that there really is no substitute for full-time clergy, and for non-stipendiary clergy with time and energy to spend, if they wish to remain connected with the communities and institutions among which their congregations find themselves. And at the same time, the clergy need to know that they will be maximally effective if they contribute to the establishment of additional mediating institutions to which lots of other individuals and organisations can contribute.

Residents' Associations and the Like

Many of the mediating institutions that we have studied have been established by congregations, or by members of congregations, and particularly by members of the clergy: but there are institutions not established in this way that can function as effective mediating institutions as well.

Since the early days of the Greenwich Millennium Village every resident and every property owner has automatically been a member of the Greenwich Millennium Village Association, the Village's residents' association. Once a year a meeting to which every resident and property owner is invited elects a committee, and throughout the following year the committee meets monthly to plan events for the Village, and to respond to issues facing the Village's residents. Soon after moving into the Village I attended an Annual General Meeting and found myself on the committee. A year later I was the secretary. By the time we left the Village three other members of the Holy Trinity congregation were on the committee, and one of them was its treasurer; and over some projects – such as the annual Big Lunch – Holy Trinity would involve itself as an organisation as well as through its individual members. The GMVA was in some ways functioning as a mediating institution, enabling Holy Trinity Church and its members to build and deepen relationships with the Village, with its institutions (such as its management company), and with its residents.

This was not the GMVA's purpose, but that does not change the fact that in relation to Holy Trinity this became one of its functions. Within a few weeks of my successor Rob Ryan moving into Becquerel Court he found himself on the residents' association committee.

The Peninsula Forum was a similar exercise. The Greenwich Millennium Village has a clear northern boundary along John Harrison Road, which runs from east to west across the Peninsula. South of the road the existing Village and the new phases being built to the south are the creation of Greenwich Millennium Village Ltd., which is owned by Countryside Properties PLC. North of the road the development is now the responsibility of Knight Dragon, which is owned by Henry Cheng Kar-Shun, who owns substantial interests in property and infrastructure in Hong Kong and China. When the first owners and tenants started to move into City Peninsula, the first block of flats north of John Harrison Way, the GMVA had to ask itself whether it wished to act as the residents' association for all of the residential property that would be built on the Peninsula. The obvious answer was no. It would end up with far too unwieldy an agenda. It would be better to encourage the residents of each new block, or each collection of blocks, to form their own residents' association. But that meant that there would be no organisation to tackle issues facing the Peninsula as a whole – a function that to some extent the GMVA had been carrying out, simply because it was the only residents' association there. The answer to that problem was to establish a Peninsula Forum: and so that it would be maximally effective, it was decided that every residents' association should be represented on it by its committee members, and that every institution on the Peninsula should be invited to send representatives. So since the beginning of 2012 meetings have been held quarterly, hosted and chaired by a representative of Knight Dragon, with the GMVA providing the secretary (initially myself, and then my successor as GMVA secretary, Shivanee Brigham, when I left). The reason for both the GMVA and Knight Dragon providing the officers was so that the organisation might be able exert a certain amount of pressure. The GMVA had always been quite successful in persuading people it wanted a discussion with to turn up at its committee meetings or at the residents' meetings held three times a year. Developers would sometimes be vigorously quizzed about their plans, and occasionally the discussion might make a difference to what was built. But there are some situations and some organisations over which a residents' association finds it has little influence, and these were sometimes situations and organisations over which Knight Dragon wished that it had more influence as well. By joining forces in the same Forum we were able to invite representatives from Transport for London to attend meetings, and they would turn up.

Because Holy Trinity and the Greenwich Peninsula Chaplaincy are both organisations working on the Peninsula, both of them can send representatives to the Forum, thus turning the Forum into a mediating institution – and in some ways that is its intention. The Peninsula Forum's purpose is to facilitate communication and relationships between different institutions on the Peninsula, so it is a mediating institution not just between religious and secular organisations, but between all of the organisations and other institutions at work on the Peninsula. Elsewhere in the Thames Gateway public, private, voluntary and religious sector institutions and representatives are doing their best to create places in which healthy communities can evolve (Perumbalath 2008; Hutson 2008). On the Greenwich Peninsula, the Peninsula Forum provides an example of the kind of mediating institution that can facilitate that process.

Other Faiths in the Thames Gateway

In Chap. 2, our discussion of religious organisations' engagement with industrial and commercial institutions offered evidence of widespread multi faith activity. Different models were in evidence, but there was no activity that did not in some way recognise the multi faith nature of our society, and the multi faith nature of religious organisations' engagement with that society.

The discussion so far of religious organisations relating to residential areas has been about Christian organisations. The reason for this is that residential areas are where we usually find congregations, and a congregation is necessarily a gathering of people belonging to a particular faith. So in residential areas it is usually single-faith congregations that create mediating institutions – either longstanding ones or temporary ones – and not multi faith organisations. In the UK the vast majority of religious organisations are Christian, so the majority of congregations establishing or working with mediating institutions will be Christian ones. But that does not mean that other faith communities are not engaging with their communities.

The Thames Gateway is home to people from most of the major world religions recognised in the UK: Baha'is, Buddhists, Christians, Hindus, Jains, Jews, Muslims, Sikhs, and Zoroastrians – and is also of course home to people of no faith. The different faith communities function very differently: In the case of the Zoroastrians, there are just a couple of formal faith groups to be found in London – the Zoroastrian Trust Funds of Europe based in Harrow, and the World Zoroastrian Organisation in South Norwood – drawing in people from across the Thames Gateway and beyond. At the opposite end of the spectrum, there are sometimes two or three Church of England congregations in each parish, and there might be fifteen or so parishes in a borough, so perhaps around 300 Church of England congregations can be found within the geographic boundaries of the Thames Gateway. The densities of most faith communities lie between these two extremes. Any study of this field of organisations would struggle to be comprehensive, so all we can do here is offer a few glimpses of the ways in which different faith communities are engaging with the communities in which they are set.

A Sikh *Gurdwara* (or temple) in East Ham and a Hindu *Mandir* (or temple) in Plumstead are typical of Sikh and Hindu religious organisations. Both are mostly focused on their own worship, and on the religious and other needs of their own faith communities; and because a great deal that goes on in the temple, and particularly the reading of the Scriptures, is not in English, visitors of other faiths or of no faith can find the proceedings somewhat inaccessible. However, Sikh and Hindu temples as a matter of principle offer a warm welcome to members of other faiths. At the heart of the building is always a kitchen, and the Sikh *langar*, a communal meal to which anyone and everyone is invited, is in practical terms as central to the faith as the reading of the Sikh Scriptures, the *Guru Granth Sahib*. The *langar* functions as a mediating institution for anyone who comes through the door. Outward-facing relationships are constituted by visits from local groups of schoolchildren, and by individuals who relate across faith boundaries and participate in civic, inter faith and multi faith organisations of various kinds. Members of the East Ham and Plumstead Temples work as volunteers for the Greenwich Peninsula Chaplaincy, so the chaplaincy functions as a mediating institution connecting the Temples with a wider community.

Much the same is true of Bromley Reform Synagogue. The liturgy is in Hebrew, and although an English translation is available, this still makes the liturgy rather inaccessible to a visitor who is not a Hebrew speaker: but again, a welcome is always given. As with the Sikh and Hindu Temples, the task is to care for the needs of that particular faith community, and to preserve its traditions. Individuals in the congregation – as with individuals in all congregations – will engage with institutions and individuals around them, and so it is the organisations to which they relate that function as mediating institutions. In the case of the Bromley Synagogue two of those organisations are the Greenwich Peninsula Chaplaincy (of which a now former Rabbi is a trustee) and local borough councils, particularly in relation to arrangements for the annual Holocaust Remembrance Day.

Greenwich is privileged to contain a small Baha'i community. Here again we find faith community members jealous of their traditions – such as the Baha'i calendar, with its nineteen months of nineteen days each: but it is a faith open to a changing world, and its members are open to compromise – so weekly or monthly meetings will sometimes be held, as well as the appropriate celebrations every nineteen days. The faith is just over a century old, and because it started in what was then the Ottoman Empire, it started in a multi faith world, and continues to regard the pursuit of unity and peace between members of different faiths, and grassroots connections with local communities, as core principles and tasks. So in Greenwich, even though the whole of the Baha'i community can fit into a member's living room, the community provides a trustee for the Greenwich Peninsula Chaplaincy, and is fully engaged with the Greenwich Faith Community Leaders meetings and committee. So here again it is multi faith organisations that function as mediating institutions.

Muslims make up the second-largest faith community in Greenwich. There is more than one Mosque, but the most visible is the one between Woolwich and Plumstead, the Greenwich Islamic Centre. Its remarkable achievement is to keep together in one Mosque an ethnically diverse Muslim community (– other boroughs have seen the Muslim community splinter into ethnic groups, each with its own Mosque). This success has presented the Greenwich Islamic Centre with a challenge. A growing Muslim population means that there is never enough space – hence the newly constructed extension, and more extensions to come. The Greenwich Islamic Centre's substantial youth project relates well to the police, to Charlton Athletic Football Club, and to Greenwich Youth for Christ; the Director of the Mosque chairs the Greenwich Faith Community Leaders' meeting, which meets once a quarter at the Town Hall; since the inception of the Greenwich Peninsula Chaplaincy, a member of the Mosque has been a trustee, and an Imam has been a member of the chaplaincy team and leads Muslim Friday Prayers at the Prayer Space every week. Engagement with the wider community thus happens at a variety of levels.

The picture that emerges from our discussion of Christian and other religious organisations is that where a religious organisation is of sufficient size it will create and manage mediating institutions to enable it to relate to the world around it. Larger religious organisations might also join together to organise more demanding mediating institutions such as foodbanks, and they might also participate in multi faith organisations when they see these as a means of serving their own faith community members at the same time as making a contribution to the wider community. Smaller religious organisations might have less energy to spend on creating their own mediating institutions, so members who wish to relate to the wider society will seek out existing mediating institutions to enable them to do that.

Four Organisations in North Kent

A relevant existing study is the Thames Gateway Kent Partnership June 2010 report on *Faith Communities and Regeneration in the Thames Gateway* (undertaken by the Grubb Institute and Whole Community Works). This is a study of four faith-based organisations: The Living Well (a partnership between a church and a GP surgery on Temple Hill in Dartford), Hope Street Community Centre (Sheerness), All Saints Community Centre (Chatham), and the Guru Nanak Football Club (Gravesend). These all 'responded to social issues and deprivation impacting on their local communities'. The researchers identified ten factors that contributed to these projects having an impact:

1. There is an identifiable community with significant deprivation and/
   or social issues where existing provision is difficult or having too limited an impact.
2. The faith community is identified with and/or is itself experiencing
   the dilemmas of its local 'community'.
3. There is a vision for the 'faith community in community' which is
   both informed by the faith and bigger than maintaining the congregation and worship space.
4. There is a strategic level enabler from the faith community able to
   link local vision to strategic concerns about delivery and opportunities for funding.
5. There needs to be a 'mobilising idea' of the project around which
   support can be built and different pressures contained – either an
   identifiable community or a shared passion (for instance, football).
6. The faith community is willing to make a significant investment in
   the regeneration over a period of time, in terms of people, buildings
   and finance.
7. A capacity to identify and get on board a sufficiently senior 'champion' in the relevant public sector bodies – local authority, primary
   care trust, etc.
8. The proposed project is an imaginative response of the right scale
   which is clearly relevant to local needs.
9. There need to be credible local leaders who know (and are known in)
   the community, have their confidence, and are felt to be able to speak
   for them.
10. If the faith community does not continue to renew its vision and
    involvement with the wider community, then changing secular agendas are likely to be the dominant influence on what develops.

The researchers conclude that

> the Findings of the Feasibility Study underline the potential difference
> which embedded faith communities can make in the social regeneration of

disadvantaged communities which the statutory agencies find hard to reach or where issues such as racism are politically sensitive. A key element in realising this potential has been the work of those we have described as strategic level enablers from within the faith communities. (Thames Gateway Partnership 2010: i–ii)

These findings cohere with our initial findings in this chapter, and particularly the tenth finding that only a faith community's continuing engagement with a mediating faith-based organisation that it has created will ensure that the organisation remains attached to its religious roots and that it remains an institution able to mediate between religious and secular institutions. I would add, on the basis of our findings so far, that a religious organisation's *structural* engagement with the mediating institution is essential to maintain the organisation as faith-based and mediating.

Conclusion

Every Sunday a Eucharist takes place on the Greenwich Peninsula, and on weekdays people gather for prayer on the Peninsula (though sometimes the gathering might be one person, and some days it doesn't happen). The numbers might be small, but worship happens. On Fridays Muslims gather for prayer; and during the week individuals use the Prayer Space for prayer. Prayer requests are written in the prayer requests book, and those who gather to pray use the book during their intercessions. Discussions take place in cafés, and plays are performed in the Village Square. Posters are put up, and a website is maintained, to tell people about services. Members of the Christian congregation serve on the residents' association committee and take part in the Peninsula Forum. There is an identifiably religious building on the Peninsula, and there are identifiable members of the clergy, both Christian and Muslim, at work on the Peninsula. Teams of clearly religious chaplains regularly visit workplaces on the Peninsula. Whatever else they are, all of these activities function as mediating institutions: as institutions through which the residential and other communities on the Peninsula can relate to religious organisations, and through which religious organisations can relate to them.

Just as a workplace chaplain functions as an individual mediating institution, so the minister of a church can function as a mediating institution (– and this can include such lay ministers as non-ordained pioneer ministers and Church Army officers). They are intimately and publicly connected with the congregation gathered for worship, and they can be intimately and publicly connected with all manner of secular and faith-based organisations. The personal relationships that they build with individuals in those organisations will often be the mechanism for the mediating effect, but those relationships will always be in the context of the minister's role within the religious organisation and of the organisational roles of the people to whom they relate. This suggests that churches need more ordained ministers, for it is ordination that publicly signals a mediating role. We clearly need to find as many methods as possible for ordaining more ministers.

But the clergy on their own will never be enough. Congregations are the first requirement; buildings are another (whether owned by the congregation or otherwise available on a long term basis); and then both temporary mediating institutions organised by the congregation, or autonomous faith-based organisations that function as longer-term mediating institutions. Research into what makes successful mediating faith-based organisations – such as the research into four faith-based organisations in North Kent discussed in this chapter – will help us to create faith-based organisations that work: so such research should be high on denominations' agendas: but every place will be different, so when mediating institutions are planned, the first priority is a careful study of the community in which they will be required, and then a careful matching of the institution to the congregation and to the community.

Bibliography

Baker, Christopher R. 2008. The wider perspective: The church in the new urban developments. In *Building utopia? Seeking the authentic Church for new communities*, ed. Laurie Green and Christopher R. Baker, 93–113. London: SPCK.
Beacon Project. 2016. https://www.facebook.com/no3atTheBridge/. Accessed 27 Jan 2016.

Beales, Chris. 2001. *The churches in Thamesmead: Their presence, interests, involvement and influence in the town.* Thamesmead: Christian Community Partnership.

Beeson, Trevor. 1963. *New area mission: The Parish in the new housing estates.* London: Mowbray.

Enoch-Onchere, Jedidah, and Simon Boxall Boxall. 2007. Congregations are mission: Building congregations in Thamesmead. In *Regeneration and renewal: The Church in new and changing communities*, ed. Malcolm Torry, 131–142. Norwich: Canterbury Press.

Fox, Michael. 2008b. The incomers' perspective. In *Building utopia? Seeking the authentic Church for new communities*, ed. Laurie Green and Christopher R. Baker, 41–56. London: SPCK.

Fox, Michael, and Sue Hutson. 2008. Shaping the church. In *Building utopia? Seeking the authentic Church for new communities*, ed. Laurie Green and Christopher R. Baker, 131–148. London: SPCK.

Harris, Margaret. 1998. *Organizing God's work: Challenges for churches and synagogues.* Basingstoke: Macmillan.

Hutson, Sue. 2008. The impact on the public sector. In *Building utopia? Seeking the authentic Church for new communities*, ed. Laurie Green and Christopher R. Baker, 77–91. London: SPCK.

Neutral Ground. 2015. www.neutralground.info/. Accessed 1 Dec 2015.

Perumbalath, John. 2008. Visionaries and strategists. In *Building utopia? Seeking the authentic Church for new communities*, ed. Laurie Green and Christopher R. Baker, 57–75. London: SPCK.

Roman Catholic Church. 1964. *Unitatis Redintegratio*, The Decree on Ecumenism, Second Vatican Council. www.vatican.va/archive/hist_councils/ii_vatican_council/documents/vat-ii_decree_19641121_unitatis-redintegratio_en.html. Accessed 15 Feb 2016.

Tabor, Tim. 2010. Community, urban environment and sustainability in urban villages: Assessing the success of the Greenwich Millennium Village, unpublished B.A. dissertation, University College London.

Thames Gateway Kent Partnership. 2010. *Faith communities and regeneration in the Thames Gateway: Feasibility study report.* London: The Grubb Institute.

4

Some More Mediating Institutions in Residential Communities

Introduction

In Chap. 3 we studied mediating institutions in residential communities in the Thames Gateway. In this chapter I have gathered case studies on mediating institutions in a variety of residential communities outside the Thames Gateway, and also some that are located within the Gateway's boundaries but are not directly related to new housing developments.

Telegraph Hill

Most of this study of mediating institutions is focused on the Thames Gateway, both because it is a definable area that contains a wide diversity of mediating institutions, and because that is where the research that led to many of the case studies was carried out. Telegraph Hill, at New Cross in South London, is not in the Thames Gateway, but I include it because, as a more settled community, it provides a useful comparison with some of the other material; because it shows evidence of a number of different mediating institutions; and because it is an area that I know

© The Editor(s) (if applicable) and The Author(s) 2016   **117**
M. Torry, *Mediating Institutions*,
DOI 10.1057/978-1-349-94913-7_4

well, and that I knew particularly well twenty years ago when I was vicar of the parish.

Telegraph Hill has undergone the kind of transition experienced by many communities in South London: from wealthy owner occupiers when it was built during the late 1800s, through a mixture of neglect and multiple-occupation during the early to mid-twentieth century, then through a highly cosmopolitan period as students and Caribbean families moved into the large houses, and now gentrification (Butler and Robson 2003: 53–5, 74–6, 99).

A survey of the voluntary organisations in the parish of St. Catherine's, Hatcham ('Hatcham' is the ancient name of the parish) revealed that most of them had been given birth by the parish church. And then, during the 1960s, the church gave birth to a 1000 m² community centre, built partly inside the church, partly on the churchyard, and partly in the vicarage garden. When I arrived as the Vicar of St. Catherine's in 1988, an independent management committee, the Telegraph Hill Neighbourhood Council, autonomously constituted, was managing the Telegraph Hill Centre on the basis of a ninety-nine year lease: but by the following year the local authority had withdrawn its grant aid, the independent management had walked out, and although legal responsibility for the building lay with two elderly trustees of the Telegraph Hill Neighbourhood Council, which continued to manage an advice centre in New Cross, the St. Catherine's Parochial Church Council (PCC) decided that it had a moral obligation to manage the Centre, even if it had no legal obligation to do so. It established a subcommittee of the PCC to manage the Centre, and let out the top two floors of the building as office space so that it could pay the bills and keep the building running. All of the Centre's activities (an elderly people's lunch club, a playgroup, a youth club, and a few occasional activities) just about fitted into the ground floor of the building. Still managed by a subcommittee of the PCC, the Centre remains at the heart of the community, hosting a wide variety of activities. Over fifteen hundred people use the Centre each week, and it continues to make a substantial contribution to the sense of community cohesion on Telegraph Hill.

The previous Telegraph Hill Neighbourhood Council management committee had been elected annually at a meeting that any member of the community could attend, and the organisation's officers were chosen at the same meeting, again by an electorate constituted by the entire residential community. The meeting was sometimes packed by groups of residents with particular agendas – whether that was maintaining a bar in the Centre, or running a campaign for speed bumps in their road. The stated aim of the Telegraph Hill Neighbourhood Council – to benefit the community of Telegraph Hill – would then come rather a long way down the agenda. So when the PCC found itself responsible for establishing a management committee, it constructed a committee with three equal parts: one third of the members were appointed by the PCC; another third by an annual meeting of the entire community; and another third by an election among user groups. The committee elected its own officers. In order for a decision to be taken, or for an officer to be elected, at least two of the constituencies had to agree. This prevented any single group of residents, or the Centre's users, or the PCC, from monopolising the committee's agenda. It is a committee structure that I would recommend to anyone establishing a similar mediating institution. The committee is now constituted in two parts: PCC members, and members elected from the community at an AGM; but one aspect of the constitution has not changed: the Centre management committee remains a subcommittee of the PCC. This was and is essential, because following the Telegraph Hill Neighbourhood Council's abandonment of the Centre, the parish agreed to be entirely responsible for the Centre and for its activities. By constituting the Centre's management committee as a subcommittee of the PCC, the PCC quite properly retains a veto – rarely used – over Centre management committee decisions.

As we might expect, the Telegraph Hill Centre functions as a mediating institution at a variety of levels. Church members involved in the committee, and perhaps in one or other of the Centre's activities, relate to committee members who are not church members, and to individuals around the Centre who do not belong to the church but are involved in Centre activities. The Centre enables religious and secular organisations to relate to each other, as the church, the Centre's user groups, and the residential community, are all fully engaged in the life of the Centre. And the committee itself is a mediating institution: an institution in which a religious organisation – the parish church – is structurally engaged with the residential community and with the organisations that use the Centre. The unusual density of relationships between religious and secular institutions exhibited by the Telegraph Hill Centre and its management committee mean that the Centre is an interesting example of a mediating institution deeply entrenched between a residential community and a religious organisation. The density of the relationship is probably one of the reasons for individuals crossing the boundary between the Centre and the congregation: a phenomenon particularly noticeable on such already mediating institutions as Remembrance Sunday and Christmas events.

Later in this chapter we shall discuss the Telegraph Hill Festival. One of the reasons that it was possible to establish the arts festival as a successful mediating institution was because the Telegraph Hill Centre was already a mediating institution, and because the parish church and organisations in the community were already well used to relating to each other through the Centre and through other organisations in which they were all involved. Where one mediating institution exists, it will be easier to establish another, and another, and another. The difficulty is in starting the process.

It is not always easy to manage a building in which a community centre is physically connected to a parish church, because secular uses can encroach inappropriately on the religious activity. For a building to function as a mediating institution, religious activities must keep their distinctively religious character, and the space in which they happen must always be available for that activity at the normal times for that activity. There have been times when the Telegraph Hill Festival, which uses the building for community drama rehearsals and productions, has made it difficult for the congregation to worship appropriately; and times when Centre activities in the Narthex, next to the church part of the building, have made life difficult for a religious event. But for St. Catherine's, and for many buildings like it, the double doors and glass screen between the two parts of the building enable people to be familiar with the church part of the building in such a way that the building can function as a mediating institution for them. A large proportion of the people who live on Telegraph Hill have been inside the church building: for school and other concerts, for General Election hustings, and for the Festival; and there will be many who have looked through the glass screen, or wandered through the doors, during their pilates class, pre- or after-school activity, parents' and toddlers' group meeting, Alcoholics Anonymous meeting, youth club meeting, ballet class, lunch for vulnerable adults, or elderly people's activity. During some of these activities they will meet participants and volunteers from the St. Catherine's congregation, adding another layer to the mediating institution. The top two floors of the Centre are now rented out as artists' studios, and here personal relationships between the artists and the Vicar, Sheridan James, add yet another layer to the mediation. Similarly, the choir and the orchestra that rent the church for rehearsals enable the building to function as a mediating institution for their members: a mediation enhanced when a relationship with the Vicar becomes part of the package – in the case of St. Catherine's a process much assisted by the Vicar being a musician. One of the choirs is a soul and gospel choir, which contributes to three services a year, and puts on a concert in the church once a year. The choir sings both secular and religious music. Here additional mediations are occurring: between religious music and secular music, and between choir members and audience members.

When the Centre was built, Lewisham Council took ownership of the southernmost part of it for use as a library. The library closed, and the parish's patron, the Worshipful Company of Haberdashers, which had built the church as well as most of the housing on Telegraph Hill, provided the funds for the purchase of the library building. There being no café on the hill, a group of residents established a charity, Bold Vision, and opened the space underneath the old library as the 'Hill Station' café. This is not as intimately connected with the church part of the building as the rest of the Centre is, but because the building belongs to the parish, and because the café's management and the Vicar of St. Catherine's and other church members have worked at creating good relationships, a number of mediating institutions have evolved. The Vicar, Sheridan James, leads an annual ukulele carol jam in the café; and the café organises the Telegraph Hill Big Lunch (as part of the annual Big Lunch initiative sponsored by the Eden Project) and the church joins in (– the church building providing the wet weather venue). The vicar participating in such events turns them into mediating institutions, but they are even more effective at mediating between the religious and the secular if other members of the congregation join in as well.

Telegraph Hill is host to a wide variety of mediating institutions: the Centre management committee (organisational), the Big Lunch (non-organisational institutional), the Vicar (again institutional but not organisational), and the building (a different kind of institution). The combination of these different mediating institutions, and the density of the relationships that many of them achieve, makes possible a multi-faceted relationship between the congregation and other Telegraph Hill organisations, between members of the congregation and other members of the community, and between the religious and the secular.

OneSpace, Kidbrooke Village

Again, not in the Thames Gateway, but significant because of the diversity of mediating institutions, the new Kidbrooke Village and its OneSpace provide a useful case study.

The Ferrier Estate, built during the early 1970s between Kidbrooke and Eltham in the London Borough of Greenwich, was once a highly sought after address. The rooms were larger than was normal for local authority properties, and only tenants with perfect rent payment records were invited to apply for flats. Forty years later the buildings had been neglected, and rather than spend money on them, Greenwich Borough Council decided to demolish the estate and replace it with 'Kidbrooke Village': 4398 new homes, 1350 of which were to be affordable rented homes and 550 shared equity dwellings. The plans were announced, including plans to disperse the existing community. The Ferrier Residents' Action Group (FRAG) was established to represent the existing five thousand or so tenants, and the 160 leaseholders who had exercised their right to buy their flats; Nick Russell, a Church Army officer, became its chair; and FRAG set about trying to protect tenants from the worst aspects of the borough council's mistreatment of them.

Ferrier Focus was a longstanding partnership between St. James's Church, Kidbrooke (Church of England), Eltham Green Christian Centre, Greenwich Youth for Christ (GYFC: running a drop-in for young people on the Ferrier Estate), Superkidz (a local Christian charity serving the needs of children), and, before its closure, Holy Spirit Church – a

Church of England congregation attached to St. James's and meeting in a leased shop on the Estate. Charlie Ingram, a Baptist minister working for the Church of England at Holy Spirit Church, estimated Ferrier Focus's contribution of voluntary labour to the Ferrier Estate to be worth £239,000 per annum, which inspired a more co-operative relationship between the Church and the borough council alongside Nick Russell's more conflictual one. A meeting with councillors discussed the Church's long history of community-making, and led to the council offering a disused community building to Ferrier Focus to use for the benefit of Kidbrooke Village's new residents.

Ferrier Focus was renamed Kidbrooke Focus and became a charitable company; money for the refurbishment of the building was raised from individual donations, grants, and the developer; the building was refurbished by the developer, Berkeley Homes; and it was then opened as 'OneSpace'. Margaret Cave, then curate of St. James's, Kidbrooke, became its first director and chaplain. The developer thought that they were providing a 'village hall' for their new 'village'. The parish church and its partners in Kidbrooke Focus thought that they were providing a location for serving the community in the diverse ways in which the Church normally does that. Both the developer and Kidbrooke Focus were clear that they wanted OneSpace to contribute to a sense of identity for the new community. As Margaret Cave put it:

> In an increasingly secular society and in a new development with no provision for community or faith spaces, how is the local church to engage with and serve the local community? As the church recognises that it is at work in an increasingly secular landscape, there is an imperative to renew connections with other structures and institutions once taken for granted and now lost. It is these connections that provide the conduit for the church to challenge and shape society. (Cave 2012: 7)

Kidbrooke Focus and OneSpace have two clear purposes: to be open to everyone in the community, and to be a Christian faith-based organisation, both at the same time. The charitable company has a religious purpose, which it fulfils through the values and ethos that it promotes at OneSpace, and by hosting a monthly gathering for worship organised by

St. James's, Kidbrooke (Kidbrooke Focus 2015): but the main purpose of OneSpace is to provide a context for Kidbrooke Focus, Greenwich Youth For Christ, Superkidz, and other organisations, to serve the needs of the community emerging in Kidbrooke Village. To this end, OneSpace hosts a regular forum to enable residents to tackle such issues as bus routes; it has facilitated the creation of a skate park in its outside space to serve the skateboarders who were using the space already; and it runs a carers' and toddlers' group. This group, the youth activities organised by GYFC, and the after school activities organised by Superkidz, are staffed mainly by volunteers drawn from local congregations: so the Christian Faith's contribution to the activity that occurs at OneSpace occurs on at least three levels: Christian personnel; Christian organisations managing the activities; and a Christian organisation managing the space in which the activities happen.

Another church that meets at OneSpace, a congregation of the Redeemed Christian Church of God, assists with the Foodbank centre that OneSpace organises, adding an ecumenical element to the mainly Church of England church involvement, but there is no multi faith organisational aspect. Individuals of any faith or none are of course welcome to participate in everything that happens at OneSpace, but institutional involvement is entirely and explicitly Christian. In the context of Kidbrooke Village, this might be legitimate. The important thing was to ensure that a mediating institution was established to enable a new community to experience a religious dimension. The organisations already working together where Kidbrooke Village was to be built were all Christian, so in order to make something happen it made sense to keep it that way. As the Village community evolves, a variety of faith communities will be represented, and the institutional involvement of other faith communities might one day be appropriate: but until then, Christian religious and faith-based organisations working together to serve the needs of the new community through Kidbrooke Focus and OneSpace is an entirely appropriate way to provide the required mediating institution and activity.

OneSpace is a temporary building, and one day it will have to be demolished to make way for more homes to be built. The developer has promised a 'community hub' in which Kidbrooke Focus will have a role. The organisation's directors and partner organisation are keeping in touch with evolving plans. Successful and communicated mediating activity will provide the best possible foundation for negotiations over how to provide the kind of permanent space that will enable Kidbrooke Focus to continue to function as an effective mediating institution.

St. Mary's, Woolwich

In 1959, Nicholas Stacey was appointed Rector of Woolwich. The St. Mary's building, just over the road from the Woolwich Ferry terminal, was decaying and damp. When the borough council compulsorily purchased Holy Trinity, Woolwich, for a road widening scheme, Stacey and the Parochial Church Council used the money to divide the vast galleries from the nave so that rooms could be created for community use. The building went from being an empty shell for most of the week, with a Sunday congregation of fifty people sitting in pews designed for seven hundred, to a community hub used by fifteen hundred people each week to pray, to buy coffee at the coffee house, to attend a local group meeting in the lounge, to seek counselling at the branch of the Samaritans located in the building, to attend the youth club in the refurbished crypt, to join the over 60s group that met in the crypt, or to visit one of the other organisations that rented space in the offices constructed on and under the balconies: Greenwich Voluntary Action Council, an Indian community health project, or the young offenders' project. The building and its activities became a bundle of formal and informal mediating institutions that together facilitated relationships between the church and its surrounding residential community (Stacey 1971: 72, 101–22). One of the community initiatives given birth in offices at St. Mary's was a housing association, which became London and Quadrant. Like the Carr-Gomm Society discussed later in this chapter, it 'wandered' in a secular direction and ceased to be the mediating institution that it had once been.

Fifty years later, the gallery partitions were gone, and most of the community initiatives with them. One long-standing community initiative survives. After the youth club closed, a preschool nursery was established in the crypt. It is still there twenty-five years later, and now occupies the south aisle as well. It brings parents, staff and children into the church building, and in contact with congregation members and with the Rector, Jesse van der Valk. It functions as a mediating institution. The 1960s innovations, and the community connections that accompanied them, were contingent upon the continuing support of the large parish staff team at the time, and faded away as the initial enthusiasts moved on to other tasks, and as the innovations became less relevant to the community's needs and less connected with the life of the congregation.

Over the years, the building itself has been a mediating institution. It is home to two Christian congregations, each of which meets several times a week in the building; and it is under the care of the Rector, the Churchwardens, and the Parochial Church Council: so the building cannot help being firmly rooted in Christian organisations and in the Christian Faith. As in any parish church, baptisms, marriages and funerals take place in the building, and these events are of course mediating institutions that facilitate relationships between the Christian Faith and the community. The building and the rites of passage function together, mutually enhancing the mediating potential of each one. The churchyard still belongs to the church and is now a public park used for a variety of religious and secular activities: so the building and the park together function as a mediating institution in relation to every organisation that uses them, every individual who comes into them, and the community around them. An added factor at St. Mary's, Woolwich, is the highly visible nature of the church building, located as it is on a hill next to a main road. The building is expensive to maintain – many of them are – but before any congregation, parish, diocese, or other denominational body, thinks about getting rid of a church building, it needs to ask not only about its function as a home for a Christian congregation, but also about its function as a mediator between the Christian Faith and the largely secular community around it.

The 1960s was a time of innovation, particularly at St. Mary's: and one further innovation was the ecumenical relationship with St. Andrew's Presbyterian Church (later St. Andrew's United Reformed Church). This congregation was struggling to maintain its building, and so moved into the St. Mary's building, in the process giving birth to the 1969 Sharing of Church Buildings Act, which made it possible for congregations to share buildings on a formal basis. The arrangement was subsequently established as a Local Ecumenical Partnership when these became available. Twelve years ago the St. Andrew's congregation ceased to thrive, and closed. There is now a good but less formal relationship with the Pentecostal church that uses the building on Sunday afternoons. Any relationship between two congregations, and particularly a relationship in which a building is shared, can represent the unity of Christians. Where this happens, an additional factor is added to the building's capacity to function as a mediating institution.

St. Mary's has seen a vast array of mediating institutions. Some of these were established by the church to enable it to relate to the wider community, and some were secular organisations occupying space in the building. Some of the clergy in Nick Stacey's time were workplace chaplains in the parish, and David Rhys, Jesse van der Valk's predecessor as Rector, acted as chaplain to the local authority: so in those capacities the clergy were mediating institutions. Jesse is often to be found in local community and church schools, making the kinds of connections still possible for the Church of England's clergy. The church building itself has functioned as a mediating institution, particularly when hosting rites of passage – and, sadly, during the vigil organised after the murder of Fusilier Lee Rigby in Woolwich in 2013, which is discussed at the end of this book.

Christ Church Forum

During the 1980s, Christ Church in East Greenwich took a somewhat different approach, and established a charitable company, Christ Church Forum, to run a Centre for Integrated Living in which people with disabilities and people without disabilities could work together in the service of the community. The parish church building was turned into offices and meeting rooms and was leased to Christ Church Forum, and a new worship area was built on the end. The vicar was chair of the Forum's management committee (although this was not a requirement of the constitution), several members of the congregation were heavily involved, and promotion of religion was one of the Forum's charitable aims. Although it would not have been conceptualised in quite these terms, the aim was to establish a permanent mediating institution that would enable the church and a variety of other charitable organisations (the Greenwich Association of Disabled People, Mencap, a toy library, and others) to work together to serve the East Greenwich community. At the beginning of the project it would have looked to the wider community and to the church as if the Forum and the church were locked securely together: after all, the promotion of religion was an aim of the Forum, there were lots of congregation members involved, and the Forum and the new worship area were in the same building and shared an entrance, foyer, toilets, and café area. It would have looked like a faith-based organisation that was an effective mediating institution between the church, the residential community, and a variety of charitable organisations active in the community.

The Forum's name is now the Forum @ Greenwich, there are no longer congregation members on the management committee, the vicar is no longer its chair, and religion does not feature among the organisation's stated objectives. The church still occupies its own part of the building by right, but in other respects it is a Forum user group, and uses spaces in the Forum building on much the same basis as any other organisation. The Forum is no longer a faith-based organisation, and it is no longer a mediating institution. What looked like a solid connection with the church turned out to be fragile and easily dismantled. In order to create a permanent mediating institution, it would have been necessary to provide a *structural* connection with the parish church, perhaps along the lines of the management arrangements at the Telegraph Hill Centre, with the management committee of the Forum being a subcommittee of the Parochial Church Council. Anything else is easy to unravel.

There is also an argument that it might have been right for the Forum to wander from its faith-based character. Managing a mediating institution can take considerable time and effort, and much of that time and effort might have to be spent by the clergy and other members of a congregation. For one mediating institution to cease to exist might provide the time, energy, and social space required to start new ones. It might sometimes be right for faith-based organisations and other mediating institutions to wander from their religious roots if the outcome might be new faith-based organisations and new mediating institutions.

Foodbanks

Prior to the recent recession the borough of Greenwich already had two local foodbanks, in Woolwich and Thamesmead. The foodbanks where places that people in temporary need of food could go to receive immediate supplies to tide them over until they could obtain other resources. There have always been domestic financial crises. When forty years ago I worked behind the public counter at Brixton's Supplementary Benefits office, administering means-tested benefits, we could provide emergency loans to claimants; and local authority social service departments used to be able to assist in times of crisis: but in this age of austerity, such emergency help is more difficult to obtain, families and friends will often have little ability to help, and the local foodbank can be the only answer. All manner of contingencies can trigger a crisis: a higher than usual heating bill might have left little money for food; or the earning partner might have left, leaving the family with no money; or someone might have gone to prison, leaving a family member with extra children to feed. Benefits and wages are falling in real terms; employment contracts are becoming less secure; and benefits sanctions, the benefits cap, and the bedroom tax (reductions in Housing Benefit where a family is deemed to have more bedrooms than it needs), have reduced the ability of the benefits system to provide a secure safety net. All of this means that families who could previously manage on their incomes are finding that they can no longer do so. As the rent and fuel bills have to be paid (particularly where the property has coin meters for gas and electricity), there could suddenly be insufficient money for food.

A group of concerned Christians in Greenwich, and then the Ecumenical Borough Deans (representatives of the different Christian denominations and categories of churches), decided to establish a borough-wide foodbank, with 'welcome centres' throughout the borough, a co-ordinated campaign to collect the necessary food, and a warehouse in which to store the food collected. A management committee sought advice from the Trussell Trust (an umbrella organisation for foodbanks throughout the country), recruited volunteers, and opened welcome centres in Plumstead, Woolwich, East Greenwich, Kidbrooke, Blackheath, Eltham, and Thamesmead: some in church premises, some not, and each one open for a couple of hours at a different time of the week, so that every day except Sunday there is a welcome centre open somewhere in the borough. At the Borough Deans' usual annual meeting with the Leader of Greenwich Council, Cllr Chris Roberts warmed to the foodbank project, heard the need for a warehouse, and committed the borough council to refurbishing a suitable building: so there is now a warehouse with lots of shelves, lots of volunteers, and lots of tinned and dried food coming in from collection points in churches, supermarkets, and elsewhere, and then going out again to the welcome centres in preparation for each centre's weekly opening time. Schools, doctors' surgeries, and other institutions, give out vouchers that can be taken to the foodbank and exchanged for food: and each claimant who brings a voucher is entitled to sufficient food for their family for three days, which is deemed to be sufficient time to enable them to sort out more permanent resources.

The foodbank is governed by a board of trustees, and is directed by Alan Robinson, who gives his time for free. The only paid member of staff is a warehouse manager. Trained volunteers sort the food at the warehouse, and yet more trained volunteers welcome people at the welcome centres, provide them with food, and discuss with then whether there are other services to which they might need to be referred. Debt counselling is frequently on the agenda. About 120 volunteers are active in any one month, and about 1500 people a year are receiving emergency food.

The Greenwich Foodbank is a classic faith-based organisation that functions as a mediating institution on a variety of levels. It mediates between the borough council, the borough's community, and the churches as organisations; it mediates between the particular church that hosts a welcome centre and that church's immediate community (not so much because that is where that community goes for emergency help with food, but because the local community knows that the church runs a foodbank welcome centre, and might therefore provide some of the volunteers); it mediates between the churches and the organisations to which foodbank clients might be signposted in pursuit of appropriate counselling and other assistance; and it mediates between the individuals who staff the welcome centres and the individual members of the community who come to the centres looking for food. While the Greenwich Foodbank is not in any sense a religious organisation, and is not structurally connected to any particular religious organisation, most of the welcome centres are hosted by churches, the trustees are church members, most of the volunteers are active church members, and the foodbank is affiliated to the Trussell Trust, which is clear that it is a Christian faith-based organisation. The Greenwich Foodbank is a faith-based organisation that is unlikely to wander towards the secular end of the religious/secular spectrum, so it promises to remain an effective mediating institution. Having said that, the foodbank's trustees and volunteers hope that it will soon be able to close. A wealthy country like the UK should not be running an economy and a benefits system that make foodbanks necessary.

Religious Drama

In English medieval cities, groups of citizens would rehearse religious plays and perform them on carts winding their way through the city streets. The Church functioned in Latin, but most people living in a town or city would have been unable to read, certainly would not have been able to read Latin, and until the printing press was invented, and Bibles were printed in English and chained in parish churches during the reign of King Henry VIII, very few people would have had the opportunity to read the Bible for themselves. This combination of circumstances kept most people largely in ignorance of the Gospels, and of the rest of the Bible's contents, apart from what the clergy chose to tell them. The mystery plays, as they were called, were created by the people of a city to provide the Christian education that the Church was not providing. The plays were highly imaginative, and sometimes quite creative with the biblical text, and were no doubt successful efforts to educate people in the contents of the Gospels, in the history of salvation from the creation to the final judgement, and in the rudiments of Christian doctrine. The mystery plays were mediating institutions: not between religious organisations and the societies in which they were set, but between the Christian Faith and the institutions and individuals of society. Recent revivals of the mystery plays from Chichester, York, Chester, and Coventry, have been most welcome.

There was something of a hiatus in religious drama in England during the Commonwealth of the seventeenth century, when drama in general had a hard time; and then a new censorship emerged, with the Lord Chancellor not permitting Jesus to be represented on the stage. Such films as *Ben Hur*, and such plays as *Christ in the Concrete City*, were the imaginative result: Jesus was always off stage, but dramatically present. Musicals about other biblical figures: *Jonah Man Jazz*, *Daniel Jazz*, and *Joseph and the Amazing Technicolor Dreamcoat*, were equally successful. Then the ban was lifted, and we could enjoy *Godspell* and *Jesus Christ Superstar*.

I had been Vicar of St. Catherine's, Hatcham, in New Cross in South London, for three years, when the Young family moved into the parish. Patrick was an assistant director at the Opera House, and Clare had been working for Kent Opera, but was taking time out to have children. I asked her if she would direct *Joseph and the Amazing Technicolor Dreamcoat* for us. We advertised around the Telegraph Hill community for an all age cast, and particularly in Edmund Waller Primary School. Clare rehearsed the cast for five weekends, and the single performance was a stunning success: fast, professional, and full of imagination. Joseph's chariot was a supermarket trolley. The fixed pews in the church had been a real constraint, so with everyone's agreement we replaced them with movable pews and chairs. From then on we alternated religious and secular themes. The single performance of *The Piper of Hamlyn* was so dangerously packed that after that we put on two performances of everything. We performed *Godspell*, *Guys and Dolls* (– is that a religious drama, or a secular one?), *The Ragged Child* (based on Lord Shaftsbury's work among the poor of London: religious or secular?), *The Passion*, from a mystery play revival that had just finished at the National Theatre: and when we could not find a modern passion play musical suitable for an all age cast, we wrote one: *Pop Goes the Passion*, based around nursery rhyme tunes and lyrics. The casts were getting bigger, the performances were as professional as ever, and additional events started to gather around the drama productions: concerts, comedy nights, a service in the church, a vast sculpture of the Holy Spirit hanging in the church – and so the Telegraph Hill Festival was born. The Telegraph Hill Festival is still going, more successful than ever, and still the biggest community arts festival in

South London. There are now a hundred different events spread across two weeks; two thousand people take part; and the community's schools, the church, and lots of other organisations, get involved.

For twenty-five years the Festival has functioned as a significant mediating institution. Church members work with non-members; and the Festival ticket booking night, and the community drama rehearsals and productions, take place in the church building, which of course functions as a mediating institution in that context. A significant event during every Festival is the Festival Service: a Sunday morning service designed to reflect the themes of that year's Festival. The service remains an entirely religious event. This is essential. The Festival, the church building, and the Festival Service, can only function as mediating institutions if it is genuinely Christian religion that is relating to a secular community, and if the community is relating to a genuinely religious event. So it is also essential that the Festival is designed to ensure that if a drama production has happened the night before the Festival Service, the building is entirely suitable for Christian worship on the Sunday morning; and the usual congregation needs to ensure that it is particularly easy for anyone not used to a church service to identify with one. Sometimes it is a momentary inspiration that enables the mediation to happen: as when at the end of the Festival Service in 2014 everyone present joined in a dance on entirely equal terms.

In 1996 we moved from Telegraph Hill to the Parish of East Greenwich, and in particular to St. George's, Westcombe Park. The congregation already had a musical and drama tradition, so we invited Clare Young to direct *Joseph and the Amazing Technicolor Dreamcoat*, and then *Godspell*; and with a variety of directors, mostly home-grown, we then put on *Pop Goes the Passion, Guys and Dolls, Jonah Man Jazz, George* (based on the St. George myths, and written by some of the church's younger members), and *A Lad in a Manger*: a pantomime based on the nativity story. And then we did *Pop goes the Passion, Joseph*, and *A Lad in a Manger*, all over again.

Putting on community drama is incredibly hard work. It takes months of preparation and administration (– obtaining permission from the rights holders, conforming to local authority rules for entertainment events, making sure that safeguarding policies and procedures are all in place, advertising for the cast), and then the drama workshops, the casting, the rehearsals – not to mention the script learning and the individual practising of soloists. But it's all worth it. Every event is a mediating institution, through which the congregation and the wider community can relate to each other, congregation members can relate to non-members, non-members can relate to the church as an institution, and, when the drama is inspired by the Christian Gospel or the biblical text, everyone involved can relate to the Christian tradition. Much the same is true of such arts festivals as the Telegraph Hill Festival. By the time we left Telegraph Hill the festival had its own autonomous committee: and this again became a mediating institution through which the church and the wider community could relate to each other, and through which church members and others could relate to each other, quite apart from the many relationships constantly facilitated by the festival itself.

And then came the really big one. In 1996, at one of my first Parochial Church Council meetings in the Parish of East Greenwich, the subject of the millennium celebrations was raised. We already knew that the Millennium Dome would be built in the parish, and we were all aware that the meridian line crossed the parish at its northern end – so we really did have a responsibility to create something significant to celebrate the turn of the millennium. Jesus was probably born three or four years before year 1 in the current calendar, but still the year 2000 was quite properly being celebrated as the two thousandth anniversary of Jesus' birth, so something had to be done. We were not a well-resourced parish in terms of congregational size or financial income or assets, but we had enthusiasm. A parish outing to the Oberammergau Passion Play was soon off the agenda when we discovered the cost: so we started to discuss putting on our own passion play. During a parish outing to Hastings we arranged to meet an old friend, Robert Wilson, whose partner John Doyle was a professional musical drama director. He had recently directed the Coventry Mystery Plays, so I asked him if he would help us to create the Greenwich Passion Play. He kindly agreed: so the planning and fundraising began. The top end of Greenwich Park was the obvious place. The Royal Parks have a 'no politics and no religion' rule, but we managed to persuade the management company that the story of Jesus' life was a story that belonged to everybody, and was as secular as it was religious. John started to write and rehearse the play with groups all over South-east London:

a Jewish Christian dance group, choirs of a variety of styles, schools, churches, and groups of churches. We ended up with eight hundred in the cast. With much help from the professionals, who gave generously of their time (– some asked for no financial reward, and some agreed reduced fees); from Edwin Shirley Staging, which loaned, constructed and dismantled eight stages for the event; a group of financial guarantors; and vast amounts of work from hundreds of people, South London's largest community drama during the millennium year took place on Good Friday 2000. The performance was the first time that the whole cast had been together. It started at noon with short plays about Jesus' life on seven different stages. Rather than the plays moving through the audience, as in a medieval city, the audience rotated around the performances. And then at two o'clock the action filled the whole space and involved the audience, and was finally focused on the central stage on which Jesus was tried and crucified. The play finished at three o'clock. The plan was that the audience should slowly depart, and then Jesus, Ben Thomas, our only professional actor, would come down from the cross. But the audience of between two and three thousand didn't leave. They were transfixed. Ben finally had to climb down while most of them were still there.

The Greenwich Passion Play was the largest single mediating institution in which I have been involved. Through it numerous religious organisations related to lots of secular institutions (the local authority, the Royal Parks, Edwin Shirley Staging, lots of other organisations that helped with the production, and the BBC); Christian and non-Christian cast members related to each other; schools related to congregations; all of them related to the longstanding English institution of passion plays; and all of these individuals and institutions found themselves relating to the story of Jesus' life and death (with a hint at the resurrection to come), and thus to Jesus himself.

Underlying all of the relationships facilitated by the mediating institutions that we have discussed so far is the genuinely religious character of a Christian congregation's activity – worship, and proclamation of the Good News of Jesus and the Kingdom of God. The greater the clarity of the religious character of the religious institution, the deeper will be the relationship between the religious and the secular that a mediating institution can facilitate when it relates to both the religious institution and secular institutions. It would be difficult to better the religious clarity achieved by congregations working together to create a highly public passion play.

Essential to the success of the Greenwich Passion Play was the establishment early in the process of an autonomous charitable trust to organise it. The Greenwich, Blackheath and East Greenwich Trust for the Arts (Greenwich BETA, or BETA for short) was set up to promote religious drama, and particularly the passion play. It sponsored some of the smaller community dramas that helped St. George's Church to prepare for the play; it sponsored a visit to the parish of the Riding Lights Theatre Company to inspire us with their own particular brand of religious drama; and it handled all of the decisions, contracts, and funding for the Greenwich Passion Play. There were both negative and positive reasons for establishing an autonomous trust. Perhaps negatively, it was important that no religious organisation should be in charge of the play, because religious organisations have an understandable tendency to want to control events put on in their name, and artistic freedom was going to be essential for a play that was to be written and rehearsed through workshops dispersed throughout South-East London. We had confidence in our Director, and he needed to be able to work without interference. More positively, we needed an organisation that could relate both to the religious and faith-based organisations that would be rehearsing and performing the play, and to the many secular organisations that would need to be involved. This was the biggest single community entertainment event for which the local authority had ever had to grant a performance licence; we needed to negotiate contracts with the companies and individuals involved with the resourcing and management of the play (for instance, we had to employ a technical manager to ensure that the cross would be safe for Ben Thomas to climb), and we needed to be able to apply to charitable trusts and to other organisations for money. All of this would have been difficult for either a congregation or an existing faith-based organisation to manage. Greenwich BETA was a mediating institution that enabled religious and secular organisations to relate to each other, religious and secular institutions of other kinds to relate to each other (– for instance, the religious and secular aspects of a passion play), and religious and secular individuals to relate to each other – and perhaps it also enabled the religious and secular aspects of every participant to relate to each other. So not only was the play a mediating institution, but the organisation constructed to put it on was a mediating institution. Both of them enabled the religious and the secular to meet in a unique event that was life-changing for many of the individuals and institutions involved.

Across Europe: Faith-Based Organisations as Mediating Institutions

As a result of the 'Welfare and Religion in a European Perspective' (WREP) research project, which set out to discover 'exactly what happens on an everyday basis in the fields of welfare and religion in Europe in the first decade of the twenty-first century, and to ask what this can tell us about the changing nature of European societies' (Bäckström and Davie 2010: 1), we have available some useful information on the ways in which churches throughout Europe undertake welfare activity. The project was not specifically about mediating institutions, but in amongst the evidence collected by the researchers we find useful material on organisations through which churches are undertaking welfare functions, and some interesting evidence of the organisations' perceived effectiveness.

For instance, in Gävle, in Sweden, the Diakonal Council (*Heliga Trefaldighets Diakoniförening*) meets 1500 requests a year for financial assistance to satisfy families' immediate needs, and works with families to try to prevent financial crises occurring in the first place (in particular through its Centre for Financial Advice) (Edgardh and Pettersson 2010: 46). In Drammen, in Norway, the Church City Mission runs a café and activity centre that mainly serve people who struggle with substance abuse. The aim is 'to make everyday life a little better for people in a difficult life situation'. The centre is financed by local government grants, individual donations, grant-making foundations, and other organisations; and in 2004 the bank that had loaned the money to get the centre built remitted the debt. Not only does the organisation serve the needs of some particularly vulnerable people, but it also represents a set of values about caring for the most vulnerable (Angell 2010: 69). In Reutlingen, in Germany, the Vesperkirche is an independent organisation that for five weeks in the winter organises a meeting place for people from a variety of social backgrounds. The church in which the activity occurs is open from 9 a.m. to 6 p.m., and there the Vesperkirche offers meals, refreshments, and volunteers, whose task it is to participate in conversation. The aim is 'to encourage interaction between people living in different circumstances' (Leis-Peters 2010: 103). In Darlington, in the UK, First Stop offers advice to homeless and unemployed people. The organisation was established by the parish church, and the church is still structurally involved with the project. Local churches have also given birth to two credit unions which they continue to support (Middlemiss Lé Mon 2010: 121). Evreux in France offers evidence of the many international and often lay-led organisations that stand between the Roman Catholic Church and the communities served by its churches, such as Caritas (an international development agency), the Catholic Committee against Hunger and for Development (*Catholique contre la Faim et pour le Développement*: a campaigning and development organisation), and the St. Vincent de Paul Conferences (a charity at international, national, and local levels, serving the needs of socially excluded people). Local branches will often co-operate with secular voluntary organisations – for instance, in serving the needs of illegal immigrants (Valasik 2010: 137). Similarly, in Vicenza, in Italy, Caritas-Diaconia is a local organisation related to the international Caritas, but separately funded, sometimes by local government grants. It is a 'pastoral organisation of social activity at the service of Christian communities. The goal of its existence is to promote solidarity towards people who are suffering from poverty and marginalisation'. It runs a shelter for homeless people, manages a project for ex-offenders, offers debt counselling, organises self-help groups among people with psychological problems, provides training and volunteering opportunities for young people, and much more (Frisina 2010: 154–5).

The WREP research project set out to discover how the relationship between religion and society is changing, particularly in relation to the provision of welfare. It draws conclusions about the different ways in which the relationship is changing in different countries, and discusses possible reasons for the differences, which often lie in the different welfare state regimes of the different countries, and also in the different ways in which the relationship between the Church and the state has evolved in different places. The researchers did not set out to study the different characteristics and effects of welfare functions carried out directly by religious organisations and by faith-based organisations – that is, by congregations keeping projects within their own governance (although generally in practice to some extent separately managed as 'projects' with their own governance structures), and by relatively autonomous organisations with firm connections with religious organisations and traditions: but some tentative conclusions are possible on the basis of the evidence to be found in the researchers' report. Faith-based organisations find it easier to access funds from a wider diversity of sources than religious organisations; they are more likely to slip in a secular direction (which congregations cannot – although projects that emerge within them clearly can); and they are more likely to be managing a diversity of activity in relation to a diversity of groups of people, whereas congregations are more likely to concentrate on a particular group that is already to some extent represented in the congregation. The faith-based organisations are often intended to supplement government and other provision by providing assistance in unusual or emergency circumstances, and by trying innovative methods, but they sometimes find themselves providing long-term solutions that other players have neglected (Frisina 2010: 155). Welfare activity more directly connected to congregations is more likely to remain temporary, focused, and innovative. In terms of impact on the total welfare provision of a place, faith-based organisations appear to have a greater effect than congregations. Researchers found that 'no other church-based agent, agency or activity is described and evaluated as favourably as the Church City Mission in Drammen' (Angell 2010: 69).

Relatively autonomous faith-based organisations are more clearly mediating institutions than are projects managed more directly by congregations, because faith-based organisations stand between religious organisations and secular organisations, mediating between them, enabling the religious and the secular to co-operate over welfare provision – even in a country like France, in which the secular and the religious are meant to be entirely separate.

Housing Associations in the UK and the USA

Until the mid-1980s, the Carr-Gomm Society was a small housing association that specialised in housing people coming out of mental hospitals. The Society provided rooms in large houses, and each house had a housekeeper. A small central staff worked from a dilapidated terraced house in Bermondsey in South London. Trustees were mostly committed Christians, and a small amount of explicitly religious activity took place. But then the Government started to close large long-stay mental hospitals so that their former patients could be cared for in the community. As there were few housing associations experienced in the field, the Carr-Gomm Society found itself expanding rapidly. Its Chief Executive was an ordained minister of the Church of England, but he had been recruited from a social services post; and large numbers of new staff, new offices, and lots of government funding, pulled the organisation in a secular direction. In 2010 the organisation merged with the larger Sanctuary Group.

The Carr-Gomm Society was a faith-based organisation that mediated between the Christian Faith and secular institutions in the housing field such as other housing associations, government funding and regulatory bodies, health service institutions, and local authorities. The Society 'wandered': that is, it moved in a secular direction along the spectrum between religious and secular organisations. But not every faith-based organisation does this (Jawad 2012: 211–17). The Southwark and London Diocesan Housing Association was established to enable church land to be used for social housing, with the land remaining under the control of the dioceses. The two co-chairs are Archdeacons, and there are other substantial links with the two Anglican dioceses of Southwark and London. While funding comes from government sources, land comes from the church; and while staff members belong to a professional housing association world, and there are close links with other housing associations, the strong links into religious organisations ensure that the organisation cannot travel very far in the secular direction. (Here I count a diocese, being a federation of congregations, as a quasi-religious organisation.) This is an example of an 'attached' faith-based organisation – though it is conceivable that future changes might enable it to 'wander'.

The Renaissance Collaborative in Chicago manages a hundred and one accommodation units designed for people who have been chronically homeless. Residents might have been previously on the street, or might have experienced a mixture of street-living and hostel accommodation. The problem has always been that the step from chronic homelessness to independent living can be a step too difficult to take – so the homelessness persists. The Renaissance Collaborative provides single rooms (each one with bathroom and kitchenette) and on-site support. The assumption underlying this approach is that people who have been chronically homeless need a safe environment in which to learn to make relationships, to manage their own lives, and to become financially self-sufficient. The organisation was founded in 1992 by four churches working together: the Quinn Chapel African Methodist Episcopal Church; St. Thomas's Episcopal Church; St. Elizabeth's Roman Catholic Church; and the Apostolic Faith Church. The original campaign was to save the Wabash YMCA (Young Men's Christian Association) building: a building of historic significance because of its role in Black empowerment throughout the twentieth century (– it was the birthplace of Black History Month). The building was rescued, refurbished, and put to use to serve some clear needs in Chicago: not only homelessness, but also many poor residents' need for health and social services of various kinds. So alongside the hundred and one housing units, the building contains the on-site support provided for the building's residents: 'employment education and training, job readiness, employment referrals and retention, health and wellness support including continued recovery support, nutrition education, mental and physical health services and general management of life skills'. The Renaissance Collaborative has taken on more projects since then: housing units for elderly people, employment training (for other members of the community as well as for the previously homeless residents), and a landscaping social enterprise that employs those whom the organisation has trained so that they can build up an employment history.

Unlike the Carr-Gomm Society, which relied on individual Christians to provide the connections with religious organisations, and like the Southwark and London Diocesan Housing Association, The Renaissance Collective Board of Directors contains among its members the ministers of the four original participating churches. As long as this continues, The

Renaissance Collaborative will remain an 'attached' faith-based organisation, closely connected to religious organisations. The purposes of The Renaissance Collective are not religious, in the sense that they are not worship, prayer, or proclamation: but they are certainly Christian in the sense that providing homes for the homeless, and enabling them to rebuild their lives, coheres with Jesus' statement that he had come to 'bring good news to the poor … to proclaim release to the captives and … to let the oppressed go free' (Luke 4: 18), and the clear expectation expressed in one of his parables that his followers would provide food for the hungry, welcome the stranger, clothe the naked, and take care of the sick (Matthew 25: 35–36).

The four churches that founded The Renaissance Collective have established a long term mediating institution to enable their congregations and office-holders to relate to a community, and particularly to its most vulnerable members, in ways that would not have been possible had each congregation been acting alone and from within the congregation as a religious organisation. The mediating institution constituted by the hundred and one housing units, the on-site services, and the employment and training initiative, enables thousands of individuals, and the community as a whole, to relate to a faith-based organisation, and therefore to the religious organisations and to the Christian Faith to which those initiatives are constitutionally firmly attached.

The three housing associations that we have discussed here have to varying degrees been mediating institutions, standing between religious and secular organisations; and, again, the mediation has been at more than one level. The housing associations as organisations have related to religious organisations and to secular organisations, and their personnel have related to the personnel of religious organisations and to the personnel of secular organisations. The Southwark and London Diocesan Housing Association and The Renaissance Collective have had strong *institutional* links with religious organisations, because church postholders hold office. The links between the Carr-Gomm Society and religious organisations were personal, temporary, and contingent. This is the difference that enabled the Carr-Gomm Society to 'wander', and therefore to cease being a mediating institution, and the Southwark and London Diocesan Housing Association and The Renaissance Collective to remain firmly 'attached' and to continue to be mediating organisations.

Conclusion

Religious organisations, up and down the country, and around the world, create mediating institutions all the time. Funerals are mediating institutions for individual and institutional mourners (– communities and organisations can mourn just as much as individuals can). Baptisms function as mediating institutions for the individuals and families involved, and so do religious weddings. Carol singing round the parish, in tube and railway stations, and in public houses, function as mediating institutions, and so do carol services and special church services for Mothering Sunday and Harvest Festival. All of these constitute both religious and mediating activity, for they are examples of the core worshipping activity of the congregation at the same as being mediating institutions, connecting the congregation with its residential community.

Some church activities are specifically designed to be mediating institutions. The highly popular 'Messy Church' – an all-age mixture of craft work, story-telling, and worship – can function as a long term mediating institution enabling a congregation to relate to a local community and its members, and also to local schools. Some activities are not designed as mediating institutions but function as highly effective ones. Jumble sales in churches and church halls can be significant mediating institutions if they are managed and run by congregation members, for they connect the congregation and its individual members to the individuals who contribute saleable stuff, to the individuals who buy it, and to the communities from which they come.

These mediating institutions are managed from within the religious organisation, often by groups of congregation members working together. A jumble sale is a project. It will have its own management structure – a temporary association of individuals who work together towards a purpose – with some formal elements, and some informal ones. Such temporary organisations are firmly rooted in religious organisations, so their behaviour will not be dissimilar to the behaviour of religious organisations: but their activity will lie somewhere on a spectrum between religious activity (worship and proclamation) and what we might call secular activity (selling clothes and other stuff). A group organising 'Messy Church' events will also be on that spectrum, but because of the worship content of Messy Church events, they will be closer in organisation, method, and ethos, to a religious organisation (Jordan 2005).

Long-term faith-based organisations that congregations might set up to fulfil a need that they have identified are rather different. Congregations across the UK, across Europe (Bäckström and Davie 2010), across the USA (Ammerman 1999: 367; Cnaan 2002), and throughout the world, work alone or with others to create faith-based organisations (whether internal to the congregation or external to it) that operate as mediating institutions. We have discussed the way in which Christ Church Forum and the Carr-Gomm Society wandered from being faith-based organisations: but this is not the only challenge facing religious organisations that set up faith-based organisations or work with existing faith-based organisations. Faith-based organisations are not religious organisations; they do not behave like religious organisations; and some of their characteristics are those of other organisational sectors. Forming an organisation or project in partnership with an organisation from the voluntary, public, or private sectors, can be quite disorienting for religious organisations, in relation both to such practicalities as buildings regulations, and to such issues as ethos and management style (Cameron 2010: 91–102, 132–47; Torry 2005: 151–64; Torry 2014b: 50–86, 112–67). But, as we have discovered, faith-based organisations can function as effective facilitators of relationships between the religious and the secular, so, whatever the difficulties, establishing such faith-based organisations should be close to the top of every church's agenda.

God is never absent, but all these mediating institutions create a thriving bridge between religious institutions and secular ones, and so contribute to the resacralisation or desecularisation of the Greenwich Peninsula and of everywhere else that they happen.

Bibliography

Ammerman, Nancy Tatom. 1999. *Congregation and community*. New Brunswick: Rutgers University Press.

Angell, Olav Helge. 2010. Sacred welfare agents in secular welfare space: The church of Norway in Drammen. In *Welfare and religion in 21st century Europe: Volume 1: Configuring the connections*, ed. Anders Bäckström and Grace Davie, 57–75. Farnham: Ashgate.

Bäckström, Anders, and Grace Davie. 2010. The WREP project: Genesis, structure and scope. In *Welfare and religion in 21st century Europe: Volume 1: Configuring the connections*, ed. Anders Bäckström and Grace Davie, 1–23. Farnham: Ashgate.

Butler, Tim, and Garry Robson. 2003. *London calling: The middle classes and the re-making of inner London*. Oxford: Berg.

Cameron, Helen. 2010. *Resourcing mission: Practical theology for changing churches*. London: SCM Press.

Cave, Margaret. 2012. *Setting up and running a faith based community centre and exploring its use as a base for new contextual Church in a new community*. Unpublished dissertation.

Cnaan, Ram A. 2002. *The invisible caring hand: American congregations and the provision of welfare*. New York: New York University Press.

Edgardh, Ninna, and Per Pettersson. 2010. The church of Sweden: A church for all, especially the most vulnerable. In *Welfare and religion in 21st century Europe: Volume 1: Configuring the connections*, ed. Anders Bäckström and Grace Davie, 39–67. Farnham: Ashgate.

Frisina, Annalisa. 2010. What kind of church? What kind of welfare? Conflicting views in the Italian case. In *Welfare and religion in 21st century Europe: Volume 1: Configuring the connections*, ed. Anders Bäckström and Grace Davie, 147–166. Farnham: Ashgate.

Jawad, Rana. 2012. *Religion and faith-based welfare: From wellbeing to ways of being*. Bristol: Policy Press.

Jordan, Stuart. 2005. Organizational studies strand—Worship and action. In *Studying local churches: A handbook*, ed. Helen Cameron, Philip Richter, Douglas Davies, and Frances Ward, 109–122. London: SCM Press.

Kidbrooke Focus. 2015. www.onespacekidbrooke.org.uk/kidbrooke–focus/faithworks–charter/. Accessed 22 Nov 2015.

Leis-Peters, Annette. 2010. The German dilemma: Protestant agents of welfare in Reutlingen. In *Welfare and religion in 21st century Europe: Volume 1: Configuring the connections*, ed. Anders Bäckström and Grace Davie, 95–112. Farnham: Ashgate.

Middlemiss Lé Mon, Martha. 2010. The "in-between" church: Church and welfare in Darlington. In *Welfare and religion in 21st century Europe: Volume 1:*

Configuring the connections, ed. Anders Bäckström and Grace Davie, 113–128. Farnham: Ashgate.

Stacey, Nick. 1971. *Who cares*. London: Anthony Blond.

Torry, Malcolm. 2005. *Managing God's business: Religious and faith-based organizations and their management*. Aldershot: Ashgate.

———. 2014b. *Managing religion: The management of Christian religious and faith-based organizations*: vol 2, 'External relationships', Basingstoke: Palgrave Macmillan.

Valasik, Corinne. 2010. Church-State Relations in France in the Field of Welfare: A hidden complementarity. In Welfare and Religion in 21st Century Europe: Volume 1: Configuring the connections, ed.Anders Bäckström and Grace Davie, pp. 129–45. Farnham: Ashgate.

5

Mediating Institutions Between Religion and Civil Society

Introduction

Allocating institutions to categories has been one of the most difficult elements of writing this book. At one stage I was tempted not to, and to write a single chapter, but that might have made the book even less manageable for the reader than it is already. As it is, the chapters are long. After experimenting with a variety of categorisations I fixed on three categories: industry and commerce – essentially private sector organisations and connected institutions; residential areas, and their related organisations and other institutions; and the institutions of civil society. This final category includes public and voluntary sector organisations that relate to areas wider than a local community (although of course the idea of a 'local community' is somewhat flexible), and also other institutions that relate to society as a whole. So in this chapter the reader will find educational and healthcare organisations, borough-wide consultative organisations, language, money, and the professions: a wide diversity of civil society institutions that have provided fertile ground for the development of mediating institutions.

© The Editor(s) (if applicable) and The Author(s) 2016   **147**
M. Torry, *Mediating Institutions*,
DOI 10.1057/978-1-349-94913-7_5

Educational Institutions

In the UK, as in many other countries, the churches were early players in the provision of education. Gradual State involvement in education in the UK, a history of local governance (by essentially voluntary boards of governors, with local authority involvement, and with central government playing a regulatory role), and the churches' continuing interest, particularly in relation to the school buildings that they own, have resulted in a highly complex web of educational institutions: local authority 'community' schools, two different categories of faith schools (mainly Christian, but there are now schools attached to other faith communities), academies (managed by academy trusts), and free schools (managed by anybody). All of these are state-funded. Alongside the public provision there are still numerous private schools that have somehow managed to hang on to their charitable status.

Faith schools are faith-based organisations: but do they function as mediating institutions? There is a variety of governance structures, but generally the board of governors will contain representatives of one or more local religious organisations, the local authority, the wider community, parents, and staff. The religious organisation is expected to contribute towards the maintenance of the building, but most of the costs will be met by the state. Senior staff members will normally be practising members of the faith community concerned. The curriculum will in most respects be the same as the curriculum taught in community schools, but religious education will generally have a higher profile, and will concentrate on the faith to which the school is attached (although not exclusively). There will usually be daily assemblies of an explicitly religious character.

There are numerous arguments for and against faith schools (Flint 2009). *For* faith schools is the view that parents should be able to choose the kind of education that their children will receive, and that because religious identity is an important aspect of a family, parents should be able to choose educational institutions that reflect their own family's particular religious identity. Another argument in favour of faith schools is the fact that faith communities can be a good source of committed school governors, which is one of the reasons for faith schools often providing high quality education.

But there are some problems. The other mediating institutions that we have studied have generally been established and paid for by members of faith communities. Where service to the community is the institution's task, either everyone will be served equally (for instance: chaplains visit every worker on a construction site, regardless of their faith commitments), or it will be the more vulnerable members of society who will be served (as with foodbanks). Faith schools are an exception to this rule, as most of their admissions policies privilege active members of the faith communities to which they are attached. There are several things wrong with this: it does not represent the attitude of Jesus, whose ministry was for everyone, and not just for his own followers; it uses state funds to privilege one particular faith community (hence other faith communities' demands for their own state-funded faith schools); it encourages dishonesty, because parents can rightly be expected to do the best for their children, and if a good quality school requires a period of churchgoing in order to get a child in, then that is what parents will do, whatever their own religious convictions; an oversubscribed church school can boost congregational size (– my anecdotal research suggests that this can be by up to a third) – so, in effect, state funds are being used to construct an institution that artificially boosts the membership and funds of a particular faith community; and it puts in a difficult position those members of the clergy who are expected to vouch for the churchgoing of school applicants. A further problem is the fact that teachers who belong to a faith community will be drawn towards a school attached to that faith community. This means that other schools will be deprived of teachers of that faith community, thus depleting the diversity and religious expertise of community schools' teaching staffs. Similarly, a congregation with a faith school attached will relate closely to its faith school, and will therefore be less likely to spend energy on relating to community schools in its neighbourhood. The beneficiaries are faith schools themselves, congregations with oversubscribed faith schools attached to them, and the children of parents who are sufficiently motivated to organise their lives around a period of churchgoing. The losers are neighbouring schools, and the children of less motivated, less organised, or more honest parents.

So are faith schools mediating institutions in their communities? That is: do they mediate between religious organisations and the residential communities in which they are set? For some families, yes: but for other families, no. Faith schools that discriminate on the grounds of attendance at a particular religious organisation can only damage that faith community's image in the eyes of the wider community. A faith school can therefore become the very opposite of a mediating institution. It can become an alienating institution. The only faith schools that would have any chance of functioning as genuine mediating institutions in relation to the *communities* in which they are set would be schools with no admissions criteria related to church attendance, and even then schools attached to one faith community might struggle to serve adequately children belonging to another.

An important question to ask is whether we seek a multicultural society, in which different ethnic, religious, cultural and other communities live alongside each other, or a more homogeneous society within which ethnic identity, religion, and culture, are essentially individual commitments with relevance to our private lives but not to society at large. I shall not attempt to answer that question here: but what I shall attempt is a social policy perspective that respects both possible answers to it.

Let us suppose that we are seeking a homogeneous society in which faith commitment is a family or individual commitment with no social implications. Faith schools will clearly not serve such an objective, because they divide the children of different faith communities from each other, and emphasise their differences rather than their common membership of a single society. We might think that entirely secular schools, within which religion is simply one more phenomenon to be studied, would be the correct policy response: but we would be wrong. If a family's or an individual's religion *is* an essential element of their identity, then if a child finds no opportunity to practice their religion in their school, an essential part of their identity has been left outside the school gate. It is not the whole person who is being educated to live in a cohesive society. Only a school that facilitates the *practice* of each child's religion will model a cohesive society in which religion might be a vital element of each person's private identity. Not to facilitate the practice of religion within the school will push religious practice and education outside the school and into religiously isolated organisations, creating the conditions for increasingly isolated faith communities.

Let us suppose, on the other hand, that we are seeking a multicultural society, characterised by tolerance and mutual understanding, in which different faith communities have lives of their own. We might think that faith schools are what is required, but again we would be wrong. A faith school can nurture the life of a particular faith community, but what it cannot easily do is generate the mutual tolerance and understanding between faith communities that a society containing different faith communities needs to foster if each of those faith communities is to experience tolerance and understanding. Entirely secular schools, within which religion is treated as an interesting phenomenon to be studied, might think that they can promote mutual tolerance and understanding between people of different faiths: but of course they cannot, because those faiths do not exist in the school in forms that could be recognised by their adherents. The only kind of school that can both nurture individual faith communities, and facilitate genuine mutual tolerance and understanding between them, is one in which the different faiths are genuinely practised alongside each other. Only schools that mirror the society that we want to see can be the correct policy prescription for the education system if we are to build a tolerant and multi faith society.

So we can see that whichever of the two kinds of society is our aim, what is required are community schools within which each child is encouraged and enabled to practise their religion. If this were to occur then faith schools would be unnecessary; and if this were to occur then every community school would function as a mediating institution between faith communities and society as a whole. Within that school religious organisations would be invited to ensure that the religious activities of their own faith communities would be properly represented within the school: for instance, by holding Muslim Friday Prayers every Friday, by holding Christian services, by representatives of the different faiths teaching the tenets of their faiths in school assemblies and during lessons, by taking religious drama, music, and other events into the school, where appropriate, and by enabling the school to celebrate religious festivals, not as cultural events, but as religious ones. All of these events and activities would be mediating institutions, enabling religious institutions to relate to the secular institution of the school, to the secular institution of education, and to wider society, as well as to every individual pupil and staff member in the school. Some of this activity happens, of course. In the UK, groups from churches rehearse and perform plays in community schools around the times of the religious festivals to which the plays relate; and members of the clergy are still occasionally invited to lead assemblies in community schools. But what is generally missing – and which needs to be central to such mediating activity – is genuinely religious activity: liturgy, prayer, and, in relation to the Christian Faith, the sacraments. To enable community schools to prepare their children for a multi faith society, schools need genuinely religious activity to happen, and not simply education about religion.

Higher education raises a rather different set of issues. Universities and other higher education establishments can appear threatening to religiously conservative families, making it difficult for them to encourage their children to enter higher education rather than the family business. The children of the family might themselves be concerned about their ability to continue to practise their faith at university, might be concerned about risking alienation from their family and its culture, and might feel their parents' anxiety and their own as a pressure not to seek higher education. The answer is to make higher education establishments more attractive to the conservatively religious by ensuring that they can continue to practise their faith once they arrive. Methods for doing this will be the establishment of multi faith chaplaincy teams, the construction of high-quality multi faith prayer rooms (designed to attract conservative members of all of the different faiths, and not just the more liberal ones), and the training of staff so that they understand students' religious needs – and the publication of these policies and of the ways in which they work. The complex policy questions arise when the desirability of attracting the conservatively religious into higher education establishments conflicts with other espoused and stated objectives, such as social cohesion and gender equality. Should separate prayer rooms be provided for women and men? Should women be permitted to wear face veils? It is when the practical policy implications of two desirable objectives conflict that the policy questions become genuinely interesting.

Established Religion

I have tackled two particular policy questions in the education field, and in each case have arrived at policy prescriptions that respect people's very different religious commitments, that create porous boundaries across which deeper understanding can travel, and that create the conditions for families and individuals to make their own transitions – culturally, occupationally, educationally, and religiously – if they wish to do so. This is a proper role for social policy: to open the boundaries of society's different 'clubs' (Jordan 1996: 8–11) so that understanding and resources can travel between them, and so that individuals, families, and communities can, if they wish, seek new situations, both within and outside their faith communities, within which disadvantages can be abandoned and new advantages can be sought (Torry 2016).

Singh and Cowden (2014: 130) would like to see secularism become the framework within which society negotiates its relationships with religion, whereas Modood would prefer active state support for relatively benign religion in the cause of marginalising less benign varieties. States in developed countries are increasingly turning to faith communities as delivery mechanisms for social welfare; and state recognition of religious identity and of religious communities can be a useful context within which to tackle disadvantage suffered by members of faith communities (Modood 2010: 8). Modood suggests that 'respect for religion is compatible with and may be a requirement of a democratic political culture' because it would encourage social pluralism rather than an 'intolerant secularist hegemony' (Modood 2010: 12, 13). This all seems entirely sensible, particularly as an established Church can function as a significant mediating institution. State recognition of a particular religious organisation can mediate between civil society institutions and religious organisations of all kinds (Bonney 2015: 131), and between individuals and institutions in government and associated organisations, individuals in the established religious organisation and its institutions, and individuals in all manner of institutions and organisations related to religious organisations.

Here the 'establishment' is an institution, but not an organisation. The establishment is not the religious organisation in question, the Church of England, but is rather a bundle of legal provisions, mutual understandings, and connections between organisations, that together form a flexible bond between the Church of England and the UK's monarch, government, parliament, and people: a bond constructed out of such a wide diversity of elements that it is often difficult to say exactly what it is. It is the establishment that functions as a mediating institution, mediating between the Church of England and society, between society and religion, and therefore between society and religious organisations in general.

But such an establishment always raises a question: To what *extent* should a religion be established? From the side of civil society, the answer has to be 'not too much so'. For an established religion to serve the useful purposes that it can serve, it must not be felt to be exercising undue influence on the Government or on society generally. There must therefore be a question as to whether Church of England bishops should continue to sit by right in the House of Lords. When we ask the same question – to what *extent* should a religion be established – of the Church of England, then the answer has to be the same: 'Not too much so'. The Church needs the freedom to establish its own ethos and rules. The compromises now in place in the UK, particularly in relation to the appointment of bishops, have created an establishment that leaves both civil society and the Church to develop in their own directions, while still preserving sufficient of a connection to enable the establishment to function as a mediating institution. Prayers are said when Parliament convenes, and can be said at the beginning of local authority meetings where council members vote for that (a provision recently reaffirmed by the Government); bishops *do* still sit in the House of Lords, but they are in practice perfectly capable of pursuing an independent view, and frequently a diversity of views. The establishment of the Church of England in the UK will no doubt continue to evolve. As it does, it will be essential to ensure that the arrangement continues to give both to the Church and to the institutions of civil society sufficient freedom of movement, and that the bond remains strong enough to enable it to function as a mediating institution between civil society and religious organisations, and between the religious and the secular: and in particular that it continues to facilitate a positive religious contribution to the shaping of social policy (Jawad 2012: 55).

Reports

During the past forty years the Church of England has produced some significant reports on the urban world. Perhaps the first was David Sheppard's *Built as a City*. While not an official report of the Church, it was by a high-profile bishop, it drew attention to the state of our cities, invited the Church to take a more active role in serving a changing urban world (Sheppard 1974: 355), and was explicitly theological, and in particular Christological.

Somewhat different was *Faith in the City* (Archbishop of Canterbury's Commission on Urban Priority Areas 1985). Canon Eric James, one of the facilitators of the Archbishop of Canterbury's Commission on Urban Priority Areas, confirmed in a discussion a few months after the publication of *Faith in the City* something that many of us had already realised: that Chap. 3, 'Theological Priorities', was an afterthought. Specifically theological reflection had clearly not been high on the Commission's agenda. This is no criticism. The situation in Urban Priority Areas, and the Church's situation in them, meant that 'to remember the poor' (Galatians 2: 10) was sufficient theological underpinning for the entire exercise. There is little Christological in the theological chapter, and nothing at all about the Eucharist, which by the end of *this* chapter we shall see as a serious omission.

Very differently, the theology of *Faithful Cities* is 'democratic' and 'contextual': it is practical, everyday, and in public. It is a theology of 'values' and 'visions' (Commission on Urban Life and Faith 2005: 14–15, 13). In 1985 *Faith in the City* would have had a similar influence on the Church as *Faithful Cities*, and as little influence on the nation, if Norman Tebbitt, a Government minister, had not accused it of being 'Marxist', which it really was not. The report was the result of the Archbishop of Canterbury's Commission on Urban Priority Areas' visits to areas of urban deprivation, and of detailed research. Its recommendations to both nation and Church were persuasive. After its publication the Government did take urban priority areas more seriously, and the Church followed up on many of the recommendations, the most obvious being the Church Urban Fund and Local Non-Stipendiary Ministry (now Ordained Local Ministry: see later in this chapter) (Archbishop of Canterbury's Commission on Urban Priority Areas 1985: 161–5, 112–17).

Faithful Cities, designed to be a follow-up to *Faith in the City*, and published jointly with the Methodist Church in 2006, represents a more hopeful age. Rather than being about urban priority areas, it is about the urban world as a whole, and its context is an economy with sufficient slack to enable 'regeneration' of communities (Commission on Urban Life and Faith 2005: 45–65). It contains much intelligent comment about long-term risks such as 'the gated community' (Commission on Urban Life and Faith 2005: 50), but there is a mood of optimism about it which would not have been possible if it had been written more recently. Some major differences from *Faith in the City* are immediately obvious. The Church is invited to seek opportunities for partnership with national and local government in place of the necessarily oppositional stance of *Faith in the City*, and a particularly clear difference is the ubiquity of other faith communities – a new ingredient that informs numerous of the report's recommendations:

> Urban-based faith communities will be important stakeholders within … discussions [with national and local government], their support and participation as partners is critical in the successful emergence of the good city. Alongside this, the churches must lead a debate with other faith communities about the provision of sacred space within our communities, not least in looking for space which could be held and used in common by all. (Commission on Urban Life and Faith 2005: 65)

Faithful Cities is a wide-ranging and useful report, and it is a pity that it did not receive the publicity that *Faith in the City* received.

All of these reports have functioned as mediating institutions: they have enabled the Church to communicate with Government and with wider society and its institutions; they have enabled the Government to respond to the Church (– *Faith in the City* in particular has enabled both Church and nation to respond to the issues raised in the report); and they have enabled Christian theology and secular narratives to relate to each other. The wide consultation behind both *Faith in the City* and *Faithful Cities*, and the reports themselves, provide a model for the writing of more such reports in the future. We do not need them very often, but every now and then gaps can occur in the relationships between the religious and the secular, and between religious organisations and civil society organisations, and the writing of a report can provide exactly the mediating institution required to fill the gap.

Chaplains

In Chap. 2 we discussed workplace chaplaincy, saw that chaplaincy organisations can function as mediating institutions, and recognised that each individual chaplain can function as a mediating institution. This suggests that chaplaincy as a generic activity can be a mediating institution. We might put the different levels at which relationships occur like this: chaplaincy as a generic activity facilitates relationships between the religious and the secular as generic realities; chaplaincy organisations facilitate relationships between religious organisations and secular organisations, and between the religious and the secular as generic realities; and each individual chaplain facilitates relationships between the religious and the secular within the people to whom they relate, between religious organisations and secular organisations, and between the religious and the secular as generic realities. It would therefore appear that the essential element is the chaplain and their activity. This suggests a requirement and a question.

The requirement is for chaplains who work hard getting to know the organisations that they visit, getting to know the people who work in them, and actively engaging with the issues that those organisations and their personnel are facing. There is little point in chaplaincy that is purely 'on demand': that is, when you only see the chaplain if you ask for them. That kind of 'chaplaincy' does not build relationships, so does not function as a mediating institution, and does not enable chaplaincy organisations and chaplaincy to function as mediating institutions.

The question then arises as to whether chaplains in different contexts function in different ways. Prison chaplains (Tyler 2006) are appointed by the Government or by a government agency to supply prisoners' religious needs, and to carry out a variety of statutory duties. For instance, in the UK the prison chaplain is obliged to visit every newly arrived prisoner. The chaplain is generally licensed by a religious organisation to carry out religious functions in the prison, but is managed and paid by the Government or by a government agency. The chaplain therefore belongs to a government bureaucracy: so in what sense might a prison chaplain be a mediating institution? Because the chaplain is clearly related to a religious tradition, he or she can mediate between that tradition and the prison as an organisation and as a community. There is also no reason why the chaplain should not use their relationships with religious organisations to facilitate relationships between congregations and the prison. The difference between a volunteer workplace chaplain and a paid prison chaplain is not that one can facilitate relationships between religious organisations and secular organisations and the other cannot: both of them can. The difference relates to the kinds of relationship that can be facilitated. By virtue of being appointed, managed, and paid by the prison service, the prison chaplain will have less freedom to organise their own activity. There might also be a difference in relation to what they might be able to say: although in practice, because a workplace chaplain needs the goodwill of the institutions that they visit in order to remain a workplace chaplain, the difference between the two chaplains' experiences of freedom of expression will be one of degree rather than one of kind.

We can locate chaplains on a spectrum. At one end will be the volunteer workplace chaplain, not paid, and usually managed by a religious or faith-based organisation. At the other will be the prison chaplain, appointed, managed and paid by the prison service, and subject to significant legal and bureaucratic constraints. Also at the same point as the prison chaplain will be the armed forces chaplain (Todd 2013); and not far off will be hospital chaplains (Flagg 2006), who are paid and managed by health service organisations. Hospital, hospice, school, and college chaplains (Collier 2006), whether volunteers or paid by religious or faith-based organisations, will be closer to the workplace chaplain's end of the spectrum: but if they are appointed, paid and managed by the hospital, hospice, school, or college, then they will be close to the point on the spectrum at which we find the hospital chaplain.

All of these chaplains can facilitate relationships between religious organisations and secular organisations, between the personnel of religious organisations and the personnel of secular organisations, and between religious and secular institutions: for instance, between healthcare and a religious ethical tradition.

If religious organisations are serious about relating to the society in which they are set then they will clearly need to establish and support as many chaplaincies as possible. Chaplains might be volunteers or paid, might be clergy or members of the laity, might be part-time or full-time, might be firmly attached to the secular institution in which they are working, or managed by an autonomous faith-based organisation or a religious or faith-based organisation firmly attached to a particular faith community. All of these different kinds of chaplain will facilitate different kinds of relationships between religious and secular institutions. What is important is that they are facilitating relationships: that they are mediating institutions.

State-Funded Mediating Institutions

'Near Neighbours' is a charitable company governed by a board of trustees, all of whom are Christians, and more than half of whom are Church of England clergy. The company's registered address is Church House, Westminster, and it is administered by the Church Urban Fund, the Church of England's urban poverty relief charity. It is government funded by the Department for Communities and Local Government. Near Neighbours has two objectives:

- Social interaction – to develop positive relationships in multi faith areas, i.e. to help people from different faiths get to know and understand each other better.
- Social action – to encourage people of different faiths and of no faith to come together for initiatives that improve their local neighbourhood. (Near Neighbours 2015).

The organisation makes small grants to local organisations to enable them to establish projects that fulfil these aims. Some of the 'local hubs' that process grant applications and monitor projects are Christian organisations, and some are organisations established purely to manage Near Neighbours grant applications.

Near Neighbours is a mediating institution that stands between the Christian Church and a multi faith society. Much of its work is useful (– it funds youth projects, dialogue projects, and much else), but whether establishing a Christian faith-based organisation was the best way to achieve the Government's stated aims is an interesting question. Like the St. Philip's Centre in Leicester (Ford 2010), and the somewhat misnamed London Interfaith Centre in Queen's Park ('We are a Christian centre working with people of all faiths and none'), it is a 'host and hosted' organisation: that is, it is an organisation firmly attached to one particular faith community that hosts events open to members of other faiths. It is not a 'level playing field' organisation like the Greenwich Peninsula Chaplaincy (discussed in Chap. 2). A Christian faith-based organisation is of course perfectly capable of carrying out Near Neighbours' two stated aims. What it cannot do is develop genuinely mutual relationships between people of different faiths in multi faith areas. That would require a 'level playing field' organisation – which would, of course, be an even more effective mediating institution, because it would mediate between all of the faiths and the totality of our multi faith and secular society. If the UK Government decides on a further initiative like the Near Neighbours project, then a reformed Inter Faith Network UK might be a useful location for its administration (on which see later in this chapter).

In 2007, the UK's Department for Communities and Local Government

facilitated the creation of a Mosques and Imams National Advisory Board (MINAB), founded by four national Muslim organisations who continue to hold vice-chair positions on an executive board of over fifty people from a wide range of backgrounds. MINAB now has over 600 mosques as members. Its purpose is to improve mosque governance and management and to enable imams to work in this country and with young people in particular. This work was funded by *Prevent* on the basis that better-governed mosques and more capable imams would increase what was then described as 'community resilience' to terrorism. (Home Office 2011: 81)

This might all be true, but at the time of writing the 'about' page on MINAB's website was unavailable, and there is no shortage of suspicion related to the fact that the organisation is government funded and is explicitly part of the 'Prevent' strategy designed to reduce the risk of terrorism.

MINAB is nominally supported by a number of Muslim umbrella organisations (none of which are in any sense properly representative of mosques or madrassas), and by six hundred mosques, so it has close links with the Muslim community. It is government funded, and so has close links with the Government. The organisation is autonomous of mosques and madrassas, but it is not autonomous of Government and was entirely the UK Government's creation. It is better seen as a quango fulfilling a government agenda than as a mediating institution.

Ecumenical Borough Deans

In theory, in every London borough, every main Christian denomination (Baptist, Methodist, United Reformed Church, the Roman Catholic Church, the Church of England, and usually the Salvation Army as well) and every other category of church (usually black majority churches, and independent evangelical churches) appoints an Ecumenical Borough Dean. In Greenwich the Ecumenical Borough Deans' meetings are attended by a Baptist minister, a Church of England priest, a Roman Catholic priest, a black majority church pastor, an independent evangelical church pastor, a Salvation Army officer, a representative of the Redeemed Christian Church of God, and a representative of the United Reformed Church. The role of a borough's Borough Deans is to work together to represent the borough's churches to the civic authorities, and to ensure that where possible the borough's churches can work together in the service of the community.

The regular meetings are at the heart of the Borough Deans' work. There will often be visitors. In Greenwich, the Borough Deans meet annually with the Leader of the Borough Council and with the Metropolitan Police Borough Commander, and occasionally with representatives of the Health Service and of other public bodies. A significant role in Greenwich and in some other boroughs is to administer the churches' involvement in the borough's major incident plan: so in Greenwich there is a meeting once a year with the relevant local authority officer, and the convenor of the Borough Deans maintains the list of those clergy willing to be called out in the event of a major emergency in the borough.

The Greenwich Borough Deans have sponsored a Street Pastors scheme (which puts trained volunteers on the street late at night to serve the needs of people out late) and a borough-wide foodbank: both in co-operation with the civic authorities – the local authority and the police in the case of Street Pastors, and the local authority in the case of the foodbank. The Greenwich Borough Deans brokered the establishment of the police chaplaincy managed by the Greenwich Peninsula Chaplaincy, and co-ordinated church activity around the Olympic and Paralympic Games. The success of the quarterly forum that the Borough Deans established to co-ordinate the churches' work in relation to the Games led to a permanent quarterly Greenwich Church Leaders meeting that members of all of the borough's churches are invited to attend. The Borough Deans have been responsible for the establishment of a new representative inter faith forum for the borough (see the account later in this chapter), and more recently for a homelessness shelter that rotates among a number of church buildings during the winter. In relation to each of these initiatives, one of the Borough Deans has been deputed to lead the project, or another minister in the borough has been asked to do so.

Is an organisation necessary to achieve these things? Might not informal relationships be just as useful? In the short term, relationships between individuals, and informal relationships among a group of people, can achieve significant projects: but if long term projects are to be established, if long term relationships between churches are to be fostered, and if deep relationships between civic authorities and the churches are to be formed, then the situation needs to be 'routinised' (Torry 2005: 79–80, 97). An organisational approach is essential. The Borough Commander and the Leader of the Council need to know who to talk to if they want to talk to the churches of the borough or to an individual denomination, and only an organisation can provide the required clarity. So if the Borough Commander wants to talk to all of the churches, then she will talk to the Convenor of the Borough Deans; and if she wants to talk to the Church of England, then she will talk to the Church of England Borough Dean.

Just as important is the kind of organisation required. Each Borough Dean is appointed by their denomination or fellowship of churches in its own way. So in the Church of England and the Roman Catholic Church, the Bishop will appoint the Borough Dean; the Methodist, United Reformed and Baptist Borough Deans are usually appointed by mutual agreement between the ministers of those denominations; and there is only one Salvation Army Citadel in Greenwich, so that decision is fairly easy. In Greenwich the black majority churches are represented by one of the pastors of the largest black majority church. Whether there was consultation with other black majority churches is a question that is difficult to answer. The independent evangelical churches' Borough Dean was appointed at a meeting of leaders of evangelical churches (which included the clergy of a variety of denominations as well as members of independent churches), and he is as representative as each independent evangelical church thinks he is. The Borough Deans are as representative as possible of the churches of the borough. They might not be perfectly representative, but it is difficult to see how they could be more representative than they are.

An organisation answerable to a twice-yearly breakfast meeting of London church leaders convenes an occasional London-wide meeting, but otherwise there is no formal structure holding different boroughs' Borough Deans together. Each borough's Borough Deans are expected to meet regularly, and they will generally appoint one of their number as their Convenor. This means that each borough's Ecumenical Borough Deans constitute an unincorporated association: a group of people with a common task and a rudimentary set of rules (Torry 2005: 32–4). First of all, this is all that is possible, as each denomination and each fellowship of churches appoints its Borough Dean in its own way; and secondly, this might be the most appropriate structure. Elaborate bureaucracy is not required. Whenever it is required – for instance, when Street Pastors are established, or a foodbank – then dedicated structures can be put together for those projects.

If the churches in a borough are to establish effective long-term relationships with the civic authorities, and with the whole community of the borough, then something like London's Ecumenical Borough Deans will be required. In a small town a 'Churches Together' group to which each church sends a couple of representatives, or that anyone who wishes can

attend, might be appropriate. Each London borough contains a population of about a quarter of a million, and hundreds of churches, so a more
robust representative structure is required. The Borough Deans structure
has evolved, and it works well where the denominations are committed to
it and the individual Borough Deans are committed to making it work.
Where it works it can achieve what no individual church could achieve.
So, for instance, just before the Olympic and Paralympic Games, an open
air service was held in the centre of Woolwich to 'welcome the world'.
Only an ecumenical body could have organised such an event. And similarly, at each General Election, Greenwich's Borough Deans organise hustings. The invited candidates attend because they know that the event is
organised by a Christian organisation that is as representative as possible
of the borough's Christian community.

The alternative to an imperfectly representative body such as the
Ecumenical Borough Deans is to rely on personal relationships between
individual clergy and individuals within civic institutions: but given
the complexity of the relationships between religious organisations and
organisations in the public, private, and voluntary sectors, the speed with
which the personnel of organisations can change, and the long term nature
of the issues that can face communities, it is only through long term
mediating institutions such as Ecumenical Borough Deans that longer
term relationships and projects can be constructed and then maintained.
Where Ecumenical Borough Deans work effectively they develop legitimacy, both with the civic authorities and with the borough's churches. In
Greenwich, and in the other boroughs in which they function effectively,
the Ecumenical Borough Deans have, over the years, facilitated a culture
of trust that enables communication and significant projects to occur.

One of the reasons for the notable effectiveness of the Ecumenical
Borough Deans is that they constitute not just one mediating institution, but three. First of all, each Borough Dean is an institution, because
they represent the denomination or fellowship of churches to which they
belong, the complex network of relationships and institutions that constitutes their denomination or their fellowship of churches, and the manner
of their appointment; and each Borough Dean is a mediating institution
because they enable the civic authorities to relate to their denomination
or fellowship of churches. Secondly, Ecumenical Borough Deans as a

London-wide network constitute a further mediating institution through which London's civic authorities can relate to London's churches: so when at their occasional London-wide meetings the Borough Deans discuss some aspect of London life, and particularly if they do that with representatives of London's civic authorities present, they mediate between the churches and London's civic authorities, and between London and the Christian Faith. Thirdly, the Ecumenical Borough Deans of a borough, as an identifiable association, constitute an effective mediating organisation, facilitating long-term relationships between the churches and the civic authorities, between the personnel of the civic authorities and the clergy and other members of the churches, between the clergy of different churches and the members of different churches, between the churches of a borough and the institutions and people of the borough, and between the Christian Faith and the borough.

Given the amount that a functioning set of Borough Deans can achieve as a mediating institution, it is surely essential that the churches of every London borough should ensure that they have a well-functioning group of Ecumenical Borough Deans, and that in other towns and cities similar structures should be established where they do not already exist.

Inter Faith Fora

For nearly twenty years Greenwich was well served by the Greenwich Multi Faith Forum. Its chair was held by Christians (Fr. Antony Plummer, a Roman Catholic priest, and then the Rev'd Jesse van der Valk, the Church of England Rector of Woolwich), but its membership and its committee were religiously diverse. The Forum built links with local faith communities, with the local authority, and with the police, and cemented relationships between individuals in different faith communities: relationships that facilitated community cohesion in the borough, and made possible some additional multi faith initiatives. When in 2003 a meeting was held on the Greenwich Peninsula to decide how the faith communities, the borough council, and the developer would relate to each other in the vast new development planned for the site, it was Greenwich Multi Faith Forum committee members who represented some of the borough's faith communities.

The Greenwich Multi Faith Forum was a constituted body that any faith community congregation and any individual could join by paying the annual membership fee. One understands why, when the Forum's constitution was under discussion, those existing members who did not in any sense represent faith community congregations, but had faithfully attended the Forum's meetings, wished to retain their individual memberships, and wished the Chair to be elected at the Annual General Meeting rather than by the elected committee. Presumably similar reasons lie behind the fact that many inter faith bodies struggle with the fact that their members are only ambiguously representative of their faith communities (Weller 2009: 77–8). In 2009 the Chair of the Greenwich Multi Faith Forum resigned after five years in the post, and an ill-administered Annual General Meeting, at which two different membership lists were circulating, broke up with two different members claiming that they had been elected as the organisation's Chair. The faith communities of the borough were left with no organisation that represented them. And then in August 2011, along with much of the UK, Woolwich experienced widespread arson and looting. The Leader of the Council called a meeting of some of the borough's faith community leaders, and at that meeting it became clear that the borough's faith communities desperately needed a new representative body. There were plenty of good relationships between individuals of different faiths (– many of them fostered by the Greenwich Peninsula Chaplaincy), but there was no structure to enable the different faith communities to consult with each other or to enable them to relate to the civic authorities.

In February 2012 the Greenwich Faith Community Leaders met for the first time. Every congregation of any faith community in the borough was invited to send its elected or properly designated leader or their representative. A committee was elected (to which each faith community could elect only a single member), and a constitution followed. Because the committee represents all of the borough's faith communities (the committee has Muslim, Sikh, Hindu, Baha'i, Jewish, and Christian members, and potentially a Buddhist), and because any congregation can send just one representative to the quarterly meetings, the Greenwich Faith Community Leaders is as representative of the borough's faith communities as it is possible to get. It is therefore supported by the Borough Council: the Leader of the Council attended its first meeting, the meetings are held in the Town Hall, and because the borough's civic authorities and other organisations recognise that the quarterly meetings are genuinely representative, the meetings have been able to welcome visitors from a variety of civic authorities and other organisations working in the borough.

Whereas within a particular faith community a minimally constituted association such as a borough's Ecumenical Borough Deans can be an effective mediating institution, Greenwich's experience suggests that a mediating institution to which a variety of faith communities can contribute in the longer term requires rather more formality in its constitution. The difference is probably because such denominations as the Church of England and the Roman Catholic Church are relatively rare among faith communities, in the sense that they have well understood methods for appointing representatives. This is less true of other Christian denominations and fellowships of churches, and it is less true of other faith communities. Each Hindu Mandir, Sikh Gurdwara, or Muslim Mosque, is an entirely autonomous organisation, and quite often there will be minimal or even zero contact between the different congregations of the same faith community. Therefore the inter faith body has to establish its own mechanism for ensuring that it is as representative as possible. Representation will always be imperfect, because each congregation will appoint its leadership in a different way, each elected or otherwise designated leader will decide whether or not to attend the meetings of the Greenwich Faith Community Leaders, and whether or not to send a representative if they do not attend: but whether or not large numbers attend, by constructing an internal method for ensuring that meetings and the committee are as representative as possible, the Greenwich Faith Community Leaders can function as a long-term mediating institution.

The Inter Faith Network UK

The Inter Faith Network for the UK (IFN UK)

> works to promote understanding, cooperation and good relations between organisations and persons of different faiths in the UK.

It does this through providing opportunities for linking and sharing of good practice, providing advice and information to help the development of new inter faith initiatives and the strengthening of existing ones. It raises awareness within wider society of the importance of inter faith issues and develops programmes to increase understanding about faith communities, including both their distinctive features and areas of common ground.

The Inter Faith Network's member bodies include national faith community representative bodies; national, regional and local inter faith organisations; and academic institutions and bodies concerned with multi faith education. (Interfaith Network for the UK 2015)

IFN UK is a charitable company managed by an Executive Committee elected by the membership at the Annual General Meeting. It is therefore representative of its members, which are an assortment of organisations with a variety of different interests in inter faith activity. When the Greenwich Peninsula Chaplaincy asked if it could become a member, it was told that there was no appropriate category. We found it difficult to understand why single faith national bodies could be members but not multi faith chaplaincy organisations deeply involved in creating good relationships between people of different faiths. The Greenwich Peninsula Chaplaincy is built on the 'level playing field' model (that is, no single faith is privileged in the constitution), rather than on the 'host and hosted' model (in which one faith is privileged, either by virtue of owning the building in which activity occurs, or having a privileged position in the constitution). Strangely, the Inter Faith Network for the UK's constitution is a compromise between the two models. It could so easily have been established on the level playing field model, but instead privileges the Christian faith community by ensuring that one of the co-chairs is always a Christian whereas the other faith communities have to take turns to provide the other co-chair.

But imperfect as it is, the Inter Faith Network UK functions as a mediating institution because it enables a variety of inter faith organisations and national faith community bodies to relate to the institutions of the UK's civil society. A significant problem, though, is that IFN might look as if it represents the faith communities of the UK whereas in fact it does not. In Greenwich, the Greenwich Faith Community Leaders is as representative of the borough's faith communities as it is possible to get. IFN is not as representative of the UK's faith communities as it is possible to get, and it is not as representative of inter faith activity in the UK as it is possible to get.

Just as it has proved extremely useful in Greenwich, and no doubt in other boroughs too, to have a body as representative as possible of the borough's faith communities to act as a mediating institution between the faith communities and the civic authorities, so it would be most helpful to have a similar body at national level. There would be two ways of doing this. Either each faith community could ensure that it was properly represented by a single organisation; or a national organisation could be constructed out of representatives of properly representative local inter faith organisations. The first route is unlikely to be productive. Where faith communities look as if they have representative bodies, they generally do not. Churches Together in Britain and Ireland does to some extent represent the main denominations in the UK, but not the independent evangelical churches (many of which join the Evangelical Alliance, or a variety of other federations) or the majority of black majority churches (some of which also ally themselves with various other federations). The Muslim Council of Britain is an umbrella body of which five hundred mosques, schools, and other Muslim organisations are members. It is as representative as possible of the Muslim community, but there are many mosques that are not members. Similarly with the British Board of Deputies: it is as representative as possible. British Sikhism has a variety of organisations that claim to be representative, and the Hindu community does not even have that. It is possible that an inter faith body to which each faith community could send a single representative of a single national representative body were to be established then each faith community would ensure that it had such a single body so that it could be represented. This would be a positive outcome. Alternatively, IFN UK could have a single category of membership in which each member organisation was as representative as possible of its local faith communities. This would require each member organisation to have congregations rather than individuals as members.

Either way, the UK would benefit from a properly representative inter faith organisation if it conformed to the level playing field model. Such an organisation would be a mediating institution, facilitating relationships between the UK's faith communities and the Government and other civil society organisations. Such a properly representative organisation would also be a useful location for a future Near Neighbours initiative, because to locate it in a genuinely representative organisation constructed on a level playing field basis would enable Near Neighbours to be a genuinely neutral meeting place between different faith communities and their members.

Other countries would benefit from similar organisations. Not that such mediating institutions would be a solution to the world's problems, but they would at least enable relationships and communication to occur where now they are absent.

Language

Language is an institution. It is organised activity that enables one individual to converse with another, or one institution to communicate with another. If language facilitates communication, and therefore relationships, between religious and secular institutions, or between two individuals, perhaps one who belongs to a faith community and one who does not, then language is a mediating institution: but if language is ambiguous, or one party's language is incomprehensible to the other party in a conversation, then it is not a mediating institution, and we might be better to call it an obfuscating institution (Cheyne 2008; Riordan 2008a, 2008b, 2009)

Ambiguous language can be either mediating or obfuscating. Where a sentence or a word can mean two different things, and both parties to a conversation understand both meanings, then the communication can be rich and interesting, and the language can be an impressive mediating institution: but where one party understands both meanings of a sentence or a word, and the other party understands only one of them, then the party who knows both meanings, and knows that they are only communicating one of them, is being economical with the truth (Torry 1980).

If two parties to a conversation are speaking the same language, and perhaps even the same dialect, but they are using different jargons, then neither will understand the other. They are speaking different languages.

Their encounters will be 'blurred' (Baker 2009b). Granted, language constantly changes, and no word ever means the same in two different contexts: but where two people in different institutions understand much the same by the words being used – that is, for both of them the words make the same connections with other words, and the same connections with institutional practices – then the two parties will understand each other, communication will occur, and the language that they use will function as a mediating institution. But if words form different linguistic connections for the two of them, or different connections with activities and events, then either no communication will occur, or, worse, miscommunication will occur. If the two conversation partners represent organisations, then if they manage to communicate, their organisations will understand each other better; if they do not understand each other, then no new inter-organisational understanding will take place; and if they misunderstand each other, their organisations will misunderstand each other, and serious consequences might result.

In our increasingly complex and interconnected world, it is crucial that we should understand each other, that organisations should understand each other, that institutions should understand each other, and that cultures should understand each other. Organisations are as much linguistic entities as they are structures and roles; institutions are often intensely linguistic; and cultures are significantly linguistic, especially if we include music, visual imagery, and bodily movement, among the languages that we use to express ourselves. Mutual understanding is going to be more and more important; and because communication channels can now convey information so quickly, it is essential that we should be able to understand each other quickly and easily.

Perhaps the greatest communication difficulties occur across the religious/secular boundary. Religious and secular individuals will often use language differently from each other; religious and secular organisations and institutions will use language differently; and different cultures will use language differently. Similarly, members of different faiths will use language differently, and the organisations and other institutions of different faith communities will use language differently. The word *jihad* can mean terrorism to one person, personal spiritual struggle to another, and strategies for religious and cultural domination to yet another.

It is a significant difficulty that only someone who has spent a life-time, or at least a number of years, committed to a faith community, will understand the nuances of that faith community's language – and then they will only understand the nuances of the language of their own particular corner of that faith community. What hope is there that someone of a different faith community, or someone with no faith, will understand? And what hope that the language of a religious organisation will be understood by a secular civil society institution, or by an organisation belonging to another faith community?

It is not just organisations that we are discussing here. Different professions will have their own languages, too. Police officers will speak the language into which they have been socialised, local authority officers will speak their own language, and each different denomination's clergy will speak their own various varieties.

A cohesive society does not require that differences should be disowned or minimised. It requires good communication and inclusive dialogue, and in particular 'inclusive dialogue on faith' (Cheesman and Khanum 2009: 59). Religious capital, spiritual capital, and social capital can only contribute together to community development, to regeneration projects, and to much else, if communication between the private, public, voluntary and faith sectors can use a shared language (Baker 2009b). Otherwise the discourse will remain 'instrumental … critical … and sceptical', and only occasionally 'aspirational' (Farnell 2009: 189–96). So what can we do to improve communication across the many organisational, institutional, and personal linguistic boundaries running through our societies, and to create widespread and permanent locations for dialogue? It is easy enough to say that we need to learn each other's languages, but that is far from easy to do. The least we can do is provide plenty of opportunities for conversation so that through constant practice we might be able to understand just a few more of the nuances of the linguistic usages in the institutions and organisations around us; and perhaps we could also provide institutions where members of different organisations could study each other's organisational structures, languages, and practices. If we wish to learn the language spoken by private sector organisations then we can study at a business school; if we want to understand public sector organisations and linguistic conventions, then we can attend one of the many courses and departments that teach public sector management; and if we want to study how voluntary sector organisations understand themselves and communicate with each other and with the world around them, then we can attend one of the many voluntary sector training courses or research institutes. If we want to understand religious and faith-based organisations and the languages that they use, then the answer is not so obvious. There are departments that study religions, religion in the public square, leadership in different religious organisations, and various other aspects of religion: but in the UK at least there is no academic department or other organisation dedicated to the understanding of religious organisations and the language that they use. (At the time of writing I was hoping that Heythrop College in London, which has at least taken an occasional interest in this area, might one day establish the necessary institution: but the college is now about to close.) There really is a massive gap here. If a local government officer or a government civil servant wants to improve their ability to relate to religious organisations and to understand better the language used in faith communities, then their only recourse is to pursue their own studies of a variety of faith communities. There is no organisation to which they can turn in order to discover the expertise that they require, and within which any research that they undertake will contribute to others' ability to understand and use the languages used by religious organisations and individuals.

This is not a book of recommendations, but perhaps one can be made here: in the UK, and in other countries, there is an urgent need for research and study centres on the characteristics, language, structures, and management of religious and faith-based organisations: institutions within which different religious organisations can learn each other's languages, structures, characteristics, and management methods, and within which representatives of civil society's institutions can learn how faith communities and their organisations understand themselves. The dialogue that would take place would be of enormous help to all of us who want to see cohesive societies develop in our increasingly complex and fast-changing world. Such a research and study centre could prove to be an increasingly important mediating institution.

Marriage

The institution of marriage has a complex history, or rather, complex histories. *Homo sapiens* have always paired up, in relationships of varying lengths, in order to bring up their children. In different cultures sexual intercourse, child rearing, same-gender couples, and couples containing individuals of different genders, have arranged themselves in a variety of ways. 'Marriage' and similar concepts and words have experienced their own diversity of meaning, but marriage has generally meant two individuals making a publicly recognised lifelong commitment to each other. An additional complexity is the diversity of relationships between marriage and religion. In some cultures marriage has been understood as deeply connected to religion, and a religious ceremony has therefore marked the beginning of a marriage. In others – including cultures that we might count as intensely religious – marriage has been an areligious and pragmatic institution constituted by a man taking a woman into his tent. In yet others, a secular ceremony marks the beginning of a marriage understood as a relationship recognised and regulated by the State.

In many societies today there will be a wide diversity of attitudes to marriage. For some individuals, and for some faith communities, marriage is at the heart of the faith. The Roman Catholic Church understands marriage as a sacrament, alongside baptism and the Eucharist. The Church of England understands the couple as marrying each other and the minister as a witness, but the couple's marriage is still understood in something like a sacramental manner, with the promises that the couple make to each other laced with religious language. In the Christian Faith, scriptural references that connect marriage with the relationship between Christ and the Church (Ephesians 5: 21–33) lie behind these religious connections; and most adherents of the world's major faiths will understand marriage as having a religious dimension, as well as a secular dimension relating to the law of the State. A couple that does not belong to a faith community will be more likely to regard marriage as a State-regulated institution that gives stability to their relationship, to their children, and to society.

If both the religious and the secular meanings of marriage are understood by a couple, then marriage can function as a mediating institution for them, connecting the religious and the secular. If a society understands the religious and secular meanings of marriage, then for that society as a whole marriage can function as a mediating institution. Where there are differences in understandings, things can get complicated. So, for instance, for the Roman Catholic Church, a marriage is normally only recognised by the Church if the marriage ceremony is conducted by a Roman Catholic priest (although a dispensation can now be granted where a Roman Catholic is marrying a member of the Church of England and a Church of England priest is to conduct the ceremony). So for the Roman Catholic Church, significant differences in religious and secular understandings mean that marriage itself cannot function as a mediating institution, because secular marriage ceremonies do not establish marriages recognised by the Church. The Church of England used to be in a different position. Here, marriage could function as a mediating institution because secular state ceremonies were recognised as establishing marriages as legitimate as those established by a Church of England ceremony. Now things have changed. In spite of the fact that many members and clergy of the Church of England might wish to recognise same-sex marriages established by the State, and might wish the Church to conduct marriage ceremonies for same-sex couples, the Government and Parliament, following (far from unanimous) pressure from the House of Bishops, have forbidden Church of England clergy to conduct marriage ceremonies for same-sex couples. The Church's stated view of marriage, and the State's view of marriage (which is also the majority view of marriage in society), have now diverged, meaning that for members of the Church of England marriage can no longer function as a mediating institution. It might be objected that a marriage between a man and woman can still be experienced as a mediating institution, and that will be true of any individual such marriage: but it remains true that marriage as an institution can no longer function as a mediating institution. There are churches that permit their clergy to perform same-sex marriages (for instance, the United Reformed Church, if the local Church Meeting agrees), but this does not change the general situation. Apart from the

Roman Catholic Church, the Church as a whole in the UK used to experience marriage as a mediating institution. It can no longer do so: and the legislation that forbids Church of England clergy to conduct same-sex marriage ceremonies means that the State no longer sees marriage as a mediating institution. Other faith communities are in much the same situation. They are generally opposed to same-sex marriage, and for them, too, marriage has ceased to be a mediating institution. Such a loss of a significant mediating institution looks like a purely national issue because there are still many countries that do not permit same-sex marriage: but that number is declining, and with the Republic of Ireland voting to change the constitution to make same-sex marriage possible, the United States of American's Supreme Court deciding in favour of the states that permit same-sex marriage, and Latin American countries now legislating for same-sex marriage, the process would seem to be unstoppable. Globally, marriage will soon cease to be a mediating institution.

This might look like a question purely about marriage, but it is not. It matters a great deal that an institution at the heart of society can no longer function as a mediating institution. There were few enough such mediating institutions as it was, and to remove such an important bridge between civil society and faith communities is a serious step. So what is to be done?

Central to the debates within faith communities has been whether or not that faith community's scriptures and traditions permit same-sex marriage. The evidence is generally ambiguous, because this would not have been a question on the agenda when the Scriptures were written and as traditions solidified. It is therefore normally possible for individuals of a conservative bent to interpret the scriptures and tradition of a faith community as forbidding same-sex marriage, and for more progressive members of the faith community to read them as permitting it. Rarely is the loss of an important mediating institution mentioned. This might be because the protagonists do not recognise the seriousness of the issue, or it might be that they recognise it but do not think it to be as important as what they take to be the principles involved. I must disagree. There is little that is more important to both society and faith communities than mediating institutions. We all need as many as we can get.

We cannot expect the world's societies' headlong rush towards permitting same-sex marriage to abate. It won't until every country permits it. This might take a while in parts of Africa and in some traditionally Muslim countries, but it will happen, just as the emancipation and empowerment of women is now an unstoppable process, however slow it might seem in Saudi Arabia, and however reactionary some countries' governments have become on this issue. This means that the faith communities will sooner or later have to find a way to accommodate same-sex marriage.

When we lived on the Greenwich Peninsula this was a particularly live issue for Holy Trinity Church. The Greenwich Millennium Village contains a very high proportion of same-sex couples, and in the gay community the Village is often referred to as 'the gay village'. We had two staff members in same-sex relationships, a non-stipendiary priest and a Reader, and St. George's Church in Westcombe Park, to the south of the Peninsula, had often welcomed same-sex couples and (just within the rules) had celebrated their civil partnerships during Sunday morning services. It was essential that Holy Trinity Church should establish its own position on same-sex marriage before Parliament voted. We held our own thorough consultation. We read the Scriptures, and asked ourselves what Jesus' attitude would have been if he had been faced with the question that we were facing. Jesus accepted marriage as he found it in his society, and made it more rigorous by forbidding either party to divorce the other unless there was adultery involved. We concluded that Jesus would have accepted marriage as he found it in our own society (including same-sex marriage), and that he would have insisted that it was a lifelong commitment that could only be broken by either party if the other committed adultery. We published our findings on the Holy Trinity website, held a café discussion based on them, sent them to the Bishop of Woolwich, and, at his suggestion, sent them to the Church of England's consultation on same-sex marriage. (The Church Council's submission can be found in the appendix of this book.)

This is a journey that the whole Church – and every church – will need to take if we are to rescue marriage as a mediating institution, which surely we should attempt to do. Mediating institutions are the bridges that we need between the Christian Faith and the communities in which we are set, and between the Church as a whole and the nation as a whole.

If we do not keep our collection of mediating institutions in good repair then the Church and civil society will find themselves increasingly distanced from each other, and less and less able to communicate. The same is true of every other faith community, and of the faith communities together. It might be that some faith communities will never regard same-sex marriage as legitimate, and so will not recognise the marriages of same-sex couples: but if a significant number of faith communities can learn to accommodate, and perhaps to celebrate, same sex marriage, then we shall have gone a long way towards repairing marriage's mediating function. Those faith communities that provide bridges into civil society for other faith communities, as the Church of England often does, have a particular responsibility in this direction.

My readers might quite legitimately object that in the case of same-sex marriage it is the State that has deprived us of a mediating institution by changing the nature of marriage, and that the State therefore has a responsibility to put the mediating institution back together by repealing legislation that permits same-sex marriage. This is a fair point, but not decisive. Marriage belongs to society as a whole, and not to any particular faith community. Some faith communities might not see it that way officially, but there are very few members of the Roman Catholic Church who would not recognise as valid the marriages of their non-Roman Catholic friends, neighbours, and family members. Jesus and the earliest Christians received marriage as they found it in their society, and it was not until the Council of Trent in the sixteenth century that the Church in the West decided that a marriage was only valid if witnessed by a priest (Council of Trent 1563). So in practice, if not always in theory, faith communities recognise that marriage belongs to society, and not only to their own faith community. This means that changes in legislation relating to marriage are perfectly legitimate if they reflect public opinion on marriage. But even more relevant is the fact that public opinion has moved decisively in the direction of same-sex marriage, that legislative change has occurred, and that it is difficult to conceive of that process ever being reversed. It would no longer be possible for the UK Government to ban same-sex marriage. This leaves the Church and other faith communities with a choice. Either they live with the destruction of an important mediating institution, or they do everything they can to repair it – which will mean recognising same sex marriage as a legitimate development, and contributing to the debate their conviction that marriage is a lifelong commitment.

Does that mean that any and every mediating institution that falls into disrepair should be put back together? No. There might be differences between civil society (as represented by Parliament) and faith communities (as represented by religious organisations) that simply cannot be bridged. There might be more of these: which is what makes it so important to mend the mediating institutions that we can mend.

The Clergy as a Mediating Institution

There is a sense in which every member of a congregation functions as a mediating institution, because they stand between the congregation and the community in which they live, and facilitate relationships between them (Atkins 2006). This can be particularly the case where an individual is commissioned by the Church to fulfil such a mediating role, as is the case in the Church of England with Readers, Church Army Officers, and other licensed and commissioned lay workers (Newman 2006; Russell 2006; Reeve 2006; Griffiths 2006); and even more so when a variety of functions meet in a single individual. When I first got to know Sukhdev Singh Marway he was the President of his Gurdwara and a borough councillor, and he had recently been Mayor of Newham. He then joined the team of Prayer Space welcomers on the Greenwich Peninsula. Sukhdev was a significant mediating institution.

In relation to the Christian Faith, the New Testament contains a diverse picture of church governance. Each congregation had its 'elders' or 'overseers', and in some places 'deacons' took care of what we would call welfare activities (Acts 6: 1–6; Philippians 1: 1–2; 1 Timothy 3: 1, 8; Torry 2014a: 44–5, 199–204; 2014b: 51–2). As the centuries passed, and particularly after Constantine turned the Christian Faith into the established religion of the Roman Empire, dioceses with multiple congregations spread across Europe and beyond. A bishop governed the diocese, and presbyters, or priests, served the parishes. The bishops and priests constituted the clergy, and it was the clergy who could read and write.

Apart from state officials, the clergy formed the first profession. They had their own admissions criteria, they governed themselves, and they possessed a knowledge-base that others did not possess: all of the marks of a profession. The clergy, along with religious orders, were often the medics, teachers, and lawyers of Europe and elsewhere: but as education spread to the laity, and as each of these fields developed a more complex knowledge base, medicine, education, and the law developed their own professions, leaving the clergy as a profession with mainly religious and pastoral tasks. During the nineteenth century, as the other professions consciously developed their knowledge bases and methods, the clergy attempted to follow suit, and so became one profession alongside others. As new occupational groups have developed their admissions criteria, internal governance, and educational methods, in order to be able to claim professional status (– nursing has professionalised in this way during the past thirty or so years), other professions have found that they now no longer have a monopoly on the skills and knowledge bases that had previously enabled them to claim a professional status, and so have become semi-professions. You do not need to be a qualified teacher to be able to teach, so teaching is now a semi-profession. Lots of people can do what clergy do, and can know what the clergy know, so the clergy too are now semi-professionals: but the clergy are still sufficiently professionalised to enable their semi-professional status to enhance their ability to be mediating institutions. Because professions share many of their criteria and methods, members of professions can relate to each other in ways in which members of unprofessionalised occupations cannot. The professional character of a denomination's clergy can therefore function as a mediating institution, enabling members of the clergy to relate more easily to members of other professions, and enabling churches as organisations to relate more easily to the organisations served by members of other professions.

But something is lost in this process. Professional clergy might find that they can relate more easily to members of other professions than they can to members of their congregations or to members of the wider community. Because a community will quite rightly regard the priest or minister as a representative of the Church, and of the particular church in their neighbourhood, a professionalised member of the clergy is in danger of distancing the church from its community. This doesn't need to happen, and members of the clergy who are alive to this possibility will work hard to avoid it: but the fact that it takes hard work to avoid it suggests that there is a problem.

The problem has been felt to be particularly acute in working class communities – that is, in communities containing few members of the professions. In more middle class communities, where the density of members of the professions will be greater, the clergy will more easily identify with a larger proportion of the community, and will therefore more closely identify with the community as a whole: but in communities containing few members of the professions, the minister can be quite isolated, can seek personal and work relationships beyond the boundaries of the parish or local community, and can increasingly distance the life of the church from the experience of the community in which it is set.

Recognition of this problem has given birth to numerous experiments. After the Second World War, a number of Roman Catholic priests in France became worker priests – that is, employees of large companies – to enable them to identify themselves and the Church with members of the working class. England also saw worker priest experiments, and then the ordination of working class church members. This required training courses specifically designed to match their previous experience with the task for which they were being trained – which was to remain rooted in their communities as representatives of the Church; and the experience of these experiments then gave birth to centrally approved Ordained Local Ministry schemes in a number of dioceses. The result is that in hundreds of parishes there are now Ordained Local Ministers whose vocations to the priesthood were recognised by their congregations, who were trained largely in the context of their congregations, and whose dedicated ministries have been carried out in the communities with which they were already closely identified. Not all of the schemes have survived: but where they have they continue to provide parishes with clergy deeply embedded both in their congregations and in their communities, and therefore uniquely placed to function as mediating institutions. The Church of England and every other church need as many mediating institutions as they can get, so the ideal situation is for members of the clergy who function in different ways as mediating institutions to work together. In both of the places where I have served as a stipendiary incumbent I have had the privilege of working in a parish that nurtured a congregation member's vocation to the Ordained Local Ministry and then received their ministry (Obiora 2006). The combination was highly effective.

Equally essential to the diversity of types of clergy is to keep as many clergy as possible located in the communities that they serve (Ahern and Davie 1987: 63). The full-time paid clergy will function effectively if they live in the communities in which the churches that they serve are set; Ordained Local Ministers will do this effectively because they are embedded in their communities already; and self-supporting ministers who travel in from outside the parish might manage to achieve this if they are constantly present in the communities in which they serve, and if they have an identifiable physical base from which to work – but conversely, they can experience frustration if they live outside the parish that they serve, and spend large parts of their lives elsewhere (Scott 2006: 59). Ministers who live where they serve can experience multiple belongings: to the local church, to the community, to the community's institutions, to mediating institutions, to the wider Church, and so on. The more engaged they become with as many institutions as possible, the more effective they will be as mediating institutions, and the more effective the congregation will be at creating and using mediating institutions to enable it to relate to its community. This is not a zero sum game. The congregation is the religious organisation that needs to relate to its community, and it will do that through multiple mediating institutions: through its own members functioning as members of the community; through temporary and more permanent mediating institutions that the congregation establishes; and through its clergy. So the more mediating institutions the better, the more clergy the better, and the more different kinds of clergy the better.

The United States of America: The Episcopal Peace Fellowship

On Armistice Day, just after the beginning of the Second World War – 11 November 1939 – the Episcopal Peace Fellowship was founded by Paul Jones, a Bishop of the Episcopal Church of the United States of America.

Members were required to sign a statement which said: 'In loyalty to the Person, Spirit and teachings of Jesus Christ, my conscience commits me to His way of redemptive love and compels me to refuse to participate in or give moral support to any war'. It supported conscientious objectors, and tried to persuade the whole Church to do so. The organisation continues to pray, study, and take action, in the cause of justice and peace in local communities, in the Church, and in the world. Currently the organisation campaigns against guns and gun crime and the death penalty, and for peace and justice in Palestine: and always the campaign includes prayer, study, and action. So in relation to guns there are suggestions as to how members and others might pray; study materials are published; 'No Guns in God's House' stickers and posters are distributed to churches; and 'Gun Free Zone' stickers and posters are delivered to businesses. The Fellowship is particularly interested in recruiting bishops to its causes, so members are encouraged to write to their bishops about them; and the organisation takes delegations to the Episcopal Church's General Conventions to attempt to persuade delegates to support resolutions in line with the Fellowship's interests.

The Fellowship is now a broader church than when it began. For instance, its Palestine Israel Network recognises that 'we will have differences about positions and strategies which we want to air openly in order to benefit from the variety of opinions within the Network'. The commitment that members have to sign is now somewhat different from the way that it was at the beginning:

In loyalty to the teaching and person of Jesus Christ, my conscience commits me to the way of redemptive love: to pray, study, and work for peace, and to renounce, as far as possible, participation in war, militarism, and all other forms of violence.

In fellowship with others, I will work to discover and create alternatives to violence and to build a culture of peace. I urge the Episcopal Church in accordance with our baptismal vows 'to renounce the evil powers of this world which corrupt and destroy the creatures of God', and to wage peace across all boundaries, calling upon people everywhere to repent, to forgive, and to love.

The Fellowship was started by a bishop, it still has a bishop on its National Executive Council, and a number of people in leadership positions in the

Episcopal Church are members, so the Fellowship retains a close relationship with the Church: but it is not part of the Episcopal Church's structure, and a mark of its autonomy is that although it still says about itself that it 'brings together Episcopalians …', its online membership form asks prospective members to state their 'faith', suggesting that people of any faith are now welcome to join.

The Fellowship's autonomy means that it can mediate between the Church and a variety of organisations and issues, between the Christian tradition and the pursuit of justice and peace, and between the Church and the various aspects of the peace movement in the United States. The Fellowship's 'Peace Partners' – congregations, dioceses, and seminaries – are expected to mediate between the Church and these same issues and movements as they are represented in their own localities. Largely because the Fellowship stands between the Church and the issues that it tackles, it can advocate change in the Church's attitudes and actions: so recently it took part in a somewhat complex General Convention debate over church investments that might relate to the occupied territories in Palestine. At the same time, the Fellowship is closely related to the Episcopal Church, and so can mobilise its resources. On the tenth anniversary of the 2003 United States invasion of Iraq, the Fellowship organised a gathering at the Episcopal National Cathedral in Washington, followed by a march to the White House.

One of the marks of a mediating institution is its flexibility in relation to the organisations and issues among which it mediates. National and local cultures evolve, issues are not the same from one year to the next, and organisations and movements change constantly, so any institution that wishes to mediate between religious organisations and secular organisations, or between religion and the issues facing a complex secular society, must constantly adapt. The Episcopal Peace Fellowship exhibits the necessary flexibility.

Conclusions: Sacraments and Mediating Institutions

This chapter has contained accounts of a variety of apparently disconnected mediating institutions. What connects them, of course, is the fact that they are all mediating institutions: that is, they all mediate between religion and the secular, religious institutions and secular institutions, religious organisations and secular organisations – as do all of those mediating institutions that we have discussed in previous chapters.

An interesting question is whether the combination is more than the sum of its parts: that is, do two mediating institutions have more than double the effect of one mediating institution? Removing a mediating institution – as we have just done in the UK in relation to marriage – appears to have done considerable damage to the relationships between the religious and the secular, between civil society and religious institutions, and between couples in society and church leaders and members. This suggests that mediating institutions really are cumulative in their effect. This means that adding a new one, or repairing an old one, might have a considerable positive effect on the functioning of existing mediating institutions. We can see why this might be the case. To take again the example of marriage: to repair that mediating institution would enable the clergy to relate more easily to other professionals, congregations to relate more easily to their communities, and chaplains to relate more easily to students in universities, thus strengthening a number of existing mediating institutions.

It is perfectly understandable that some churches and many Christians regard marriage as a sacrament – that is, as an outward and visible sign of a spiritual reality. Sacraments in general, and particularly baptism and the Eucharist, provide a bridge across which people can relate to the Christian Faith. Every mediating institution is to some extent a sacrament, but the Eucharist and baptism, being sacraments established by Jesus, have a particularly clear and representative sacramental role to play. It is therefore essential that they should be able to function as sacraments – as mediating institutions – which implies that all barriers to participation in them should be removed. If parents bring a child for baptism, then that child should be baptised. If someone arrives in church during a Eucharist, then they should be invited to share in the bread and wine along with the rest of the congregation, whatever their faith commitment; and if a secular organisation arrives in church during a Eucharist then every member should be welcome to participate if they wish. We need to cherish and nourish the sacraments so that they become the mediating institutions that Jesus intended them to be: and if, as Philip Sheldrake suggests, we are to 'live eucharistically beyond the church doors' (Sheldrake 2010: 176; cf. Sheldrake 2001: 170), then the Eucharist in church needs to be entirely open and hospitable, so that the Christian community's mediating institutions and activity will be of that character.

The conclusion to draw is that we need to treasure and nourish every mediating institution that we can, and build as many new ones as we can think of. Of course, where a matter of principle is clearly and necessarily involved, the Church might need to demolish a mediating institution: but before it does so, it should put maximum effort into finding a way to square essential principles with keeping the mediating institution intact. Mediating institutions are essential to the life and work of the Church, and of every other religious organisation and faith community. This means that if ever there is a conflict between a principle and a mediating institution, we are not looking at a choice between an essential principle and an expendable mediating institution, but rather at a choice between an essential principle and an essential mediating institution. That will not make for easy decision-making, but it ought to concentrate minds on how existing mediating institutions might be maintained, and on how new ones might be constructed.

Bibliography

Ahern, Geoffrey, and Grace Davie. 1987. *Inner city God*. London: Hodder and Stoughton.

Archbishop of Canterbury's Commission on Urban Priority Areas. 1985. *Faith in the city: A call for action by church and nation*. London: Church House Publishing.

Atkins, Ann. 2006. A variety of gifts: The people of God. In *Diverse gifts: Varieties of lay and ordained ministries in the Church and community*, ed. Malcolm Torry, 14–25. Norwich: Canterbury Press.

Baker, Christopher. 2009b. Blurred encounters? Religious literacy, spiritual capital and language. In *Faith in the public realm: Controversies, policies and practices*, ed. Dinham Adam, Furbey Robert, and Lowndes Vivien, 105–122. Bristol: Policy Press.

Bonney, Norman. 2015. The sacred state: Religion, ritual and power in the United Kingdom. In *Is God back?* ed. Titus Hjelm, 118–131. London: Bloomsbury.

Cheesman, David, and Nazia Khanum. 2009. "Soft" segregation: Muslim identity, British secularism and inequality. In *Faith in the public realm: Controversies, policies and practices*, ed. Adam Dinham, Robert Furbey, and Vivien Lowndes, 41–62. Bristol: Policy Press.

Cheyne, Angela. 2008. Lost in translation: Faith-based charities and "public benefit" in the eyes of the state, 7–51 in *The institute series*, no.6. London: Heythrop Institute for Religion, Ethics and Public Life.

Collier, Paul. 2006. Serving in a learning community: The chaplain in higher education. In *Diverse gifts: Varieties of lay and ordained ministries in the Church and community*, ed. Malcolm Torry, 157–170. Norwich: Canterbury Press.

Commission on Urban Life and Faith. 2005. *Faithful cities: A call for celebration, vision and justice*. London: Methodist Publishing House, and London: Church House Publishing.

Council of Trent. 1563. *Canons and decrees*. www.documentacatholicaomnia. eu/03d/1545-1545,_Concilium_Tridentinum,_Canons_And_Decrees,_ EN.pdf, 24th session. Accessed 14 Dec 2015.

Farnell, Richard. 2009. Faiths, government and regeneration: A contested discourse. In *Faith in the public realm: Controversies, policies and practices*, ed. Adam Dinham, Robert Furbey, and Vivien Lowndes, 183–202. Bristol: Policy Press.

Flagg, David. 2006. Serving in a healing community: The hospital chaplain. In *Diverse gifts: Varieties of lay and ordained ministries in the Church and community*, ed. Malcolm Torry, 171–184. Norwich: Canterbury Press.

Flint, John. 2009. Faith-based schools: Institutionalising parallel lives? In *Faith in the public realm: Controversies, policies and practices*, ed. Adam Dhinham, Robert Furbey, and Vivien Lowndes, 163–182. Bristol: Policy Press.

Ford, Mandy. 2010. St. Philip's Church and Centre, Leicester: Presence and engagement. In *Crossover city: Resources for urban mission and transformation*, ed. Andrew Davey, 139–143. London: Mowbray.

Griffiths, Peter. 2006. Commissioned to care: The Southwark Pastoral Auxiliary. In *Diverse gifts: Varieties of lay and ordained ministries in the Church and community*, ed. Malcolm Torry, 65–77. Norwich: Canterbury Press.

Home office. 2011. *Prevent strategy*, Cm 8092. London: Her Majesty's stationery office.

Inter Faith Network for the UK. 2015. www.interfaith.org.uk. Accessed 31 Aug 2015.

Jawad, Rana. 2012. *Religion and faith-based welfare: From wellbeing to ways of being*. Bristol: Policy Press.

Jordan, Bill. 1996. *A theory of poverty and social exclusion.* Cambridge: Polity Press.

Modood, Tariq. 2010. Moderate secularism, Religion as identity and respect for religion. *Political Quarterly* 81(1): 4–14.

Near Neighbours. 2015. www.cuf.org.uk/how-we-help/near-neighbours. Accessed 26 Aug 2015.

Newman, Liz. 2006. Making connections: The reader. In *Diverse gifts: Varieties of lay and ordained ministries in the Church and community,* ed. Malcolm Torry, 26–39. Norwich: Canterbury Press.

Obiora, Arthur. 2006. Here to stay: The ordained local minister. In *Diverse gifts: Varieties of lay and ordained ministries in the Church and community,* ed. Malcolm Torry, 78–84. Norwich: Canterbury Press.

Reeve, Gillian. 2006. Professionals between the church and the world: Licensed lay workers. In *Diverse gifts: Varieties of lay and ordained ministries in the Church and community,* ed. Malcolm Torry, 85–94. Norwich: Canterbury Press.

Riordan, Patrick. 2008a. Facing the challenges: Faith-based charities and the legislative context, 53–62 in *The institute series,* no.6. London: Heythrop Institute for Religion, Ethics and Public Life.

———. 2008b. At a loss for words, 31–42 in *The institute series,* no.11. London: Heythrop Institute for Religion, Ethics and Public Life.

Riordan, ——— (ed.). 2009. *Words in action: In ten thousand places,* The institute series, no.12. London: Heythrop Institute for Religion, Ethics and Public Life.

Russell, Nick. 2006. A different kind of soldier: The church army officer. In *Diverse gifts: Varieties of lay and ordained ministries in the church and community,* ed. Malcolm Torry, 40–50. Norwich: Canterbury Press.

Scott, Sara. 2006. Balancing roles: The non-stipendiary minister. In *Diverse gifts: Varieties of lay and ordained ministries in the Church and community,* ed. Malcolm Torry, 51–64. Norwich: Canterbury Press.

Sheldrake, Philip. 2001. *Spaces for the sacred: Place, memory and identity.* London: SCM Press.

———. 2010. *Explorations in spirituality: History, theology, and social practice.* New York: Paulist Press.

Sheppard, David. 1974. *Built as a city.* London: Hodder and Stoughton.

Singh, Gurnam and Stephen Cowden. 2011. Multiculturalism's New Fault Lines: Religious Fundamentalisms and Public Policy. *Critical Social Policy.* 31 (1): 343–64.

Todd, Andrew. 2013. *Military chaplaincy in contention: Chaplains, churches and the morality of conflict*. Farnham: Ashgate.

Torry, Malcolm. 1980. Two kinds of ambiguity. *King's Theological Review* 3(1): 24–28.

———. 2005. *Managing God's business: Religious and faith-based organizations and their management*. Aldershot: Ashgate.

———. 2014a. *Managing religion: The management of Christian religious and faith-based organizations*: vol 1, 'Internal relationships', Basingstoke: Palgrave Macmillan.

———. 2014b. *Managing religion: The management of Christian religious and faith-based organizations*: vol 2, 'External relationships', Basingstoke: Palgrave Macmillan.

———. 2016. Religious advantage and disadvantage. In *Social advantage and disadvantage*, ed. Hartley Dean and Lucinda Platt, 285–303. Oxford: Oxford University Press.

Tyler, Alison. 2006. Serving in a walled community: The prison chaplain. In *Diverse Gifts: Varieties of lay and ordained ministries in the Church and community*, ed. Malcolm Torry, 143–56. Norwich: Canterbury Press.

Weller, Paul. 2009. How participation changes things: 'Inter-faith, 'multi-faith' and a new public imaginary. In *Faith in the public realm: Controversies, policies and practices*, ed. Adam Dinham, Robert Furbey, and Vivien Lowndes, 63–81. Bristol: Policy Press.

6

Mediating Institutions: A Task for the Church

Introduction

The argument of this book can be understood two different ways round: firstly, as an exploration of the place that mediating institutions might play in enabling the religious and the secular to relate to each other, faith communities and the institutions of civil society to relate to each other, and individuals in many different institutions to relate to each other – and especially in enabling faith communities to relate to diverse new developments; and secondly, as a discussion of the ways in which the Church and other faith communities relate to diverse new developments, and the role that mediating institutions play in that process.

During our discussions of a wide variety of developments and mediating institutions, we have discovered the many different ways in which mediating institutions can enable the religious and the secular to relate to each other, religious organisations to relate to secular organisations, religious institutions to relate to secular ones, and members of religious organisations to relate to non-members; we have discovered that mediating institutions can enable different religious organisations to relate to each other, different religious institutions to relate to each other, and

© The Editor(s) (if applicable) and The Author(s) 2016
M. Torry, *Mediating Institutions*,
DOI 10.1057/978-1-349-94913-7_6

members of different faith communities to relate to each other; and we have discovered how mediating institutions have enabled the Church and other faith communities to relate to diverse new urban developments.

The hope that lies behind this exploration is the hope that Jesus expressed when he spoke of the Kingdom of God: a community of justice and peace that God will bring about, and that was already coming to birth through his own ministry. Perhaps all that we can hope for in this life is signposts towards that Kingdom of God: in which case, those of us who are followers of Jesus surely have an obligation to seek and to create such signposts. This is where the two foci of this book come together. Mediating institutions have the potential to enable peace and justice between the religious and the secular, between religious institutions and secular institutions, and between members of religious institutions and members of secular institutions; and mediating institutions have a particular role to play in enabling the religious and the secular to work together in diverse new developments so that those developments might become communities of justice and peace, and therefore signposts towards the Kingdom of God.

This first concluding chapter must therefore ask how mediating institutions (whether organisational or non-organisational ones) function as mediators, that is, as facilitators of relationships; how we might enhance those institutions' ability to mediate; and how we might create more such institutions. Much of the book has been about institutions understood as organised activity, but in a number of our case studies we have also found buildings functioning as mediating institutions: so an additional task must be to ask about the characteristics of such buildings, how they function as mediating institutions, and how we might enhance their ability to function in this way.

Figure 6.1 represents the picture of mediating institutions that we have discovered.

Our final task will be to ask a more theological question: What is it to which the mediating institutions can be signposts, and how might we fashion institutions (whether organisations, non-organisational institutions, or buildings) that will point our society and our society's institutions in that direction? That will be the subject of our second concluding chapter.

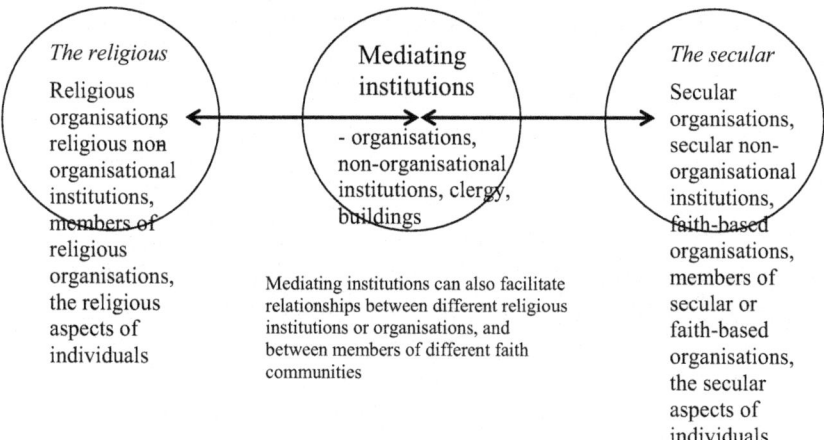

Fig. 6.1   Mediating institutions: including conclusions from chapters 2 to 5

Mediating Institutions

Mediating Institutions Between Religion and the Workplace

In Chap. 2 we studied institutions that mediate between the economy and faith traditions, between the workplace and faith communities, and between individuals in faith communities and individuals in secular workplaces. A long tradition of workplace chaplaincy has facilitated such relationships between the religious and the secular, and on the Greenwich Peninsula, at Bluewater, at Stratford, and at Canary Wharf in the UK, we have asked how different approaches function as mediating institutions. Workplace chaplaincy embeds chaplains in the secular institutions in which they both belong and do not belong, enabling them to experience in their own persons the tensions between the secular and the religious, and to become the place where mediation occurs. This is a highly personal approach that to some extent mirrors in the pastoral field the Christian doctrine that Jesus is both human and divine. As well as the chaplains themselves functioning as mediating institutions, we have also found chaplaincy organisations functioning as mediating institutions:

standing as organisations between religious and secular organisations, enabling both kinds to relate to the chaplaincy organisation, and therefore facilitating relationships between secular and religious organisations, and between the secular ethos of workplaces and the faith traditions of faith communities. It is of course true that a representative of a faith community can be a workplace chaplain without belonging to a chaplaincy organisation: however, constructing a chaplaincy organisation enables relationships to be created on multiple levels: institution to institution, person to institution, person to person: so wherever possible an organisation should be constructed, and chaplains should belong to it. In this way a more dense, and potentially more consistent, mediation can occur.

In the Gossner Mission we have discovered a somewhat different institutional approach. Here we find an organisation and a pastoral figure relating to individuals working in industrial organisations, so that those individuals can then function as mediators between their workplaces and the Christian Faith. Different again is Interfaith Worker Justice in the United States. Here a more confrontational approach pits the Christian Faith against a flawed workplace ethos, and invites workplaces to relate their practices to the character of the Kingdom of God.

In all of these case studies, the institutions that mediate between the secular and the religious are organisational. In some places, the institutions manage spaces designed for prayer. In some of those cases the prayer space is close to the heart of the organisation's activity (as on the Greenwich Peninsula), in some cases it is peripheral (as in Canary Wharf), and in some cases there is no prayer space (as in much of the UK's workplace chaplaincy, and in the work of Interfaith Worker Justice). In the Gossner Mission, what we might call a temporary prayer space emerges when required. In no case is the management of a place for prayer essential to the task. What is essential is the organisation of chaplaincy relationships, and events and other activities ancillary to that.

The lesson here is that if faith communities wish to relate to workplaces purely as collections of individuals, then of course that happens all the time. Members of faith communities work in workplaces. Their activity within those workplaces will necessarily be tightly constrained by the organisations within which they work, but there will nevertheless be relationships between individuals, and relationships between those individuals and their workplaces, through which faith traditions will relate to workplaces. The presence of a chaplain will have a complementary effect. The chaplain both belongs to the workplace (by virtue of the welcome offered by the workplace's management) and usually does not belong (because generally they are not part of the organisation's structure): so they can stand between their faith community and the workplaces that they visit. (I say 'generally' here because, as we have discovered, secular organisations are increasingly contributing towards chaplains' salaries and co-opting them into management teams, thus drawing them into the workplace's own structures, and to some extent compromising the chaplain's ability to mediate between the workplace and the faith community's ethos and convictions.) The chaplain therefore functions in an institutional fashion in ways in which the workplace's employees cannot, and can therefore provide a mediating function that complements that of the worker who belongs to a faith community. But if faith communities wish to relate to secular organisations as organisations, then constructing chaplaincy organisations is essential. Such organisations can create and then mature institutional relationships in ways in which isolated chaplains cannot. This means that if the Christian Church and other faith communities are serious about relating to the institutions of a secular urban world, then in every place in which workplaces exist, chaplaincy organisations need to be created and sustained. If it is a priority to enable secular institutions to relate to the Kingdom of God, as surely it should be, then congregations of different faiths, and where possible different faiths' regional organisations, need to work together to create the necessary institutions, and to appoint the necessary chaplains, preferably with at least a few paid posts to co-ordinate the activity of well-trained volunteers.

Mediating Institutions in Residential Areas

When we study residential areas, and the mediating institutions that churches and other faith communities construct in them, we find greater diversity and more significant change than we find in the workplace context. This is mainly because the faith-based organisations that congregations create – whether formally constituted ones, or projects still within the congregation's management structures – experience secularising pressures that frequently carry them in a secular direction. There are both advantages and disadvantages to this process. The disadvantage is that a secularised former faith-based organisation can no longer function as effectively as a mediating institution (although there will often be some elements of it that do). The advantage is that if one faith-based organisation wanders, then the congregation might have the social and financial space to establish another one that might more closely relate to the needs of the community than the one that has wandered.

We have learnt some particular lessons while studying organisational mediating institutions in residential areas. In Thamesmead, the churches' clergy and congregations have put effort into organisations that were never intended to be faith-based: and in that context it was the individuals involved who functioned as mediating institutions. On Telegraph Hill and in Kidbrooke, careful constitutions have ensured that the intention to create 'attached' faith-based organisations has been realised in practice. In the Beacon Project we find both of these approaches. At St. Mary's, Woolwich, a variety of mediating institutions have evolved in a secular direction or have closed, but the building continues to constitute the mediating institution that it has always been; and in East Greenwich, Christ Church Forum has taken a secularising journey to become the Forum at Greenwich, giving the congregation the space to involve itself in new activities, one of which is the Greenwich Foodbank, itself a significant mediating institution. In the Greenwich Millennium Village, establishing a congregation was the priority, because in a residential community a relationship between the religious and the secular requires there to be a congregation to which secular institutions and individuals can relate: but once a congregation exists, mediating activity is required; and, in the case of the Greenwich Millennium Village, this has been constituted by a variety of often temporary institutions within the congregation (such as café discussions and community drama), and by the clergy and other congregation members involving themselves in secular institutions.

We have found that multi faith and inter faith organisations can be important mediating institutions, enabling a variety of faith communities to work together as they relate to complex new residential developments; that across Europe a wide variety of welfare organisations, attached in a variety of ways to faith communities, are mediating relationships between faith communities and residential areas; and that in the UK and in Chicago, housing associations can enable churches to relate to some significant needs in the community. The North Kent list of characteristics of effective faith-based organisations is well worth pondering.

The lesson here, in both established and new communities, is that there are always two connected requirements: congregations, and mediating institutions established by congregations. This requires decision-making and action. Wherever there is no congregation, a congregation needs to be established, and existing congregations need to supply a core of members to enable this to happen. It is not essential for the new congregation to own its own building immediately, but if it is to survive and be useful in the longer term, then a permanent place to meet is a subsequent requirement. The permanent location of a pastoral figure in the community is a connected necessity, both to serve the congregation, and to relate to the community – for, as we have discovered, the clergy function as mediating institutions in their own right. As soon as a congregation is established in a new place, it needs to establish mediating institutions. To start with, these will generally be temporary or occasional, and managed directly by the congregation: but later on attention will need to be given to more permanent constituted organisations through which the congregation will relate to its context in the longer term. Such institutions will either 'wander' or remain 'attached'. It will be essential to make an early decision as to which is intended, because different intended outcomes will require different constitutional arrangements.

In among the mediating institutions that we have discovered we have found organisations, such non-organisational institutions as café discussions, and buildings, functioning as mediating institutions. In each context it might be helpful for congregations to ask themselves precisely which kinds of mediating institution are required, and then to create them.

Mediating Institutions Between Religion and Civil Society

When we take a view wider than particular workplaces and particular residential communities, and ask about how relationships between faith communities and secularising societies might be facilitated, we again find considerable diversity. The Episcopal Peace Fellowship functions as a nationwide organisational mediating institution; faith schools are organisations constitutionally situated around the middle of the religious-secular spectrum and suffering the tensions that that involves; established religion is a complex mixture of organisational and non-organisational institutional activity, again full of ambiguities; and reports and their associated activity are perhaps too little studied as mediating institutions. Each chaplain in a prison, hospital, university, or airport, functions as a mediating institution where they work, each chaplaincy organisation mediates relationships in its own context, and chaplaincy as a whole functions as a significant mediating institution. Perhaps more attention needs to be paid to the total effect of chaplaincy as a mediating institution standing between faith communities and a secularising society.

We have found state-funded institutions designed to facilitate relationships between different faith communities, between faith communities and government, or between faith communities and the wider community, to be somewhat compromised in their ability to be mediating institutions; we have found borough deans' networks to be effective mediating institutions; and we have found both local and national inter faith organisations to be useful mediating institutions, and especially useful when they are properly representative of congregations, because then they can mediate between faith communities and wider society rather than between individual members and society. Of the non-organisational institutions that we have studied, we have found marriage to be an increasingly problematic mediating institution that needs to be made a lot less problematic; and we have found language to be a vital mediating institution, and one on which a great deal more work needs to be done. The clerical profession lies between the organisational and the non-organisational, and is perhaps a more significant mediating institution than we realise. As in the workplace and residential contexts, society as a whole needs mediating institutions. Congregations are the primary religious organisations, and it is right that they should focus on their localities: but it is also essential for faith communities to attend to the bigger picture. Some faith communities have longstanding organisational structures that enable them to work at societal level as well as at the local level. Where faith communities do not possess such structures, they need to develop them. A second requirement is that at every level – at the local, regional, and national levels – bodies genuinely representative of the faith communities are required. Without this, organisations intended to mediate relationships between faith communities and society will not mediate them because there will be no organisational representation of faith communities to which to relate.

Where such society-wide representative structures already exist, they have an obligation to maintain the mediating institutions that already exist, and to create mediating institutions where they do not. It is particularly important to notice where mediating institutions are failing. Reconstructing faith communities' relationships with marriage is an urgent priority; and, in the longer term, serious consideration needs to be given to the language in which faith communities relate to society and to its institutions.

Places

Religious Buildings

We have discovered buildings that function as mediating institutions, facilitating relationships between religious organisations and secular organisations – and particularly between faith communities and secular organisations that use church buildings together. They can also facilitate relationships between religious aspects and secular aspects of non-organisational institutions, such as marriage – for the building in which a wedding takes place can be an important element in the mediating function of marriage. Religious buildings can facilitate relationships between secularising individuals and religious individuals – for instance, when shoppers use a staffed prayer room; and relationships between different faith traditions, particularly where different faith communities make use of the same prayer space. For the individual using a religiously significant building, the most profound effect can be the mediation of a relationship between their own secular and religious elements as they experience 'an absorption that like worship requires no further justification' (Brown 2004: 36), and a 'sense of what we are lacking and [an evocation of] possibility and hope' (Sheldrake 2010: 177).

But what is it that enables a building to function as a mediating institution? There are several possibilities: If religious activity takes place in the building, then that activity gives a religious character to the building in the mind of the person who understands the religious nature of the activity. Similarly, religious symbolism can give a religious character to a building. David Brown locates the effect in the ability of the architecture to balance transcendence and immanence, as gothic does (– it is both a secular and a religious style); and as Gaudí's Sagrada Familia in Barcelona does, forming the shapes of the natural world into evocations of transcendence (Brown 2004: 204–6).

It is not impossible that regular religious use of a building changes the physical fabric of it: a phenomenon more likely to be experienced in buildings used for prayer across many centuries (White 1995: 39). This last characteristic cannot be manufactured, but the others can be. The new prayer space at the London School of Economics has stained glass windows: an indication to its users that it has a religious purpose. The entirely plain prayer space on the Greenwich Peninsula – entirely without decoration so that the most conservative members of any faith community can feel at home in it – announces itself as a religious building by the large 'Prayer Space' notices on three sides of the building, and a noticeboard that lists the religious activities that take place in the building. The noticeboard also makes it clear that the building is available to individuals for prayer and reflection – again making clear its character as a place in which religious activity takes place. As the very ordinary Peninsula Prayer Space rather proves: 'sacred place is ordinary place, ritually made extraordinary' (Lane 1988: 15).

A further way in which a building can function as a mediating institution – mediating faith traditions to a secular world – is the presence of a religious person in the building. The person staffing the building might be a minister, and might wear a symbol of their office; or the person welcoming users of the building might announce themselves as a religious person by wearing a badge that says 'Prayer Space Welcomer' or 'Chaplain'. Where a church minister lives next to a church building, a particularly clear indication is given that the building is a religious place.

Essential to a building functioning as a mediating institution is that it must offer a clear and unhindered welcome. What such buildings must *not* do is charge for admission. A cathedral can be a sign that the whole city can be sacred (Sheldrake 2014: 130), and its architecture, location and activity can draw people into an experience of the transcendent. It is a

utopian space in which an idealized harmony, to be realized only in heaven, is anticipated in the here and now: (Sheldrake 2010: 189)

but if it charges for admission then it has ceased to evoke the hospitality and generosity of the Kingdom of God, it is charging people to enter a private museum rather than a religious building, and it ceases to be a mediating institution.

A residual sense of the sacred or spiritual even in apparently secular cultures not only draws large numbers of visitors to such buildings [as cathedrals], but also makes them uncomfortable with entry charges (Sheldrake 2010: 179)

– not to mention the fact that today's admission charges exclude the poor from so many cathedrals (Brown 2004: 412). It is people's longing for mediating institutions that makes it such a disaster that so many cathedrals now charge for admission and so cannot fulfil that need.

Religious buildings are perhaps now more needed than they ever were before.

They show a God present and actively concerned throughout his world, a world in which experience of the divine was once the norm and not the exception, and can be so again; (Brown 2004: 413)

so providing a plentiful supply of welcoming religious buildings has to be a significant priority.

Do buildings having multiple uses compromise their religious character? No, as long as the religious use remains clear. For instance, at St. George's, Westcombe Park, a meeting of a Neighbourhood Watch committee, or a jumble sale, or an entirely secular after-school educational event, might be taking place: but the religious symbolism is still present. But what of secular buildings in which religious activities take place? On the Greenwich Peninsula, the Holy Trinity congregation's first meeting place was the school hall in a secular community school. The congregation meeting on a Sunday morning was the only religious activity, and after we had cleared everything away there was no sign that the building had a religious use. However, posters on the noticeboards in every foyer in the Greenwich Millennium Village announced the school hall to be the meeting place of the congregation. Whether this permanent reminder of a religious use meant that the hall remained to some extent a mediating institution throughout the week is an interesting question.

Creating a Sense of Place

Perhaps a more important question for us is the extent to which a building that functions as a mediating institution can influence the nature of the place in which it is set; and this in turn raises the question as to the nature of the places in which we live and work. Are they places, or are they simply boundaried sections of space?

Words have fluid meanings, and sometimes 'space' is used to represent a place (– the Prayer Space on the Greenwich Peninsula is a place): but here we shall follow Sheldrake's usage – that 'place' is 'location with particular significance' (Sheldrake 2014: 117) – and Inge's suggestion that

> what begins as undifferentiated space becomes place as we get to know it better and endow it with value. (Inge 2003: 1)

Thus each place in which people live or work has its own distinctive character, not only in relation to the way in which each individual who inhabits it experiences it, but also in relation to the unique characteristics of the place, the activities that happen in it, and the activities that have happened in it. If we live or work in a place, then we change its land-scape; the landscape in turn changes us, forms our identity, and takes on value for us (Malpas 1999: 13; Inge 2003: 15, 20, 83; Sheldrake 2010: 20–24); and then the newly understood place becomes a place in which we become active agents and creators of community (Malpas 1999: 136). It is the characteristics of the environment, and the psychologies of the inhabitants, that together constitute the place (Inge 2003: 16). So in the Old Testament, the places in which God was encountered became significant places, and Israel found itself defined by a complex relation-ship between the land, the people, and God (Inge 2003: 38–45). The incarnation – God becoming flesh in Jesus Christ – happened in a place (Lane 1988: 38), thus relativising the Jerusalem temple, and locating the importance of place at the heart of the Christian tradition.

Every religious experience happens in a place.

> Personal narratives of religious experience, knowing God, like falling in love or living through a near-death experience, is inescapably contextual; (Lane 1988: 5)

and every religious experience in a place will contribute to that place's story and thus to its religious and mediating character (Inge 2003: 52). For the Christian, Jesus is the place in which we encounter God (Inge 2003: 51–4), and so Jesus is *the* sacrament – *the* outward and visible sign of an inward and spiritual reality. The Church is a sacrament; the Eucharist and baptism (and perhaps other significant actions) are sacraments; particular places can be sacraments, if they are places of encounter with God and therefore become outward and visible signs of inward and spiritual reali-ties (Inge 2003: 60–81, 90); and our cities can be sacraments: outward signs of the future reality of the City of God (Sheldrake 2014: 203–204).

The Eucharist might not be a place, but it is a story and a set of actions that change the places in which it happens (Inge 2003: 108): so the build-ings in which the Eucharist takes place are changed, and might properly be termed 'sacraments': but whether we should call buildings created and used by different faith communities working together 'sacraments' is an interesting question. We can certainly recognise multi faith buildings as mediating institutions that fulfil similar functions to single-faith buildings, and as having an additional function as well, because they both enable and represent constructive relationships between different faith communities, enable faith communities to relate together to the community in which they are set, and therefore turn the places in which they are situated into places in which different faiths relate to each other.

Buildings can function as mediating institutions because they relate both to a faith community or communities on the one hand, and to the community around them on the other, so that the whole place becomes a place in which God is encountered. A church building *can* therefore function as a sacrament, and a multi faith building similarly: they enable a place to become a genuine place – a place that we endow with value. It is in such places that community can be built: a process to which the presence and activity of a Christian community, as well as its building, can contribute (Inge 2003: 122, 131). As John Inge writes:

> The Christian community can witness to the fact that roots, place and destination are all important to human existence. It needs to help the rest of the world to recover some recognition about what place can be, for how we imagine communities and places of the future becomes part of what our future is. (Inge 2003: 137–8)

It is perhaps no surprise that the gathered Christian community on the Greenwich Peninsula has both debated the kind of place that the Greenwich Peninsula is going to be, and has encouraged such debate among the Peninsula's institutions. To take two examples: it has debated, and facilitated debate, about the importance of retaining the entire development as mixed tenure, with social housing and owner-occupation in every block; and it has debated and facilitated debate about the name of the tube station. There was once a place called 'North Greenwich' to the north of the Thames, but there is now no such place as 'North Greenwich', except in such phrases as 'lack of school places in North Greenwich', meaning that the northern half of the Borough of Greenwich lacks school places. The station needs to be called 'Greenwich Peninsula'. Then everyone who lives and works on the Peninsula will know that they live and work in a place: a place called the Greenwich Peninsula.

An essential Christian task – and one that other faith communities might wish to pursue as well – is to create places: places in which God can be encountered: that is, places that mediate between the religious and the secular. We need places in which to live: places that 'engage with our identity, with our relationships, and with our history' (Sheldrake 2010: 160; cf. Sheldrake 2014: 122). Our cities must not be simply undifferentiated space:

> If cities are to be places that reinforce a sense that human life is sacred ... they must embrace all dimensions of human existence – functional, ethical, and spiritual. (Sheldrake 2010: 160)

In our increasingly ethnically, religiously, and culturally diverse cities, places will never be simple, and 'geographical literacy' will be essential: an understanding of the ways in which global currents influence and change the local, and vice versa (Davey 2001: 39–42). Communication between people with different ethnic, religious and cultural roots, with different presuppositions and experiences, will always be complex and problematic, and will function in a 'third space' between communication and non-communication. In places characterised by extreme diversity, the reality might be multiple places in the same segment of space. Civil society is now 'liquid' rather than 'solid', requiring constant negotiation and translation between different experiences of life and different religious and cultural worldviews (Baker 2009a: 42, 53, 133). In these circumstances, 'local community' is not enough (Brown 2004: 166–7). The local has such permeable boundaries that it constantly dissolves. Community as ethnic, class, or religious, is not enough either, because it fails to serve the cohesion that a complex urban area requires. The minimum requirement in a city that is 'liquid' rather than 'solid' is tolerance: the ability of people with very different roots and experiences to live side by side. But more is possible. If we are to benefit from the radical diversity now all around us, then a positive social cohesion will be required: one in which we are mutually enriched by diversity, rather than one in which diversity makes us constantly anxious and therefore too likely to close our social boundaries against people different from ourselves. If a positive living together is to be achieved, then we shall need places that enable the many different layered places to relate to each other: places for casual congregating, cultural places, and religious places (Sheldrake 2010: 160, 168, 172). In this way, the many different activities of human life, and the many different ethnic, religious, and cultural experiences of life, can happen in a place, within which community can form, within which the community's story can evolve, and from which a place with a story can emerge (Sheldrake 2010: 170). In this task, mediating institutions will be essential: many different ones, each one undertaking diverse activities in diverse ways: and all of those mediating institutions will need to be constantly adapting as they relate to changing faith communities, and to a constant changing urban 'mixity' (Green 2010: 7). Particularly important will be those mediating institutions that enable people of different ethnicities, cultural backgrounds, and faiths, to work together in the service of their complex communities. Religious buildings will be essential to the process: buildings in which religious activity takes place, and that evoke the transcendence at the heart of religion – and particularly buildings in which people of different faiths can worship separately but in the same place, thus offering a sacrament that enables the many layered places within a place to relate to each other. Whereas the Christian Church used to regard the provision of a building for worship as a priority in new developments – as in Thamesmead during the 1970s – in new urban developments today the Church has often regarded the provision of a building as a low priority: as in West Thamesmead. Developers and local authorities routinely ignore the need for religious buildings, or only admit the need under pressure. Both the Church and developers are making a mistake. Religious buildings – whether single faith buildings, or multi faith buildings – function as mediating institutions; and they can make a significant contribution to place-making. They must return to being the priority they once were.

In our final chapter we shall discuss the Christian vision of the Kingdom of God as a community and as a place that God will achieve. The Christian Faith is all about the place: the place that God has created; the place in which the incarnation has taken place; the places in which the Church is the body of Christ; and the place that we call the Kingdom of God. It is therefore more than appropriate for the Christian Church to create places that mediate between that vision and a secular world, and to work with others to create within this world some signposts towards the Kingdom of God for which we hope.

Multi Faith and Multiple Mediations

The mediating institutions that we have been discussing are designed to relate the religious and the secular, members of faith communities and people who are not members of faith communities, religious institutions and secular institutions: but we have also discovered mediating institutions – organisations, other institutions, and buildings – that enable people of different faiths to relate to each other as they work together to create mediating institutions. We have discussed the 'level playing field' Greenwich Peninsula Chaplaincy; 'host and hosted' chaplaincies as at Canary Wharf, Bluewater, and Stratford; and the Greenwich Multi Faith Forum, the Greenwich Faith Community Leaders, and the Inter Faith Network UK. Prison, hospital, university, airport, and hospice chaplaincies, whether 'level playing field' or 'host and hosted', also function as mediating institutions that enable people of different faiths to relate to each other while they are relating to their secular institutions. There are of course countless examples of temporary and permanent institutions designed to relate the secular and the religious to each other, and that enable the people of different faiths who work through them to relate to each other while they do that: institutions that bring together faith schools of different faiths; faith forums that construct events that respond to local, national, and global crises; women's groups, interest groups, and all sorts of other groups, through which members of different faith communities are active in their communities; events and other institutions through which congregations of different faith communities work together; and joint purposeful pilgrimages (Torry and Thorley 2008).

Institutions in which people of different faiths, ethnicities, and experiences of life, work together in creating relationships between the religious and the secular, will achieve multiple mediations: between the religious and the secular, between people of different faiths, between institutions of different faiths, and between the different faiths themselves. The aim is not to deny or to diminish the differences – between the religious and the secular, or between different faiths – and, as we have seen in relation to people of different faiths working together, one effect might be to make the differences between different faiths clearer. The aim is rather to enable institutions attached to different faiths to understand each other, value each other, and enrich each other; and to enable people of different faiths to understand, value, and enrich each other. Such mediation contributes to the community of peace and justice for which we hope, and enables mediating institutions more effectively to relate the religious to the secular so that they can facilitate the complex networks of understanding that we need, and can create the multiple layers of peace and justice that we need so much.

The Church's Task

Here I address the Christian Church. Much of what I have written, and much of what I shall write in the rest of this chapter and in the next one, could be adapted so that it would apply to other faith communities. However, there are significant differences between the different faiths, and those differences create differences in their organisations and other institutions, and so differences in the ways in which those religious and faith-based institutions relate to secular institutions. Because only someone committed to a particular faith will know how the institutions of their own religion work, and how they relate across the religious/secular boundary, I must leave it to members of other faiths to ask themselves to what extent the rest of this book applies to their religion's institutions, and to what extent what I say has to be amended in order to be relevant.

Graham Ward describes the Church's response as one which

listens to many voices, the many claims for attention in the postmodern city. It risks encounter, knowing that its own voice is never pure, never innocent. It also speaks: announcing to the postmodern city its own vision of universal justice, peace and beauty, and it criticises the structural injustices, violence and uglinesses which resist and hinder the perception of that vision. (Ward 2000: 70)

The Church's voice is certainly never pure, and neither are the plans that it makes or the institutions that it builds. Whether at the level of the congregation, or at the level of the denominational structures that serve federations of congregations, plans are made and they are sometimes carried out. The Church's primary authority is God, and by the Holy Spirit God leads the Church into truth: so any plans or strategies that we create must always be tentative and constantly revisable. In each place, the local gathering of Christians will face a unique set of circumstances, a unique set of resources, and unique challenges, so only locally-made plans will be useful: and then next year, next month, next week, new plans will have to be made.

But having said all that, our discovery of the importance of mediating institutions might provide the Church in each place with some useful general guidance as it creates tentative and revisable plans for its activity. Our discoveries suggest that in each place the Church needs to ask itself what the mediating institutions are, how today they should be maintained and renewed, and what new mediating institutions might usefully be created. The task of a regional or national leader, such as a bishop or a moderator, is to encourage local churches to undertake this task, to communicate good practice across geographical boundaries, and to value the many different mediating institutions that will evolve. In places where there are no congregations, nearby congregations will need to create them. Again, this is not something that regional leaders can do – although they might be able to broker some necessary financial resources. Again, the task of such regional leaders will be to encourage congregations to start new congregations, to communicate good practice where they find it, and to value the many different approaches that will be tried. But they, and the congregations active in this task, will need to be clear that the purpose is not to create congregations for their own sake, but rather so that congregations can engage confidently in the complex new communities in which they are set (Green and Baker 2008: 170), and can create the mediating institutions that they will need – whether temporary ones that congregations continue to manage, or autonomous ones to which they continue to relate – so that faith communities can relate to the communities in which they are set, and to the many different institutions that they contain.

One aspect of this task to which the Church is particularly well suited is the multi-layered nature of it. Community exists at many levels: at the level of family and neighbours, the level of the town or borough, the regional level, the national level, and the global level. Community is not limited to the 'local' (Clements et al. 2008). The Church's fundamental unit is the congregation, but congregations relate to congregations in a vast network that constitutes the Church as the Body of Christ throughout the world. Some mediating institutions need to be created at the local level, such as café discussions; some at borough or town level, such as food banks; and some at national level, such as marriage – but all of them will have implications beyond the primary level at which they operate. So a café discussion might hone a contribution that relates to a national institution (see the appendix); and an institution such as language will have implications at local, regional, national, and global levels. The Church and other faith communities are some of the few institutions that can handle this diversity of levels, and perhaps they are the only ones that can do so.

The purpose of creating mediating institutions, and of working at the relationships that they will facilitate, is to evangelise, to tell good news: the good news that the Kingdom of God is promised to us, and that salvation both now and then is constituted by 'wholeness … liberation … forgiveness … [and] personal affirmation' (Kuhrt 2010: 76–9). If we create mediating institutions then we shall be evangelising by creating signposts, in the Church and in the cities in which we live, that will constitute lived promises of the Kingdom of God that is to come. In order to be signposts to the Kingdom of God, the institutions and activities that we create will need to be of the character of that Kingdom: they will need to be good news to the poor; they will need to be communities of justice and peace; and they will need to be communities located in particular places (Inge 2003: 137). The mediating institutions that we create will also need to be communities of justice and peace; and the relationships that the mediating institutions facilitate will need to be of that character as well, so that the institutions of our society, and not just religious institutions, will become the signposts towards the Kingdom of God that they need to be.

So what characteristics should we expect to see in the signposts to the Kingdom of God that our mediating institutions will both become and facilitate? For the Christian Church, the place to start to answer that question must be what the Church's Scriptures – both the Old and New Testaments – have to say about the Kingdom of God, and about the cities in which we live in the light of the Kingdom of God. It is to this task that we turn in our final chapter.

Bibliography

Baker, Christopher. 2009a. *The hybrid church in the city: Third space thinking*, 2nd ed. London: SCM Press.

Brown, David. 2004. *God and the enchantment of place: Reclaiming human experience*. Oxford: Oxford University Press.

Clements, Dave, Alastair Donald, Martin Earnshaw, and Austin Williams (eds.). 2008. *The future of community*. London: Pluto Press.

Davey, Andrew. 2001. *Urban Christianity and global order: Theological resources for an urban future*. London: SPCK.

Green, Laurie. 2010. "I can't go there!" The urban vocation. In *Crossover city: Resources for urban mission and transformation*, ed. Andrew Davey, 2–13. London: Mowbray.

Green, Laurie, and Christopher R. Baker. 2008. Urban visions and urban values. In *Building utopia? Seeking the authentic Church for new communities*, ed. Laurie Green and Christopher R. Baker, 149–172. London: SPCK.

Inge, John. 2003. *A Christian theology of place*. Farnham: Ashgate.

Kuhrt, Jon. 2010. What does salvation mean in the urban context. In *Crossover city: Resources for urban mission and transformation*, ed. Andrew Davey, 73–82. London: Mowbray.

Lane, Belden C. 1988. *Landscapes of the sacred: Geography and narrative in American spirituality*. New York: Paulist Press.

Malpas, J.E. 1999. *Place and experience: A philosophical topography*. Cambridge: Cambridge University Press.

Sheldrake, Philip. 2010. *Explorations in spirituality: History, theology, and social practice*. New York: Paulist Press.

———. 2014. *The spiritual city: Theology, spirituality, and the urban*. Chichester: Wiley Blackwell.

Torry, Malcolm, and Sarah Thorley (eds.). 2008. *Together and different: Christians engaging with people of other faiths*. Norwich: Canterbury Press.

Ward, Graham. 2000. *Cities of God*. London: Routledge.

White, Susan. 1995. The theology of sacred space. In *The sense of the sacramental*, ed. David Brown and Ann Loades, 31–43. London: SPCK.

7

Signposts Towards the City of God

Introduction

Mediating institutions have a purpose: to enable religious institutions to relate to secular institutions; to enable members of religious institutions to relate to members of secular institutions; and, more generally, to facilitate relationships between the Christian Faith and a secular world. But to what purpose? Different readers of this book will give different answers to that question. For some, good relationships between different institutions are essential to a peaceful society, so to understand how such relationships might be facilitated is sufficient of a reason for studying case studies about mediating institutions. Some Christian readers, and some readers who belong to other faiths, will have a more theological motive: and it is that motive that is addressed in this final chapter.

Religious organisations do not exist for their own sake. In the case of Christian organisations, they exist to worship God, and to proclaim the Kingdom of God that Jesus both promised and lived out (Torry 2014a, 2014b).

Jesus used the term 'the Kingdom of God' to express the realm of peace, healing and justice for which he hoped (Mark 1: 14–15; Luke

© The Editor(s) (if applicable) and The Author(s) 2016   **213**
M. Torry, *Mediating Institutions*,
DOI 10.1057/978-1-349-94913-7_7

4:16–21): but kingdoms imply monarchs, and not everyone is comfortable with that imagery. The term 'City of God' can express the same as Jesus' 'Kingdom of God', it does not imply any particular contemporary governance model, and it reflects the fact that much of this book has been about the urban world. I shall therefore use the term 'City of God' to express the community of peace and justice for which we hope. We already find this terminology in the Christian tradition (Neville 1971), and it is at least possible that it will not be alien to those other faith traditions that express the hope that God will bring about a community of peace and justice.

One of the Greenwich Peninsula Chaplaincy's most useful rules is that chaplains and Prayer Space welcomers are not to proselytise – that is, they are not on their own volition to attempt to persuade someone with whom they are holding a conversation of the truth or virtue of their own faith: but they are able to respond to questions about their faith, and they are encouraged to employ the resources of their faith to meet expressed need if that might be helpful. In the same spirit I shall in this chapter employ the Christian scriptures and the Christian tradition to explore the notion of the City of God, and to ask how we might give expression to that City in the communities in which we live and work, and in particular to ask how mediating institutions might contribute to this task. A further useful rule of the Greenwich Peninsula Chaplaincy is that chaplains and Prayer Space welcomers should not attempt to explain any faith other than their own. This is simply sensible, because someone who does not belong to a faith community is going to struggle to explain its beliefs and practices accurately: and it is also unnecessary to attempt to explain someone else's faith tradition, because it is always possible to find someone of the faith community concerned to offer the required explanations. In the same spirit, I shall not explore the concept of the City of God through the scriptures and traditions of any other faiths. I would not be competent to do so. I must therefore leave it to readers who belong to other faith communities to find in their own scriptures and traditions the resources required to explore the City of God and how together we might be able to give the world hope for that City's coming.

In the meantime, the task of this chapter is to ask about the character of the City of God in the Christian scritpures, to ask how mediating institutions can enable both the Church and our cities to become signposts towards the City for which we hope, and to ask about the possibility of a new Christendom (Torry 2009). This is not a suggestion that the Church will seek to exert power in the political realm: it is rather a suggestion that a Church shaped by Jesus, who came 'not to be served, but to serve' (Mark 10: 45), should serve the society in which it is set in such a way that that society takes on the character of the City of God.

The City in the Christian Tradition

As David Sheppard puts it:

> Belief in the City of God which will be made perfect one day, leads me to say that God has a purpose for the big city now. Our programme must learn something from the terms of reference of Jesus's mission. Its marks are the mending of broken lives and the proclaiming of good news to the poor. He set Himself alongside those who didn't have influence with the authorities, with the victims of principalities and powers. He was a realist about the evil influences in the world, as we have to be if we are serious about winning some battles in the city. He expected no cheap victories. His way was through suffering and death to a Resurrection which was only known to a minority. He promises that His Resurrection is only the first fruits of a harvest to come. (Sheppard 1974: 355)

So the first question must be: Can God be found in the city – in the urban world? Isn't God rather to be found among the mountains and the trees? Isn't that why posters with biblical texts on them, and powerpoint presentations designed to aid meditation, offer us sunsets over forested hills? Didn't the Psalmist say: 'I lift up my eyes to the hills ...' (Ps. 121: 1). Yes: but in this psalm the pilgrims were lifting their eyes to the hills because they were about to leave the city where they had met with God, and on their way home they would have to cross bandit-infested hills. The words that follow are a question with an answer: 'From where will my help come? My help comes from the Lord, who made heaven and earth' (Ps. 121: 1–2).

But didn't Adam and Eve live in the countryside? No. The garden in which the drama of Adam and Eve is played out is a city garden, or a garden near to a city (it is a 'garden' or 'park' (Schaper 2010: 18)). This is the garden in which God invites Adam and Eve to dwell, it is that privilege that they betray, and it is *out* of that garden that God casts them (Gen. 3: 22–24).

It is not one or the other, of course. God is to be encountered both within and outside the city. Moses led God's people out of Egypt, to Sinai, in the desert, to receive the law (Exodus 19, 20); Elijah heard God's voice on the mountain (1 Kings 19: 11); and Jesus went out to the hills to pray (Luke 9: 28). But God's temple was built in the city (2 Chronicles 3); 'cities of refuge' were cities to which those pursued by the relatives of people they had killed could flee in order to escape lynch-mob justice (Numbers 35:6); Elijah turned away from the mountain and towards political action and conflict (1 Kings 19, 21); and after Jesus had prayed and been transfigured on the mountain, he began his journey towards his death in Jerusalem (Luke 9: 51).

How does God see the city? Does God see it as a threat? After all, God destroys the tower of Babel and diversifies its builders' languages (Genesis 11: 1–9) so that such architectural co-operation would become more difficult – as anyone who has experience of a modern construction site will recognise. Does God want a home in the city, or not? (2 Samuel 7; 1 Kings 5: 5) Does God want to save recalcitrant cities, or to transform them? (Nahum 3; Jonah 1: 2; 3:10; 4)

Tim Gorringe sums up the Christian tradition's ambivalence towards the city:

> On the one hand the city is understood as a focus of violence and human hubris – this is the significance of the fact that both Cain and Nimrod are said to be the founders of cities. On the other hand the city is the model of what will finally be redeemed, the paradigm of the human home and the focus of human creativity. The city is both Babylon, the place of alienation, exile, estrangement and violence, and Jerusalem, the place where God dwells, sets God's sign, and invites humankind to peace. This twofold imaging of the city calls for a dialectic. Any city is always at any one time both Babylon and Jerusalem, as we are reminded by Jesus' description of Jerusalem, the city of peace, as the one who stones the prophets (Luke 19: 41). (Gorringe 2002: 140)

Jesus' attitude to the city is therefore one of both longing and sorrow:

> Jerusalem, Jerusalem, the city that kills the prophets and stones those who are sent to it! How often have I desired to gather your children together as a hen gathers her brood under her wings, and you were not willing! (Luke 13: 34)

I take this to be God's attitude to the city: an attitude of both longing and sorrow. Thus when the City of God finally comes, a new city is required:

> the holy city, the new Jerusalem, coming down out of heaven from God, prepared as a bride adorned for her husband. I heard a loud voice from the throne saying,
>
> 'See, the home of God is among mortals.
> He will dwell with them;
> they will be his peoples,
> and God himself will be with them;
> he will wipe every tear from their eyes.
> Death will be no more;
> mourning and crying and pain will be no more,
> for the first things have passed away.'
>
> I saw no temple in the city, for its temple is the Lord God the Almighty and the Lamb. And the city has no need of sun or moon to shine on it, for the glory of God is its light, and its lamp is the Lamb. The nations will walk by its light, and the kings of the earth will bring their glory into it. Its gates will never be shut by day – and there will be no night there. People will bring into it the glory and the honour of the nations. But nothing unclean will enter it, nor anyone who practises abomination or falsehood, but only those who are written in the Lamb's book of life. (Revelation 21: 2–4, 22–27)

John's vision was not intended as an escape from this complex world, but rather as an invitation to live the life of the City of God in our own time, and so to 'shape the communities around [us] in new urban areas so that they can be a foretaste of God's eschatological Kingdom' (Castle 2008: 119).

Transforming the City

So what has to happen to our cities to enable them to model and to promise the City of God?

First of all, something that does not have to happen: there is no need for our cities to cease to be secular. Harvey Cox's *The Secular City* describes the urban world as a ferment of values, as pragmatic, as hollowed out, and, during the 1960s, as experiencing significant renewal. Above all, the city is *secular*: a global phenomenon, and not just a Western one (Cox 1968: 50, 82, 108, 98). Cox traces the roots of secularisation in the Christian tradition itself, and in particular to the doctrine of creation, and to the prophets' and Jesus' insight that God is not spatially located. After all, witnesses stated that Jesus wanted to see the temple destroyed (Mark 14: 58), and they might have been right. Cox has no problem with a secular city, and we don't need to have a problem with it, either. As he suggests, religion can thrive in a secular state (Cox 1968: 101). That is why Kenneth Leech calls London an 'unsecular city' (Leech 2006: 118, 123). Pentecostal and mainstream denominational congregations are increasingly active because of inward migration from highly religious Africa and elsewhere, and the growing uncertainties of urban life are generating new opportunities for evangelism for churches of a variety of kinds. But none of this is a counterargument to the secularisation of the city. All of the different secularisations that I listed in Chap. 1 can be found in today's cities, and particularly institutional secularisation: 'a drawing apart and declining integration of religious and secular institutions and their personnel' (Torry 2010: 15). In this situation one of the tasks of the Church has to be to communicate in ways that address and engage with secularisations, wherever they are found; and, as we have already recognised throughout this book, a related task is to create mediating institutions so that the religious and the secular can relate to each other. Across this bridge the City of God will inform and transfigure both the secular city and religious organisations themselves. The religious will not cease to be religious, and the secular will not cease to be secular. The hope is that both will work together to turn the city into a signpost to the City of God.

But something that *does* have to happen is that some of the characteristics of our cities that are inimical to the City of God will have to be changed. Some of those characteristics go back a long way. King Solomon built God a house in Jerusalem, but he spent even longer building a costly house for himself (1 Kings 7). He built them both with slave labour, a practice which his son Rehoboam chose to continue, and which caused the division of the kingdom (1 Kings 12).

In the eighth century before Christ, Amos prophesied:

Therefore, because you trample on the poor
and take from them levies of grain,
you have built houses of hewn stone,
but you shall not live in them;
you have planted pleasant vineyards,
but you shall not drink their wine.
For I know how many are your transgressions,
and how great are your sins –
you who afflict the righteous, who take a bribe,
and push aside the needy in the gate. (Amos 5: 11, 12)

Amos lived in a time of growing inequality. This isn't a problem restricted to cities, but just as cities intensify most aspects of our society, so they intensify inequality. In the UK, society as a whole is becoming more unequal, London is becoming more unequal, and in boroughs like Tower Hamlets – with high levels of deprivation alongside the wealth on display at Canary Wharf – inequality is becoming extreme (Hamnett 2003).

Our cities can also be places of suffering. War and invasion affect everyone, but particularly a country's cities:

All who pass along the way
clap their hands at you;
they hiss and wag their heads
at daughter Jerusalem;
'Is this the city that was called
the perfection of beauty,
the joy of all the earth?' (Lamentations 2: 15)

Cities struck by earthquake, flood, or war, are places of intense suffering, and the intensification of suffering in the devastated city is one of the most harrowing of the ways in which cities are places of intensification. Much of *Faith in the City* (Archbishop's Commission on Urban Priority Areas 1985) is taken up with the suffering that the Commission found in the urban world. The Church's ministry and mission are properly directed towards individual conversion, the desecularisation of the city, the Christianisation of institutions, and its own life of worship: but if Christian theology or the Church should ever forget that Jesus came to

> bring good news to the poor…
> … to proclaim release to the captives
> and recovery of sight to the blind,
> to let the oppressed go free,
> to proclaim the year of the Lord's favour (Luke 4: 18, 19)

then it will have missed its vocation to work for a city in which there shall be no more poverty, no more insecurity, and no more suffering, in which no-one will be oppressed, and in which everyone will be able to realise their potential as children of God.

The City of God will be a new creation in which the whole created order will be renewed (Romans 8: 18–25), so in our own cities we should seek the health of the natural world. In the first creation account in the book of Genesis, the earth, the sea, plants, and animals, are created before human beings appear (Genesis 1), and in the second account Adam is told to 'till and keep' the garden in which God has placed him (Genesis 2: 15). Jesus marvelled at God's creation – 'Consider the lilies of the field, how they grow; they neither toil nor spin, yet I tell you, even Solomon in all his glory was not clothed like one of these' (Matthew 6: 28–29). Just as it took many centuries to understand that Paul's 'There is no longer Jew or Greek, there is no longer slave or free, there is no longer male and female; for all of you are one in Christ Jesus' (Galatians 3: 28) meant a ban on slavery, racism, and sexism, so now we are slowly recognising that the creation narratives, and Jesus' attitude to the created order, mean that to 'have dominion over the fish of the sea and over the birds of the air and over every living thing that moves upon the earth'

(Genesis 1: 28) means that we are responsible for sustaining the earth and its creatures – for how can we exercise dominion over them if we destroy them?

Just before Jesus' words on the lilies of the field, he says this: 'Look at the birds of the air; they neither sow nor reap nor gather into barns, and yet your heavenly Father feeds them. Are you not of more value than they?' (Matthew 6: 26) It is a truism to say that every person is unique, every person is a unique miracle, every person is valued by God: but it is these truisms that constitute the Christian pursuit of human dignity: the requirement that every person should be *treated* as a unique individual, and of infinite and eternal worth. The consequence is that in our social policy we need to express both our fundamental equality and our radical diversity. This is not easy, but it must be done. And in our communities we need to ensure the dignity of every member, too. That is the character of the City of God, so it must be the character of our cities today.

The inherent dignity of every human person deserves the best possible community and environment, and if we foster those then we shall be pointing our communities towards the City of God. In the cause of doing that we shall need to create mediating institutions, including sometimes campaigns against what is not right in existing and new communities. And so as the residents of the Ferrier Estate in South East London approached their estate's demolition, a Church Army officer was at the heart of a campaign to get the best possible deal for existing tenants – which they were not getting. His colleague was at the same time building constructive relationships with the local authority and the developer so that, as the regeneration of the estate progressed, the Church would be in a position to contribute to community-building (Russell and Ingram 2007). One of the outcomes of that positive engagement is OneSpace, which we discussed in Chap. 3. The necessarily somewhat confrontational campaign was a mediating institution, and OneSpace continues to function as a mediating institution. Both of them were designed to enhance the dignity of every member of the old and new communities, and to create signposts towards the City of God.

Transformation in Practice

The city is a place of *intensification*: a place where both good and evil are intensified, where questions and conflict are at their most intense, where sin, suffering, and inequality, are intensified, and where we find the greatest challenges to human dignity, the roots of climate change, and causes of the degradation of the created order. Here also we find the pursuit of peace and justice intensified. So if we want to discover what God is doing, then let us by all means go to the mountains and the hills in order to listen: but for the most direct experience, we need to go to the city. The city is the place of bitter conflict, but that also means that if diversity can be reconciled in the city, then it can be reconciled anywhere. We need mediating institutions above all in the cities, so that the religious and the secular can be reconciled with each other, and the different faith communities can be reconciled with each other, as a sign that other broken relationships can be healed as well.

If mediating institutions can facilitate a deeper relationship between God and the city – whether the city recognises that relationship or not – then the society in which the city is set can experience that relationship too; and if a city can come to reflect the character of the City of God, then the whole of the society in which it is set will experience that character, both in anticipation now, and in its perfection when the City of God finally comes. Harvey Cox goes too far to suggest that 'Jesus Christ comes to his people not primarily through ecclesiastical traditions, but through social change' (Cox 1968: 159), because Christ comes to us through both. Sometimes mutual criticism between social change and the Christian tradition can be appropriate. As Kenneth Leech suggests, where we see the city reflecting the character of the City of God, then we must participate (Leech 2006: 214); and, as Peter Robinson suggests, where we find lifestyles and philosophies inimical to the City of God, it is our responsibility to work for the city's conversion (Robinson 2010: 40). But the Church's task is also proactively to ask about the character of the City of God, to employ mediating institutions to build bridges into the secular city – into its communities and into its institutions – and to cross those bridges. It is also the Church's responsibility to understand where God is at work in the secular city, to permit that understanding to travel across the bridge formed by mediating institutions, and to allow its own life to be transfigured by what God is doing in the urban world. If we do these things, then what the Church experiences of the City of God will be offered to the secular city; and what God is doing in the secular city will be offered to the Church.

This requires that the Church should be present in the urban world, and if it isn't present then it should go there. If the Pentecost after Jesus' resurrection is the birth of the Church (Acts 2), then the Church was born in a city: Jerusalem. The early Church's greatest missionary, Paul, was a city person: he was born and brought up in Tarsus (Acts 21: 39), was a rabbi in Jerusalem, was converted on his way to Damascus (Acts 9), and the churches that he founded were located in many of the Roman Empire's cities. He ended up in Rome (Acts 28: 14). We only find him anywhere other than in a city when he is travelling between one city and another. Between then and now the Church has been as much a city institution as a rural one (Sheldrake 2014: 69–73); and today it is essential that the Church should be firmly located in the urban world, not only for ministry and mission among our cities' populations, but also because 'here we have no lasting city, but we are looking for the city that is to come' (Hebrews 13: 14), and only by being in the city can we shape the modern city into a signpost towards that City of God for which we hope.

The passage that we have already quoted from Revelation 21: 22–27 is not just about individuals in the city: it is about the city itself. Our cities are made up of organisations as well as of residential communities, and residential communities themselves are as much constituted by such organisations as schools, health centres, residents' associations, community centres, organisations for children and young people, and other voluntary organisations, as they are by the communities' residents. It is not just individuals who can be invited to live now the life of the 'city that is to come': institutions can be invited to do so as well. So local congregations can aim at the Christianisation of institutions as well as at the conversion and discipleship of individuals; and particularly appropriate in diverse new developments, like many of those in the Thames Gateway, will be a chaplaincy approach – chaplains for workplaces, chaplains for visitor venues, and chaplains for the institutions that we find in residential communities. Chaplains are there to serve the spiritual and other needs of individuals, and also to relate to the institutions in which those individuals work and among which they live. The workplace chaplaincy movement still has much to offer to the urban world: so forming and maintaining teams of workplace chaplains must be a high priority for the Church, and for other faith communities too.

All of this requires the Church to remain committed to the urban world. In the UK, the Church has now learnt a great deal about how to serve the needs of more deprived areas in our cities, and how to serve religiously diverse communities. Maybe it now needs to concentrate on serving the needs of new communities, and those of the vast diversity of communities in the modern city. The Church needs to be there early so that it can be involved from the beginning and, where possible, can shape emerging institutions so that they serve the needs of people living and working in the new community. It also needs to be there early so that it can create the religious infrastructure – including buildings – within which the Church can undertake its ministry and mission and so continue to serve as the development matures.

When many Israelites were taken into exile in Babylon, the prophet Jeremiah wrote to them:

> Build houses and live in them; plant gardens and eat what they produce. Take wives and have sons and daughters; take wives for your sons, and give your daughters in marriage, that they may bear sons and daughters; multiply there, and do not decrease. But seek the welfare of the city where I have sent you into exile, and pray to the Lord on its behalf, for in its welfare you will find your welfare. (Jeremiah 29: 5–7)

The city in which we live and/or work might not be the City of God, but it is a city that God loves. We are to seek its welfare, and to turn it into a signpost to the city that we hope for.

Grahame Neville, in his *City of our God*, traces the development of the idea of Jerusalem in the Hebrew Scriptures and in the Christian tradition. It is always 'the appointed meeting-place, the place of worship, the place of revelation, and the symbol of unity' (Neville 1971: 104): but there is an evolution from understanding it as a place, to understanding it as a community. In both the place and the community, the Church needs to serve the cities in which it is set by embodying in its own life the character of the City of God for which we hope (Neville 1971: 108).

This means that the Church needs to be itself, and to ensure that, whatever else it does in the service of the city in which it is set, it does the things that constitute it as the Church. For instance, prayer is a vital core function of the Church, and by praying for the city, the Church transforms the city (Brown 2004: 177, 215). As David Brown suggests, pilgrimage gave to Rome and Jerusalem their character as holy places. Those focal cities, and all of the medieval cities throughout Europe to which pilgrimage gave birth, 'acquired an enhanced value, for each embodied what was seen as a higher reality, the transforming presence of God mediated sacramentally to humankind' (Brown 2004: 244; cf. Sheldrake 2014: 69–72).

So perhaps the Good Friday prayer walks on the Greenwich Peninsula have contributed to the hallowing of the Peninsula. The reason for the prayer walks was somewhat accidental. Good Friday is a Friday, and between 1 p.m. and 2 p.m. on Fridays the Prayer Space is full of Muslims praying: so if the Holy Trinity congregation is to hold a three hour service in the Prayer Space then it has to vacate the building for the second hour. The tradition of a prayer walk around the northern end of the Peninsula thus evolved, with the different parts of the narrative of the last week of Jesus' life being read in different places, enabling members of the congregation to make their own connections between the places and the narrative (the bus stops and the entry into Jerusalem, Tesco and the disciples preparing for the Passover meal, Costa Coffee and the Last Supper …). For those of us on that pilgrimage, the Peninsula became a holy place, and perhaps was changed by the Church at prayer.

Above all, the Church is constituted by the Eucharist – by taking bread and wine, giving thanks, breaking the bread, and sharing the bread and wine – as Jesus asked us to do. By doing this, we create an inclusive celebration of the City of God. It is therefore essential that in every place, and particularly in every new development, creating a gathering of Christians to pray regularly and to celebrate the Eucharist must be a priority – not so that the congregation can seek its own health, but so that it can seek the health of the secular city. It is equally essential that every church should turn its mind to making its Eucharist entirely inclusive. Only if *every-*

one is welcome to participate can we represent the inclusive community of justice and peace for which we hope; and only by such an inclusive Eucharist will the Church be empowered to work for an inclusive community of justice and peace today.

The Church Among Other Faith Communities

From playing walk-on parts in *Built as a City* (Sheppard 1974) and *Faith in the City* (Archbishop's Commission on Urban Priority Areas 1985), the many different faith communities that are now active and highly visible in our society play a major role in *Faithful Cities* (Commission on Urban Life and Faith 2005). This is as we would expect. Any Christian activity in institutions, in communities, and particularly in new housing and other developments, will need to position itself in relation to other faith communities. This inevitably adds an additional layer to our individual and institutional activity, because not only must each Christian community relate to communities of Christians of other denominations, but as individuals and communities we must relate to individuals and communities of faith very different from ours. For such relationships to be meaningful and constructive, they need to be rooted in the intense differences between the theologies of the different faiths, and not just in the desire to be good neighbours and to do something useful together, important though those commitments are.

Clarity is required, both about what we share and about where we cannot agree: and experience on the Greenwich Peninsula suggests that the closer to each other we become in our activities and in our friendships, the clearer we become that those areas where we differ fundamentally relate to the very hearts of our respective faiths. There can be no compromises here. Given these radical differences, it would be misleading for Christians and Muslims to pray or to worship together, for the God whom Christians worship is actually different from the God whom Muslims worship, however much we might recognise that in the end God is One and that we possess a common theological heritage in Judaism.

I am aware that in other places other ways of managing these relationship are attempted. All I can say is that this way works on the Greenwich

Peninsula, and it enables conservative Muslims and Christians, as well as more liberal ones, to work together – for pastoral care is something that we *can* do together, provided we show courtesy towards one another, and keep to a handful of guidelines which encourage us to use the resources of our faiths to serve the spiritual and other needs of people we work among, which permit us to answer direct questions about our faith, and which forbid us to proselytise.

What consequences do these positions hold for Christian theology? They preserve for us an expressed distinctiveness in relation to the location of God's self-revelation, and that is crucial. They also leave to one side the issue of how God relates to people of different faiths. Given that 'now we see in a mirror, dimly, but then we will see face to face. Now I know only in part; then I will know fully, even as I have been fully known' (1 Corinthians 13:12), to maintain a certain reserve about such issues is surely appropriate.

Conclusion: Mediating the City of God

So what does all of that mean for new cities and new developments in our cities? What does it mean for the Thames Gateway, which is, after all, a massive extension of London eastwards to Southend and the Medway towns? And is it the Church's business anyway?

Yes, it is. As Graham Ward has pointed out,

> Because human beings are made by God to live in communities, their happiness is possible only within communities … . To provide the urban context in which such living is possible is to provide the theological conditions for human flourishing as God ordained it … . (Ward 2009: 210)

But what is meant by 'community'? The Department for Communities and Local Government's website defines 'sustainable communities' as

> … *places* where people want to live and work, now and in the future. They meet the diverse needs of existing and future residents, are sensitive to their environment, and contribute to a high quality of life. They are safe and

inclusive, well planned, built and run, and offer equality of opportunity and good services for all. [Emphasis added.] (Department for Communities and Local Government 2008)

While places are important – as we have discovered – they are not what communities are. Communities are communities of people, relating to each other: and in the modern urban world, communities are layered and intensely complex. The places in which communities are set need to serve this complexity, but they are not themselves communities; and, as Tim Gorringe puts it, places need to be 'ensouled' by the people who live in them (Gorringe 2002: 178; cf. Sheldrake 2014: 139): so the Church and other faith communities will need to facilitate that 'ensoulment' both by themselves being communities (Sheldrake 2014: 107–12) and through the mediating institutions that they create.

The activity will often be highly particular and detailed. For instance, if those planning new developments in the Thames Gateway and in other places are willing to hear Amos's prophecy, then they will build for equality: they will build mixed tenure developments, they will build tenure-blind developments, they will ensure that the quality of the housing is the same for owner occupiers and for social housing tenants, that the same services will be offered to owner occupiers and to social housing tenants, and that the same rules will apply. As Gorringe suggests, 'if reconciliation is to go beyond pious talk it needs to take shape in the built environment where social justice is, quite literally, made concrete' (Gorringe 2002: 49): so reading the weekly list of planning applications is as much a part of the Church's task as holding café discussions on what the prophet Amos teaches us about godly cities.

The extent to which different faith communities might want to model a hoped-for City of God together, and the extent to which each faith community might want to model their own vision, will always be an important question to ask. Working together will always be important: but it will also be important for each faith community to offer its own insights and to act accordingly. The *Christian* vision is that the God whose City of God it is is a God revealed as Trinity, meaning that God is community, and is 'a relational being' (Zizioulas 1997: 17). Just as God is community, and just as community is essential to our identity as human beings (Sheldrake 2014: 201), so is the Church a community: so rather than being something that the Church does, the Eucharist *constitutes* the Church (Zizioulas 1997: 21). There is of course much more than this that the Church contributes to the cities in which we live and work, but if it does not celebrate the Eucharist, then it is not being itself, and it is not contributing the most effective effectual sign of the coming City of God; and if its Eucharists are not open to everyone participating, then those Eucharists cannot create the reconciliation that we need them to create (Sheldrake 2014: 172–3), and they are not the sacraments of the City of God that we need them to be.

In the book of Isaiah God says to the prophet:

> I will give you as a light to the nations,
> that my salvation may reach to the end of the earth. (Isaiah 49: 6)

Israel was not God's Servant for its own sake, but for the sake of the 'nations'. Similarly, the Church is not God's Servant for its own sake. Even when it looks as if it is most concerned with itself, when it is at worship, it is doing what it does for the sake of the community in which it is set. *Everything* which the Church does must be not for itself, but for the world in which it lives. The Church in the Thames Gateway worships God and conducts its ministry so that the Thames Gateway can become a sign that the City of God is coming. We need to be today 'an eschatological community' (Cox 1968: 159) – a community of the last times – living today the life of the City of God, in order that the Thames Gateway might know that City and live it too.

The Psalmist calls us to

> walk about Zion, go all around it,
> count its towers,
> consider well its ramparts;
> go through its citadels,
> that you may tell the next generation
> that this is God,
> our God for ever and ever.
> He will be our guide for ever. (Psalm 48: 12–14)

It might or might not be relevant that the Thames Gateway has its fair share of towers, ramparts, and citadels. The primary school and health centre in the Greenwich Millennium Village are designed to look like citadels; much of the Docklands Light Railway is built on ramparts; and gated communities are today's equivalent of towers and citadels – and perhaps they should not be: but what is important is that anyone walking through the Gateway's communities should gain a vision of God and envisage something of God's purpose. Admittedly, no earthly city has ever achieved that, and we shall not: but there is no harm in aiming high. If it is the City of God that we intend to model in the cities in which we live, then we need to be involved in every aspect of the life of the city, and particularly in every aspect of the life of new cities and of new communities within our cities. It is for this purpose that we need mediating institutions: organisations that create relationships between the Church and organisations of many different kinds; institutions that enable the Christian Faith to connect with every aspect of our society; and buildings that will point institutions and individuals towards the City of God. It is across the relationships brokered by these mediating institutions that our society will discover the City of God to which the Church looks forwards; and it is across these relationships that the Church will discover the cities in which we live, their possibilities, and their constraints, and across which our churches and our cities will together negotiate ways for our cities to become signposts towards the City of God.

Mediating institutions are not simply channels, though. They act as signposts themselves, pointing towards the City of God because they relate both to the cities in which we live and to the Christian Faith that expresses our hope for the City of God. So the more mediating institutions we can maintain and construct, the more signposts there will be. By facilitating relationships between the cities in which we live, and the Church that hopes for the City of God, mediating institutions will enable many more signposts to be created in our cities and in the Church: that is, institutions and activities that point us towards the City of God. For both of these reasons, the more mediating institutions that we can construct and maintain, the more numerous and the more robust will be the signposts towards the City of God, and the closer we shall be to turning our cities into something closer to the City of God.

Bibliography

Archbishop of Canterbury's Commission on Urban Priority Areas. 1985. *Faith in the city: A call for action by church and nation*. London: Church House Publishing.

Brown, David. 2004. *God and the enchantment of place: Reclaiming human experience*. Oxford: Oxford University Press.

Castle, Brian. 2008. Gaining theological perspective. In *Seeking the authentic Church for new communities*, ed. Laurie Green and Christopher R. Baker, 115–130. London: SPCK.

Commission on Urban Life and Faith. 2005. *Faithful cities: A call for celebration, vision and justice*. London: Methodist Publishing House, and London: Church House Publishing.

Cox, Harvey. 1968. *The secular city*. Harmondsworth: Penguin (first published by the Macmillan Company, New York, in 1965).

Department for Communities and Local Government. 2008. Communities and neighbourhoods. http://webarchive.nationalarchives.gov.uk/20120919132719/http://www.communities.gov.uk/communities/sustainablecommunities/whatis/ [archived on 7 Sept 2008 and Accessed 1 Sept 2015.

Gorringe, Timothy. 2002. *A theology of the built environment: Justice, empowerment, redemption*. Cambridge: Cambridge University Press.

Hamnett, Chris. 2003. *Unequal city: London in the global arena*. London: Routledge.

Leech, Kenneth. 2006. *Doing theology in Altab Ali Park*. London: Darton Longman and Todd.

Neville, Graham. 1971. *City of our God: God's presence among his people*. London: S.P.C.K.

Robinson, Peter. 2010. New platforms for outreach: Developing a wider view of evangelism. In *Crossover city: Resources for urban mission and transformation*, ed. Andrew Davey, 37–51. London: Mowbray.

Russell, Nick, and Charlie Ingram. 2007. In the middle of it: Co-operation and resistance on the Ferrier Estate. In *Regeneration and renewal: The Church in new and changing communities*, ed. Malcolm Torry, 49–61. Norwich: Canterbury Press.

Schaper, Joachim. 2010. The Messiah in the garden. In *Paradise in antiquity: Jewish and Christian views*, ed. Markus Bockmuehl and Guy G. Stroumsa, 17–27. Cambridge: Cambridge University Press.

Sheldrake, Philip. 2014. *The spiritual city: Theology, spirituality, and the urban*. Chichester: Wiley Blackwell.

Sheppard, David. 1974. *Built as a city*. London: Hodder and Stoughton.

Torry, Malcolm. 2009. On building a new Christendom: Lessons from South London parishes. *Theology*, CXII(870): 435–43.

———. 2010. *Bridgebuilders: Workplace chaplaincy—A history*. Norwich: Canterbury Press.

———. 2014a. *Managing religion: The management of Christian religious and faith-based organizations*: vol 1, 'Internal relationships', Basingstoke: Palgrave Macmillan.

———. 2014b. *Managing religion: The management of Christian religious and faith-based organizations*: vol 2, 'External relationships', Basingstoke: Palgrave Macmillan.

Ward, Graham. 2009. *The politics of discipleship: Becoming postmaterial citizens*. London: SCM Press.

Zizioulas, John D. 1997. *Being as Communion*. Crestwood: St. Vladimir's Seminary Press.

Postscript

There is really only one two-part conclusion to draw: that we need mediating institutions, and we particularly need them in such diverse new developments as the Thames Gateway. Where they exist we need to keep them in good repair; and where they do not exist we need to create them – for the sake of the Church, and for the sake of the many diverse communities in which the Church finds itself; and in particular so that the Church and our cities can become signposts towards the City of God for which we hope.

Having concluded so briefly, I have space for an account of a tragedy:

On the afternoon of 22 May 2013, Fusilier Lee Rigby was brutally murdered in a Woolwich street by Michael Adebolajo and Michael Adebowale, two radicalised Muslims. News spread rapidly. We knew that even though the Muslim community of Woolwich had nothing to do with the murder, there would be some in the community who might cause problems for Greenwich's Muslims: so many of us immediately offered our support to the Director of the Greenwich Islamic Centre, Dr. Tariq Abbasi, and to its Imams. The next morning the Prime Minister wanted to visit Woolwich and to meet leaders of the faith communities, so our Member of Parliament, Nick Raynsford, asked me to organise the

© The Editor(s) (if applicable) and The Author(s) 2016   **233**
M. Torry, *Mediating Institutions*,
DOI 10.1057/978-1-349-94913-7

meeting. I had an hour to get together representatives of the Greenwich Islamic Centre, the Sikh Gurdwaras, and a variety of churches. It was a constructive meeting between the Prime Minister, the faith communities, representatives of the local authority, and our MP. The next day we had to do the same for Ed Miliband, the Leader of the Opposition.

The press were camped outside the Greenwich Islamic Centre – the Woolwich Mosque – and heckled one of the Imams when he read out a statement condemning the murder. After that, representatives of the Mosque quite understandably refused to talk to the press. But some things had not been said that needed to be said, so when the opportunity arose for a slot on Radio 4's *Sunday* programme, Tariq Abbasi and I were interviewed together by Trevor Barnes. Tariq was able to explain the lengths to which the Greenwich Islamic Centre had gone during the previous few years to exclude radical elements from the Mosque, and had had to spend thousands of pounds on court injunctions to achieve its aim. It was vital that this significant fact should be in the public domain.

Most of the Greenwich Faith Community Leaders committee members managed to get to a meeting convened by the Leader of Greenwich Council and the Metropolitan Police Borough Commander; we had our photograph taken together after the meeting so that the unity of the faith communities could be vigorously publicised; and we all signed the book of condolence that would go to Lee Rigby's family.

A quarterly meeting of the Greenwich Faith Community Leaders had by chance been organised for the week following the murder. A well-attended meeting discussed relevant issues with invited speakers, and then accepted the invitation of the Rector of St. Mary's, Woolwich, to hold a peace vigil in the church. Because the structures and relationships were already in place, the borough's faith communities were able to work closely together. Hostile journalists did their best to drive wedges between the different faith communities, but met with no success.

Nothing that we did together could bring Lee Rigby back, or reduce the horror of his murder: but the fact that over the years the different faith communities in the borough had got to know each other well, and had a history of working together, of meeting together, and of meeting together with representatives of the civic authorities, meant that a terrible situation did not get worse. Things would all have been a lot more difficult without the mediating institutions that many of us had put together over the years.

Both during that crisis and more generally, the Greenwich Faith Community Leaders, and its predecessor, the Greenwich Multi Faith Forum, have functioned as effective mediating institutions. The Greenwich Faith Community Leaders continues to enable different faith communities and their personnel to relate to each other; it facilitates good relationships between the borough's civic authorities and its faith communities, and between individual faith community leaders and individuals within the borough's institutions; and it enables the faith communities to respond together to issues facing the wider community, and to challenges that they themselves might face. The very different Greenwich Peninsula Chaplaincy – designed for a task, rather than for representation and dialogue – has enabled members of different faith communities to work closely together in the service of the Peninsula's large and diverse new community. These two different mediating institutions have between them served the faith communities and the borough's communities and institutions well. We commend the approach.

As we have seen, the Thames Gateway has experienced a variety of significant mediating institutions. These have enabled the Church to serve communities and institutions, and those communities and institutions to relate to the Church – and they have therefore enabled the religious and the secular to relate to each other, and the Church to make its contribution to the Thames Gateway becoming a signpost to the City of God.

This book has been largely descriptive. It is not a statement that other places, other organisations, and other institutions should create institutions identical to those that we have discovered in the Thames Gateway, elsewhere in South-east London, in Mainz-Kastel, and in Chicago. However, it is a statement that if the Christian Faith is to relate to a secular world, if the faith communities together are to relate to it, and if the faith communities are to relate to each other, then we shall be considerably helped in this process if we create mediating institutions to facilitate the necessary relationships. Our world will not stop changing, our cities will become more diverse, secularisations will continue to jostle with desecularisations, and in the midst of all of this we shall be trying to create out of our cities signposts towards the City of God that God will bring about. Yes, faith communities can sometimes relate directly to society's institutions, and congregations can of course relate directly to communities, but increasingly these relationships will be difficult to form and difficult to sustain, particularly in relation to industrial and commercial organisations and to the institutions of our secular society. We shall increasingly need mediating institutions – we shall need to nurture the ones that we have, and we shall need to create them where we do not have them. This will be one of the Church's major tasks in the years ahead. We should start now.

Appendix

Relationships and Sexuality

In 2012 a meeting of the Greenwich Faith Community Leaders asked the borough's faith communities for responses to a set of questions on relationships and sexuality. On 12 April 2012 the Holy Trinity Church Council held an initial discussion on the questions, and the Council agreed that Malcolm Torry should try to summarise the discussion in a draft paper for discussion at the next meeting. The draft was discussed at the Council's meeting on the 14 June 2012 and amendments were agreed. (This was before the UK Government legislated for same sex marriage.) The final version of the Council's response to the questions follows. It is included in this book as an appendix in the hope that it might contribute to maintaining marriage as a mediating institution.

© The Editor(s) (if applicable) and The Author(s) 2016   **237**
M. Torry, *Mediating Institutions*,
DOI 10.1057/978-1-349-94913-7

In What Kinds of Relationship Does Sexual Activity Belong?

For the Christian, Jesus is God incarnate and is therefore the primary revelation of God and of God's will. So in all matters of conduct, Jesus' words and actions are our highest authority.

Jesus said nothing directly about the kinds of relationship within which sexuality belongs, and, as far as we know, he himself provided no model of such a relationship.

The New Testament is our primary witness to Jesus. The Gospels are therefore particularly authoritative for us – but, again, they contain no direct answer to our question.

First of All: *Does Sexual Activity Belong Only in Heterosexual Relationships, or Does It Also Belong in Homosexual Relationships?*

Paul's letters can be interpreted in at least two different directions:

In Romans 1: 26–27, Paul describes one of the manifestations of rebellion against God like this: 'Women exchanged natural intercourse for unnatural, and in the same way also the men, giving up natural intercourse with women, were consumed with passion for one another. Men committed shameless acts with men and received in their own persons the due penalty for their error.' If the New Testament letters are regarded in every detail as our primary authority in relation to Christian conduct, then homosexual sexual activity is not a Christian option; but if the letters are a witness to early Christian understanding, and authoritative for us if we reinterpret them in relation to our own times, then the requirements that women should not speak in the Church (1 Cor. 14: 35), that women should cover their hair when they pray (1 Cor. 11: 13), and that sexual activity belongs only within heterosexual relationships (the passage above), are all culturally determined views from which we might be able to learn, but which we no longer need to regard as ultimately authoritative.

For Paul, 'there is no longer Jew or Greek, there is no longer slave or free, there is no longer male and female; for all of you are one in Christ Jesus' (Galatians 3: 28). This echoes Jesus' equal valuing of Jews and Gentiles, women and men, slave and free. Passages in the New Testament letters which reflect Jesus' words and actions are particularly authoritative for us for that reason. In our different context, this passage from the Letter to the Galatians is a warrant for adding that 'there is no longer heterosexual or homosexual, there is no longer straight couple or gay couple: for all of you are one in Christ Jesus', and for suggesting that this would have been Jesus' attitude in our own time.

We therefore conclude that it is legitimate for Christians to come to different decisions as to the kinds of relationship within which sexual activity belongs. On the basis of their theological commitments, some will believe that sexual activity belongs only in heterosexual relationships; and others, on the basis of their theological commitments, will believe that sexual activity belongs in both heterosexual and homosexual relationships.

The view of the Holy Trinity Church Council is that Jesus is our primary authority, that the New Testament is our primary witness to him, that the New Testament is authoritative for us when it reflects his words and actions, and when culturally determined passages are reinterpreted for our own time: and therefore that sexual activity belongs in both heterosexual and homosexual relationships.

Secondly: *Does Sexual Activity Belong Only Within Marriage, or Can It Also Belong Within Non-married Relationships?*

Again, Jesus said nothing that might help us with this precise question. Jesus' culture, like ours, valued the institution of marriage, understood as a public declaration of commitment; but the relationship between sexual activity and marriage has often been somewhat ill-defined, and Jesus did not specifically address the question.

What we can say is that Jesus commanded his followers to love one another (John 13: 34; 15: 12, 17), and Paul offered a careful description of love in 1 Corinthians 13: 'Love is patient; love is kind; love is not envious or boastful or arrogant or rude. It does not insist on its own way; it is not irritable or resentful; it does not rejoice in wrongdoing, but rejoices in the truth. It bears all things, believes all things, hopes all things, endures all things.' Sexual intercourse is a deep physical bond, and that bond can be both a great joy and an opportunity for exploitation and damage. It is therefore essential that the kind of love which Jesus exemplified, which Jesus commanded, and which Paul described, should characterise any relationship within which sexual activity occurs.

Jesus blessed a marriage ceremony with his presence (John 2: 1–11) and, as we shall see below, clearly regarded marriage as a serious and life-long commitment both for the man and for the woman. The fact that he used Genesis 2: 24 – 'Therefore a man leaves his father and his mother and clings to his wife, and they become one flesh' – in his argument for the permanence of marriage suggests that he believed that marriage is where sexual activity belongs.

We therefore believe that marriage is the ideal context for sexual rela-tionships, and that we should encourage any couple in a long-term, lov-ing and committed relationship within which sexual activity occurs to be married if that is a possibility for them. (Currently for same gender couples only the legal contract of civil partnership is available to meet this need.)

Is It Essential for Such Relationships to Be in Intention Lifelong?

The Old Testament recognised a man's right to divorce his wife by writ-ing her a certificate of divorce and sending her away (Deuteronomy 24: 1). Jesus was clear that this was not God's intention, and that marriage was to be lifelong (Mark 10: 9). His motives could have been threefold: that lifelong marriage was God's original intention (Mark 10: 6–8), that divorce of a woman by a man left the woman without means of subsis-tence, and that women had no right to divorce a man so men should not be able to divorce women.

If Jesus is our primary authority, then we too should regard marriage as a lifelong commitment.

Consistent with Jesus' words on lifelong marriage is his statement that 'whoever divorces his wife and marries another commits adultery against her; and if she divorces her husband and marries another, she commits adultery' (Mark 10: 11–12) (– an important example of Jesus' commitment to equality between women and men). The problem here is that in Matthew's Gospel a slightly different statement appears: 'anyone who divorces his wife, except on the ground of unchastity, causes her to commit adultery; and whoever marries a divorced woman commits adultery' (Matthew 5: 32 and 19: 9). Whether this text reflects Jesus' understanding that things can go wrong and that marriages can end, or the early Christians' revision of Jesus' teaching, we shall never know; but the way in which Jesus freely forgave sin (Mark 2: 5) suggests that he recognised that we get things wrong and that starting again is a possibility.

Paul, too, believed that there were situations in which divorce could be right, and in particular if one member of a couple became a Christian and the other did not: 'If the unbelieving partner separates, let it be so; in such a case the brother or sister is not bound. It is to peace that God has called you' (1 Cor. 7: 15). Paul was giving himself a certain liberty in relation to Jesus' explicit words, because the needs of the Church of his time required that: which suggests that we too should ask about the needs of the Church of our day and then ask how Jesus' words should be interpreted in our own context.

But Jesus' words about divorce suggest that however much we might recognise that marriages can end, the ideal remains marriage within which husband and wife love one another until death parts them, so that should remain the ideal for Christians.

Given our view that homosexual relationships are a possibility for homosexual Christians, and that sexual activity is possible within them, we believe that we should interpret Jesus' words about marriage for the context of our own time by saying that homosexual relationships should be in intention lifelong, that the privileges and responsibilities of marriage should be available to homosexual couples, and that Jesus' words about marriage, and our interpretation of them, should apply equally to heterosexual and homosexual relationships.

The view of the Holy Trinity Church Council is that sexual activity belongs within loving relationships, that marriage is the ideal, that marriage is a lifelong commitment, that because of our human frailty marriages sometimes end, that sin is forgiven, and that a new relationship after divorce is always a possibility; and that the privileges and responsibilities of marriage should be available to homosexual couples in the same way as they are available to heterosexual couples.

Bibliography

Ahern, Geoffrey and Grace Davie (1987) *Inner City God*, London: Hodder and Stoughton

Ahmed, Maqsood, Ted Cantle, Dilwar Hussain, and Vivien Lowndes (2009) 'Faith, Multiculturalism and Community Cohesion: a policy conversation', pp. 83–103 in Adam Dinham, Robert Furbey and Vivien Lowndes (eds) *Faith in the Public Realm: Controversies, policies and practices*, Bristol: Policy Press

Alinsky, Saul (1971) *Rules for Radicals: A Pragmatic Primer for Realistic Radicals*, New York: Random House

Ammerman, Nancy Tatom (1999) *Congregation and Community*, New Brunswick, New Jersey: Rutgers University Press

Angell, Olav Helge (2010) 'Sacred Welfare Agents in Secular Welfare Space: The Churhc of Norway in Drammen', pp. 57–75 in Bäckström, Anders and Grace Davie (eds) *Welfare and Religion in 21st Century Europe: Volume 1: Configuring the connections*, Farnham: Ashgate

Archbishop of Canterbury's Commission on Urban Priority Areas (1985) *Faith in the City: A Call for Action by Church and Nation*, London: Church House Publishing

Arise (2015) http://arisechicago.org/ [accessed 26/11/2015]

Atkins, Ann (2006) 'A Variety of Gifts: The people of God', pp. 14–25 in Malcolm Torry (ed.) *Diverse Gifts: Varieties of lay and ordained ministries in the Church and community*, Norwich: Canterbury Press

© The Editor(s) (if applicable) and The Author(s) 2016   **243**
M. Torry, *Mediating Institutions*,
DOI 10.1057/978-1-349-94913-7

Bäckström, Anders and Grace Davie (2010) 'The WREP Project: Genesis, structure and scope', pp. 1–23 in Bäckström, Anders and Grace Davie (eds) *Welfare and Religion in 21st Century Europe: Volume (1: Configuring the connections*, Farnham: Ashgate

Baker, Christopher R. (2008) 'the Wider Perspective: The Church in the new urban developments', pp. 93–113 in Laurie Green and Christopher R. Baker (eds) *Building Utopia? Seeking the authentic Church for new communities*, London: SPCK

Baker, Christopher (2009a) *The Hybrid Church in the City: Third space thinking* (2nd edition) London: SCM Press

Baker, Christopher (2009b) 'Blurred Encounters? Religious literacy, spiritual capital and language', pp. 105–22 in Adam Dinham, Robert Furbey and Vivien Lowndes (eds) *Faith in the Public Realm: Controversies, policies and practices*, Bristol: Policy Press

Beacon Project (2016) https://www.facebook.com/no3atTheBridge/ [accessed 27/01/2016]

Beales, Chris (2001) The Churches in Thamesmead: Their presence, interests, involvement and influence in the town (Thamesmead: Christian Community Partnership)

Beeson, Trevor (1963) *New Area Mission: The Parish in the new housing estates*, London: Mowbray

Bell, Catherine (1997) *Ritual: Perspectives and dimensions*, New York and Oxford: Oxford University Press

Berger, Peter L. (1999) *The Desecularization of the World*, Grand Rapids, Michigan: Eerdmans

Berger, Peter L. and Richard John Neuhaus (1977) *To Empower People: The role of mediating structures in public policy*, Washington, D.C.: American Enterprise Institute for Public Policy Research

Billis, David (1993) *Organising Public and Voluntary Agencies*, London: Routledge

Billis, David (2010) *Hybrid Organizations and the Third Sector: Challenges for practice, theory and policy*, Basingstoke: Palgrave Macmillan

Blumer, Herbert (1969) *Symbolic Interactionism*, New Jersey: Prentice Hall

Bonney, Norman (2015) 'The Sacred State: Religion, ritual and power in the United Kingdom, pp. 118–31 in Titus Hjelm (ed.) *Is God Back?* London: Bloomsbury

Brown, Callum G. (2001), *The Death of Christian Britain*, London: Routledge

Brown, David (2004) *God and the Enchantment of Place: Reclaiming human experience*, Oxford: Oxford University Press

Bruce, Stephen (ed.) (1992), *Religion and Modernization: Sociologists and historians debate the secularization thesis*, Oxford: Clarendon Press

Bruce, Stephen (1995) *Religion in Modern Britain*, Oxford: Oxford University Press

Burdett, Ricky and Deyan Sudjic (eds) (2007) *The Endless City*, London: Phaidon Press

Butler, Tim, with Garry Robson (2003) *London Calling: The middle classes and the re-making of inner London*, Oxford: Berg

Cameron, Helen (2010) *Resourcing Mission: Practical theology for changing churches*, London: SCM Press

Castle, Brian (2008) 'Gaining Theological Perspective', pp. 115–30 in Laurie Green and Christopher R. Baker (eds) *Building Utopia? Seeking the authentic Church for new communities*, London: SPCK

Cave, Margaret (2012) *Setting up and Running a Faith based Community Centre and Exploring its Use as a Base for New Contextual Church in a New Community*, unpublished dissertation

Chadwick, Owen (1975) *The Secularization of the European Mind in the Nineteenth Century*, Cambridge: Cambridge University Press

Chapman, Rachael (2009) 'Faith and the Voluntary Sector in Urban Governance: Distinctive yet similar?' pp. 203–22 in Adam Dinham, Robert Furbey and Vivien Lowndes (eds) *Faith in the Public Realm: Controversies, policies and practices*, Bristol: Policy Press

Cheesman, David and Nazia Khanum (2009) ' "Soft" segregation: Muslim identity, british secularism and inequality', pp. 41–62 in Adam Dinham, Robert Furbey and Vivien Lowndes (eds) *Faith in the Public Realm: Controversies, policies and practices*, Bristol: Policy Press

Cheyne, Angela (2008) 'Lost in Translation: Faith-based charities and "public benefit" in the eyes of the state', pp. 7–51 in *The Institute Series*, no.6, London: Heythrop Institute for Religion, Ethics and Public Life

Church of England (1918) *Christianity and Industrial Problems, being the Report of the Archbishop's Fifth Committee of Inquiry*, London: SPCK

Church of England, Lord Green Steering Group (2014) 'Talent Management for Future Leaders and Leadership Development for Bishops and Deans: A New Approach', www.churchofengland.org/media/2130591/report.pdf [accessed 18/12/2015]

Church of England, Research and Statistics Department (2014) *Statistics for Mission 2013*, Archbishop's Council, Church of England, London, www.churchofengland.org/media/2112070/2013statisticsformission.pdf [accessed 18/12/2015]

Citizens UK (2015) www.citizensuk.org/what_we_do [accessed 26/11/2015]

Clements, Dave, Alastair Donald, Martin Earnshaw and Austin Williams (eds) (2008) *The Future of Community*, London: Pluto Press

Cnaan, Ram A. (2002) *The Invisible Caring Hand: American congregations and the provision of welfare*, New York: New York University Press

Collier, Paul (2006) 'Serving in a Learning Community: The chaplain in higher education', pp. 157–70 in Malcolm Torry (ed.) *Diverse Gifts: Varieties of lay and ordained ministries in the Church and community*, Norwich: Canterbury Press

Commission on Urban Life and Faith (2005) *Faithful Cities: A call for celebration, vision and justice*, London: Methodist Publishing House, and London: Church House Publishing

Council of Trent (1563) *Canons and Decrees*, www.documentacatholicaomnia. eu/03d/1545-1545,_Concilium_Tridentinum,_Canons_And_Decrees,_ EN.pdf, 24th session [accessed 14/12/2015]

Cox, Harvey (1968) *The Secular City*, Harmondsworth: Penguin (first published by the Macmillan Company, New York, in 1965)

Crockett, Alasdair, and David Voas (2006) 'Generations of Decline: Religious Change in 20th century Britain', *Journal for the Scientific Study of Religion*, vol 45, no 4, pp. 567–84

Cuttell, Colin (1962) *Ministry without Portfolio*, London: Toc H

Davey, Andrew (2001) *Urban Christianity and Global Order: Theological resources for an urban future*, London: SPCK

Davey, Andrew (2010) *Crossover City: Resources for urban mission and transformation*, London: Mowbray

Davie, Grace (1994) *Religion in Britain since 1945: Believing without belonging*, Oxford: Blackwell

Davie, Grace (2002), *Europe: The Exceptional Case: Parameters of faith in the modern world*, London: Darton, Longman and Todd

De la Bedoyere, Quentin (2015) 'The Plot to Eradicate Faith Schools', *Catholic Herald*, 30th July 2015, www.catholicherald.co.uk/issues/july-31-2015/the-plot-to-eradicate-faith-schools/ [accessed 18/12/2015]

De Tocqueville, Alexis (2003 / 1840) *Democracy in America*, first published in 1840, translated by Gerald E. Bevan, with an introduction and notes by Isaac Kramnick, London: Penguin

den Dulk, Kevin R. and Elizabeth A. Oldmixon (2014) *Mediating Religion and Government: Political institutions and the policy process*, New York: Palgrave Macmillan

Department for Communities and Local Government (2008) 'Communities and neighbourhoods', http://webarchive.nationalarchives.gov.uk/20120919132719/ http://www.communities.gov.uk/communities/sustainablecommunities/whatis/ [archived on 07/09/2008 and accessed on 01/09/2015]

Department for Communities and Local Government (2012) 'Eric Pickles gives councils back the freedom to pray', www.gov.uk/government/news/eric-pickles-gives-councils-back-the-freedom-to-pray--2 [accessed, 18/12/2015]

Department for Education (2014) *School Admissions Code*, London: Department for Education, www.gov.uk/government/publications/school-admissions-code--2 [accessed 18/12/2015]

DiMaggio, Paul and W. Powell (1983), 'The Iron Cage Revisited: Conformity and Diversity in Organisational Fields', *American Sociological Review*, vol 48, pp. 147–60

Dinham, Adam and Vivien Lowndes (2009) 'Faith and the Public Realm', pp. 1–19 in Adam Dinham, Robert Furbey and Vivien Lowndes (eds) *Faith in the Public Realm: Controversies, policies and practices*, Bristol: Policy Press

Durkheim, Emile (1915) *The Elementary Forms of the Religious Life*, London: George Allen and Unwin

Durkheim, Emile (1938) *The Rules of Sociological Method*, Chicago: University of Chicago Press

Edgardh, Ninna and Per Pettersson (2010) 'The Church of Sweden: A church for all, especially the most vulnerable', pp. 39–67 in Bäckström, Anders and Grace Davie (eds) *Welfare and Religion in 21st Century Europe: Volume 1: Configuring the connections*, Farnham: Ashgate

Enoch-Onchere, Jedidah and Simon Boxall (2007) 'Congregations are Mission: Building congregations in Thamesmead', pp. 131–42 in Torry, Malcolm, *Regeneration and Renewal: The Church in new and changing communities*, Norwich: Canterbury Press

Episcopal Peace Fellowship (2015) http://epfnational.org [accessed 27/11/2015]

Erlander, Lillemor (1991) *Faith in the World of Work: On the theology of work as lived by the French worker-priests and British industrial mission*, Uppsala: Uppsala University

Farnell, Richard (2009) 'Faiths, Government and Regeneration: A contested discourse', pp. 183–202 in Adam Dinham, Robert Furbey and Vivien Lowndes (eds) *Faith in the Public Realm: Controversies, policies and practices*, Bristol: Policy Press

Financial Times, (2008), 'Requiem for a Dream Home' http://www.ft.com/cms/s/0/41524d5c-91ac-11dd-b5cd-0000779fd18c.html

Flagg, David (2006) 'Serving in a Healing Community: The hospital chaplain', pp. 171–84 in Malcolm Torry (ed.) *Diverse Gifts: Varieties of lay and ordained ministries in the Church and community*, Norwich: Canterbury Press

Flint, John (2009) 'Faith-based Schools: Institutionalising Parallel Lives?' pp 163–82 in Adam Dinham, Robert Furbey and Vivien Lowndes, *Faith in the Public Realm: Controversies, Policies and Practices*, Bristol: Policy Press.

Ford, Mandy (2010) 'St. Philip's Church and Centre, Leicester: Presence and engagement', pp. 139–43 in Andrew Davey (ed.) *Crossover City: Resources for urban mission and transformation*, London: Mowbray

Fox, Michael (2008a) 'The Receiving Community', pp. 23–39 in Laurie Green and Christopher R. Baker (eds) *Building Utopia? Seeking the authentic Church for new communities*, London: SPCK

Fox, Michael (2008b) 'The Incomers' Perspective', pp. 41–56 in Laurie Green and Christopher R. Baker (eds) *Building Utopia? Seeking the authentic Church for new communities*, London: SPCK

Fox, Michael and Sue Hutson (2008) 'Shaping the Church', pp. 131–48 in Laurie Green and Christopher R. Baker (eds) *Building Utopia? Seeking the authentic Church for new communities*, London: SPCK

Frisina, Annalisa (2010) 'What Kind of Church? What Kind of Welfare? Conflicting views in the Italian case', pp. 147–66 in Bäckström, Anders and Grace Davie (eds) *Welfare and Religion in 21st Century Europe: Volume 1: Configuring the connections*, Farnham: Ashgate

Furbey, Robert (2009) 'Controversies of "public faith"', pp. 21–40 in Adam Dinham, Robert Furbey and Vivien Lowndes (eds) *Faith in the Public Realm: Controversies, policies and practices*, Bristol: Policy Press

Gorringe, Timothy (2002) *A Theology of the Built Environment: Justice, empowerment, redemption*, Cambridge: Cambridge University Press

Gossner Mission (2015) www.gossner-mission.de/pages/deutschland.php [accessed 30/11/2015]

Graf, Arnie (2015) 'Community Organising and Blue Labour', pp 71–83 in Ian Geary and Adria Pabst (eds) *Blue Labour: Forging a new politics*, London: I.B. Taurus

Grant, Don, Kathleen M. O'Neil and Laura S. Stephens (2003) 'Neosecularization and Craft Versus Professional Religious Authority in a Nonreligious Organization', *Journal for the Scientific Study of Religion*, vol 42, no 3, pp. 479–87

Green, Laurie (2008) 'Postcards from Utopia', pp. 1–21 in Laurie Green and Christopher R. Baker (eds) *Building Utopia? Seeking the authentic Church for new communities*, London: SPCK

Green, Laurie (2010) ' "I Can't Go *There!*" The urban vocation', pp. 2–13 in Andrew Davey (ed.) *Crossover City: Resources for urban mission and transformation*, London: Mowbray

Green, Laurie and Christopher R. Baker (2008) 'Urban Visions and Urban Values', pp. 149–72 in Laurie Green and Christopher R. Baker (eds) *Building Utopia? Seeking the authentic Church for new communities*, London: SPCK

Griffiths, Peter (2006) 'Commissioned to Care: The Southwark Pastoral Auxiliary', pp. 65–77 in Malcolm Torry (ed.) *Diverse Gifts: Varieties of lay and ordained ministries in the Church and community*, Norwich: Canterbury Press

Hamnett, Chris (2003) *Unequal City: London in the global arena*, London: Routledge

Harris, Margaret (1998) *Organizing God's Work: Challenges for churches and synagogues*, Basingstoke: Macmillan

Harris, Margaret and Malcolm Torry (2000) *Managing Religious and Faith-based Organizations: A guide to the literature*, Birmingham: Aston Business School

Hirschle, Jochen (2010) 'From Religious to Consumption-related Routine Activities? Analyzing Ireland's Economic Boom and the Decline in Church Attendance', *Journal for the Scientific Study of Religion*, vol 49, no 4, pp. 673–87

Hjelm, Titus (2015) 'Is God Back? Reconsidering the new visibility of religion', pp. 1–16 in Titus Hjelm (ed.) *Is God Back?* London: Bloomsbury

Home office (2011) *Prevent Strategy*, Cm 8092, London: Her Majesty's Stationery Office

Hutson, Sue (2008) 'The Impact on the Public Sector', pp. 77–91 in Laurie Green and Christopher R. Baker (eds) *Building Utopia? Seeking the authentic Church for new communities*, London: SPCK

Iannaccone, Laurence R. and Sean F. Everton (2004) 'Never on Sunny Days: Lessons from Weekly Attendance Counts', *Journal for the Scientific Study of Religion*, vol 43, no 2, pp. 197–207

Inge, John (2003) *A Christian Theology of Place* (Farnham: Ashgate)

Institute of Ideas (2014) 'Keeping the faith schools?' *Battle of Ideas*, London: Institute of Ideas, www.battleofideas.org.uk/2014/session_detail/8990 [accessed 18/12/2015]

Inter Faith Network for the UK (2015) www.interfaith.org.uk [accessed 31/08/2015]

Interfaith Worker Justice (2015) www.iwj.org [accessed 26/11/2015]

Jawad, Rana (2012) *Religion and Faith-based Welfare: From wellbeing to ways of being*, Bristol: Policy Press

Jordan, Bill (1996) *A Theory of Poverty and Social Exclusion*, Cambridge: Polity Press

Jordan, Stuart (2005) 'Organizational Studies Strand – Worship and Action', pp. 109–22 in Helen Cameron, Philip Richter, Douglas Davies and Frances Ward (eds) *Studying Local Churches: A handbook*, London: SCM Press

Katz, Bruce, Andy Altman and Julie Wagner (2007) 'An Agenda for the Urban Age', pp. 474–81 in Ricky Burdett and Deyan Sudjic (eds) *The Endless City*, London: Phaidon Press

Kendall, Jeremy and Martin Knapp (1995) 'A Loose and Baggy Monster: Boundaries, definitions and typologies', pp. 65–94 in Justin Davis Smith, Colin Rochester and Rodney Hedley (eds.) *An Introduction to the Voluntary Sector*, London: Routledge

Kettell, Stern (2015) 'Illiberal Secularism? Pro-faith discourse in the United Kingdom', pp. 65–76 in Titus Hjelm (ed.) *Is God Back?* London: Bloomsbury

Kidbrooke Focus (2015) www.onespacekidbrooke.org.uk/kidbrooke–focus/faithworks–charter/ [accessed 22/11/2015]

Klimon, William M. (1992) 'Mediating Institutions', *Religion and Liberty*, vol 2, no 3, May/June 1992, Acton Institute for the Study of Religion and Liberty, www.acton.org/pub/religion-liberty/volume-2-number-3/mediating-institutions [accessed 18/12/2015]

Kuhrt, Jon (2010) 'What does Salvation Mean in the Urban Context', pp. 73–82 in Andrew Davey (ed.) *Crossover City: Resources for urban mission and transformation*, London: Mowbray

Lane, Belden C. (1988) *Landscapes of the Sacred: Geography and narrative in American spirituality*, New York: Paulist Press

Leech, Kenneth (2006) *Doing Theology in Altab Ali Park*, London: Darton Longman and Todd

Leis-Peters, Annette (2010) 'The German Dilemma: Protestant Agents of Welfre in Reutlingen', pp. 95–112 in Bäckström, Anders and Grace Davie (eds) *Welfare and Religion in 21st Century Europe: Volume 1: Configuring the connections*, Farnham: Ashgate

Malpas, J.E. (1999) *Place and Experience: A philosophical topography*, Cambridge: Cambridge University Press

Mantle, John (2000) *Britain's First Worker-Priests*, London: SCM Press

Martin, David (1969), *The Religious and the Secular*, London: Routledge and Kegan Paul

Martin, David (1978) *A General Theory of Secularization*, Oxford: Blackwell

Martin, David (2005) *On Secularisation: Towards a revised general theory*, Aldershot: Ashgate

Mason, Rowena (2014) 'Councils to be allowed to hold prayers at meetings under new bill', *The Guardian*, 18/12/2014, www.theguardian.com/society/2014/dec/18/local-councils-pray-meetings-bill [accessed 18/12/2015]

Micklethwaite, John and Adrian Wooldridge (2009) *God is Back: How the global rise of faith is changing the world*, London: Penguin

Middlemiss Lé Mon, Martha (2010) 'The "In-Between" Church: Church and welfare in Darlington', pp. 113–28 in Bäckström, Anders and Grace Davie (eds) *Welfare and Religion in 21st Century Europe: Volume 1: Configuring the connections*, Farnham: Ashgate

Modood, Tariq (2010) 'Moderate Secularism, Religion as Identity and Respect for Religion', *Political Quarterly*, vol 81, no 1, pp. 4–14

Mosques and Imams National Advisory Board (2015) www.minab.org.uk [accessed 26/08/2015]

Mumford, Lewis (1961) *The City in History: Its origins, its transformations, and its prospects*, London: Secker and Warburg

Near Neighbours (2015) www.cuf.org.uk/how-we-help/near-neighbours [accessed 26th August 2015]

Neutral Ground (2015) www.neutralground.info/ [accessed 1/12/2015]

Neville, Graham (1971) *City of our God: God's presence among his people*, London: S.P.C.K.

Newman, Liz (2006) 'Making Connections: The Reader', pp. 26–39 in Malcolm Torry (ed.) *Diverse Gifts: Varieties of lay and ordained ministries in the Church and community*, Norwich: Canterbury Press

Obiora, Arthur (2006) 'Here to Stay: The Ordained Local Minister', pp. 78–84 in Malcolm Torry (ed.) *Diverse Gifts: Varieties of lay and ordained ministries in the Church and community*, Norwich: Canterbury Press

Olson, Paul J. and David Beckworth (2011) 'Religious Change and Stability: Seasonality in Church Attendance from the 1940s to the 2000s', *Journal for the Scientific Study of Religion*, vol 50, no 2, pp. 388–96

Oxford English Dictionary (2015) www.oed.com/view/Entry/97110?redirectedFrom=institution#eid [accessed 2/12/2015]

Oxford University Press (2015) *Oxford English Dictionary*, Oxford: Oxford University Press, www.oed.com

Perrin, Henri (1965) *Priest and Worker: The autobiography of Henri Perrin* (translated and with an introduction by Bernard Wall) London: Macmillan

Perumbalath, John (2008) 'Visionaries and Strategists', pp. 57–75 in Laurie Green and Christopher R. Baker (eds) *Building Utopia? Seeking the authentic Church for new communities*, London: SPCK

Presser, Stanley, and Mark Chaves (2007) 'Is Religious Service Attendance Declining?' *Journal for the Scientific Study of Religion*, vol 46, no 3, pp. 417–23

Reeve, Gillian (2006) 'Professionals between the Church and the World: Licensed Lay Workers', pp. 85–94 in Malcolm Torry (ed.) *Diverse Gifts: Varieties of lay and ordained ministries in the Church and community*, Norwich: Canterbury Press

Reiss, Robert (2013) *the Testing of Vocation: 100 years of ministry selection in the Church of England*, London: Church House Publishing

Renaissance Collaborative (2015) www.trcwabash.org/housing.html [accessed 27/11/2015]

Riordan, Patrick (2008a) 'Facing the Challenges: Faith-based charities and the legislative context', pp. 53–62 in *The Institute Series*, no.6, London: Heythrop Institute for Religion, Ethics and Public Life,

Riordan, Patrick (2008b) 'At a Loss for Words', pp. 31–42 in *The Institute Series*, no.11, London: Heythrop Institute for Religion, Ethics and Public Life

Riordan, Patrick (ed.) (2009) *Words in Action: In ten thousand places*, *The Institute Series*, no.12, London: Heythrop Institute for Religion, Ethics and Public Life

Robinson, Peter (2010) 'New Platforms for Outreach: Developing a wider view of evangelism', pp 37–51 in Davey, Andrew (ed.), *Crossover City: Resources for urban mission and transformation*, London: Mowbray

Rochester, Colin and Malcolm Torry (2010) 'Faith-based Organizations and Hybridity: A special case?' pp. 114–33 in David Billis (ed.) *Hybrid Organizations and the Third Sector: Challenges for practice, theory and policy*, Basingstoke: Palgrave Macmillan

Roman Catholic Church (1964) *Unitatis Redintegratio*, The Decree on Ecumenism, Second Vatican Council, www.vatican.va/archive/hist_councils/ii_vatican_council/documents/vat-ii_decree_19641121_unitatis-redintegratio_en.html [accessed 15/02/2016]

Russell, Nick (2006) 'A Different Kind of Soldier: The Church Army Officer', pp. 40–50 in Malcolm Torry (ed.) *Diverse Gifts: Varieties of lay and ordained ministries in the Church and community*, Norwich: Canterbury Press

Russell, Nick and Charlie Ingram (2007) 'In the middle of it: Co-operation and resistance on the Ferrier Estate', pp 49–61 in Torry, Malcolm, *Regeneration and Renewal: The Church in new and changing communities*, Norwich: Canterbury Press

Ryan, Ben (2015) *A Very Modern Ministry: Chaplaincy in the UK*, London: Theos, www.theosthinktank.co.uk/files/files/Modern%20Ministry%20combined.pdf [accessed 3/12/2015]

Salamon, Lester M. and Helmut K. Anheier (1993) 'Measuring the non-profit sector cross-nationally: A comparative methodology', *Voluntas*, vol 4, no 4, pp. 530–54

Schaper, Joachim (2010) 'The Messiah in the Garden', pp 17–27 in Markus Bockmuehl and Guy G. Stroumsa, *Paradise in Antiquity: Jewish and Christian views*, Cambridge: Cambridge University Press

Scott, Sara (2006) 'Balancing Roles: The non-stipendiary minister', pp. 51–64 in Malcolm Torry (ed.) *Diverse Gifts: Varieties of lay and ordained ministries in the Church and community*, Norwich: Canterbury Press

Sheldrake, Philip (2001) *Spaces for the Sacred: Place, memory and identity*, London: SCM Press

Sheldrake, Philip (2010) *Explorations in Spirituality: History, theology, and social practice*, New York: Paulist Press

Sheldrake, Philip (2014) *The Spiritual City: Theology, spirituality, and the urban*, Chichester: Wiley Blackwell

Sheppard, David (1974) *Built as a City*, London: Hodder and Stoughton

Singh, Gurnam and Stephen Cowden (2011), 'Multiculturalism's New Fault Lines: Religious Fundamentalisms and Public Policy', *Critical Social Policy*, vol 31, no 1, pp. 343–64

Sky news (2006) 'New Row over Casino Dome' http://news.sky.com/story/450818/new-row-over-casino-dome

South Yorkshire Workplace Chaplaincy (2015) www.sywc.org.uk [accessed 18/12/2015]

Spittles, David (2015) 'The new world in Zone 2: Olympicopolis', *Evening Standard*, 18/112015, pp. H&P 6–7

Stacey, Nick (1971) *Who Cares*, London: Anthony Blond

Starbuck, Robert (1966) 'Introduction: Servant Witnesses of the Servant Lord', pp. 11–29 in Horst Symanowski (1966) *The Christian Witness in an Industrial Society*, London: Collins

Stewart-Darling, Fiona (2016) *Multifaith Chaplaincy in the Business Community* (working title) London: Jessica Kingsley, forthcoming, 2016

Tabor, Tim (2010) 'Community, Urban Environment and Sustainability in Urban Villages: Assessing the success of the Greenwich Millennium Village', unpublished B.A. dissertation, University College London

Taylor, Charles (2007) *A Secular Age*, Cambridge, Massachusetts: The Belknap Press of Harvard University Press

Thames Gateway Kent Partnership (2010) *Faith Communities and Regeneration in the Thames Gateway: Feasibility study report*, London: The Grubb Institute

Thatcher, Margaret (1987) 'Interview for *Women's Own*', London: Margaret Thatcher Foundation, www.margaretthatcher.org/document/106689 [accessed 3/12/2015]

Thorley, Barry (2004) 'Growing a Black Church: The multicultural parish', pp. 49–61 in Malcolm Torry (ed.) *The Parish: People, place and ministry: A theological and practical exploration*, Norwich: Canterbury Press

Todd, Andrew (2013) *Military Chaplaincy in Contention: Chaplains, churches and the morality of conflict*, Farnham: Ashgate

Torry, Malcolm (1980) 'Two Kinds of Ambiguity', *King's Theological Review*, vol 3, no 1, pp. 24–8

Torry, Malcolm (2004) 'Being and Doing: The priest in the parish', pp. 160–71 in Malcolm Torry (ed.) *The Parish: People, place and ministry: A theological and practical exploration*, Norwich: Canterbury Press

Torry, Malcolm (2005) *Managing God's Business: Religious and faith-based organizations and their management*, Aldershot: Ashgate

Torry, Malcolm (2006) 'While We're Here, We Belong: The stipendiary incumbent', pp. 185–203 in Malcolm Torry (ed.) *Diverse Gifts: Varieties of lay and ordained ministries in the Church and community*, Norwich: Canterbury Press

Torry, Malcolm (2007) 'Starting from Scratch: The Greenwich Peninsula', pp. 114–27 in Malcolm Torry (ed.) *Regeneration and Renewal: The Church in new changing communities*, Norwich: Canterbury Press

Torry, Malcolm (2008) 'Voluntary, Religious and Faith-Based Organizations: Some Important Distinctions', pp.13–26 in *Words in Action: Finding the right words*, The Institute Series, no.11, London: Heythrop Institute for Religion, Ethics and Public Life

Torry, Malcolm (2009) 'On Building a New Christendom: Lessons from South London Parishes', *Theology*, vol CXII, no 870, November/December 2009, pp. 435–43

Torry, Malcolm (2010) *Bridgebuilders: Workplace chaplaincy – a history*, Norwich: Canterbury Press

Torry, Malcolm (2011) 'The Church's Relationship to New Housing and Other Developments in the Thames Gateway: Draft Report', unpublished report based on research sponsored by the Diocese of Southwark and funded by the Church Commissioners.

Torry, Malcolm (2012) 'Is there a Faith Sector?' *Voluntary Sector Review*, vol 3, no 1, pp. 111–17

Torry, Malcolm (2014a) *Managing Religion: The management of Christian religious and faith-based organizations*: vol 1, 'Internal relationships', Basingstoke: Palgrave Macmillan

Torry, Malcolm (2014b) *Managing Religion: The management of Christian religious and faith-based organizations*: vol 2, 'External relationships', Basingstoke: Palgrave Macmillan

Torry, Malcolm (2016) 'Religious Advantage and Disadvantage', pp. 285–303 in Hartley Dean and Lucinda Platt (eds) *Social Advantage and Disadvantage*, Oxford: Oxford University Press

Torry, Malcolm and Deborah Dukes (2014) 'Faith communities engaging with new and changing communities: A report on a research project on faith communities in the Thames Gateway', unpublished report based on research sponsored by the M.B. Reckitt Trust

Torry, Malcolm and Jeffrey Heskins (eds) (2006a) *Ordained Local Ministry: A new shape for ministry in the Church of England*, Norwich: Canterbury Press

Torry, Malcolm and Sarah Thorley (eds) (2008) *Together and Different: Christians engaging with people of other faiths*, Norwich: Canterbury Press

Tyler, Alison (2006) 'Serving in a Walled Community: The prison chaplain', pp. 143–56 in Malcolm Torry (ed.) *Diverse Gifts: Varieties of lay and ordained ministries in the Church and community*, Norwich: Canterbury Press

United Nations News Centre (2014) 'More than half of world's population now living in urban areas', UN survey finds, United Nations News Centre, www.un.org/apps/news/story.asp?NewsID=48240# [accessed 18/12/2015]

Valasik, Corinne (2010) 'Church-State Relations in France in the Field of Welfare: A hidden complementarity', pp. 129–45 in Bäckström, Anders and Grace Davie (eds) *Welfare and Religion in 21st Century Europe: Volume 1: Configuring the connections*, Farnham: Ashgate

Ward, Graham (2000) *Cities of God*, London: Routledge

Ward, Graham (2009) *The Politics of Discipleship: Becoming postmaterial citizens*, London: SCM Press

Weber, Max (1922) 'The Three Types of Legitimate Rule', pp. 6–15 in Etzioni, Amitai and Lehman, E. (eds) (1980) *A Sociological Reader on Complex Organisations*, 3rd edition, Austin, Texas: Holt, Reinhart and Winston

Weller, Paul (2009) 'How Participation Changes Things: 'inter-faith, 'multifaith' and a new public imaginary', pp. 63–81 in Adam Dinham, Robert Furbey and Vivien Lowndes (eds) *Faith in the Public Realm: Controversies, policies and practices*, Bristol: Policy Press

White, Susan (1995) 'The Theology of Sacred Space', pp. 31–43 in David Brown and Ann Loades (eds) *The Sense of the Sacramental*, London: SPCK

Wickham, E.R. (1957) *Church and People in an Industrial City*, London: Lutterworth Press

Wickham, E.R. (1964) *Encounter with Modern Society*, London: Lutterworth Press

Wigfall, Valerie G. (2008) *Thamesmead: A social history* (2nd edition) Stroud: The History Press

Wuthnow, Robert (2009) *Boundless Faith: The global outreach of American churches*, Berkeley: University of California Press

Zizioulas, John D. (1997) *Being as Communion*, Crestwood, New York: St. Vladimir's Seminary Press

Index

© The Editor(s) (if applicable) and The Author(s) 2016   **257**
M. Torry, *Mediating Institutions*,
DOI 10.1057/978-1-349-94913-7

Printed by Printforce, the Netherlands